Boot Camp For
Your Brain

Boot Camp For Your Brain

*A No-Nonsense Guide
to the SAT*

Fifth Edition

M. Denmark Manning

To order additional copies of this book, contact:
Xlibris
1-888-795-4274
www.Xlibris.com
Orders@Xlibris.com
551324

Contents

Lovingly dedicated: John, Justin, my math whiz father, my mother who recommended Latin & did NY Times crosswords in ink, math teacher C. Garrett, Latin's M. Work, Friedmans, AES whose 800 V spurred me to raise my score, friends, other family, my students.

Introduction and Welcome

Welcome to the best curriculum available to prep for the SAT. It is a good sign that you are planning to prepare for the test, for it shows you understand that your performance on this important college admissions exam can be improved by effort.

The SAT does not really test ability or aptitude; it has a very strong achievement component that you can influence by working with our up-to-date, comprehensive, innovative, and just plain phenomenal materials. We focus on giving you all the tools you need to excel on the SAT. Your job is to put the material into your brain by studying it intensively and diligently on a regular-preferably daily-basis. There will be some repetition of material throughout the book; this is deliberate, since long-term memorization is aided by repetition.

It will not be fun. It will not be exciting. But think of this program as Boot Camp for Your Brain™. Most people find that, if they can make themselves sit down and study this material regularly and go over it a number of times, they will in fact learn it. The SAT is not identical from administration to administration, but very similar kinds of material are tested over and over again. So if you learn the material on the exam that you don't already know, you will answer more questions correctly and your scores will go up.

Welcome aboard. You've chosen well. Soon you will take the SAT armed only with your brain, No. 2 pencils, and what you have learned herein. And if you've studied hard and followed our suggestions, you should be absolutely ready.

How To Use This Book

This is the official textbook of The World's Best Prep Course, Inc., used in all our classes.

For those of you who are not taking the actual course with a teacher: the book can be used on its own with great results, but I believe that the best method of employing it is to use it in conjunction with the book *The Official SAT Study Guide* (the current title, but they may change it back to *10 Real SATs* or another title; always make sure it's by The College Board, which oversees the SAT.) The College Board books are the only collections of actual SATs available commercially, so please be sure you see the acorn logo and the College Board designation on any book of SATs you buy. Other books are ersatz SATs, and many of them bear little resemblance to the real thing. They are harder, or easier, or just different, so using them gives you a distorted sense of your status and progress. Actual SATs will allow you to get real feedback on your status and progress.

If you choose not to buy the College Board's book, you can still make substantial progress, but you will not have an easy way of measuring that progress prior to getting actual SAT scores returned to you. Being able to tell how you're doing ahead of time has obvious advantages. There is no way to suppress SAT scores as of this writing, and all SAT scores from the last two years of high school go to all colleges to which you apply.

Once you have the College Board's book, take the first exam on a timed basis, as directed. The answers are behind the test, along with directions for scoring and grading it. That is your baseline score. Whatever it is, *do not panic!* It's just a starting point. Even if it's so low you're embarrassed, it doesn't mean you can't go to college. It just means you need to work!

Once you've done an exam, it's time to look at the material herein and study it.If you were to learn every piece of information in this book and in the College Board's book, you would quite possibly score over

1500 on a bad day on the SAT! These books are quite comprehensive and are packed with the curricular knowledge tested on the SAT.

But you do not need to learn everything in the two books. It is a huge amount of material to cover. For most people, if you learn a third of the material, you'll go up significantly and change your test score profile for the colleges to which you're applying.

The most important parts to study in this book are: MathFacts™ 1 - 7; the Top 100 Words list; Math Worksheets I and II; New Math; the Grammar . . . Etc. chapter and Worksheet; Essay information; Mnemonics; Word Building and Discovery™ and WB&D Worksheets. If you have time, study the Latin dictionary and learn words in boldface and also the words in Words You Must Know. You'll have to count on going over the material 5 - 6 times or more. Do the worksheets on separate pieces of paper at least 6 - 8 times and look at the answers and explanations. When you've done it that many times, you will have memorized important facts and methods, and you'll know how to handle similar material on your test.

Difference Between Short-term and Long-term Memory

Repetition is critical in long-term memorization, which is what's tested on the SAT. A good analogy might be your best friend's phone number or your own cell phone number (as long as you don't have it on speed dial!). You don't need to look it up anymore, because you've dialed it so many times that it's imprinted on your brain. But when you first meet a person, you probably have to look up the number the first eight, ten or fifteen times you dial it. At a certain point, however, you realize you know the number and don't have to look it up. Likewise, material you're studying for the SAT needs to be repeated many times to put it into long-term memory.

Schools do a good job on a lot of things, but one thing that many are weak on is long-term memorization-the methods of how you study something so that you know it not just three minutes from now, but two months from now and six years from now. Repetition is the key to this.

The problem with repetition is that it's boring. So I apologize in advance for the fact that you are going to have to embark on something that isn't fun, exciting, or scintillating. You can probably come up with a list of 500 things you'd rather do!

But it will pay off if you do it. Not only is this material important for the SAT, but the problem-solving skills and vocabulary will serve you well in college and beyond. You'll use it in graduate or professional school (and yes, much of this material will come back to haunt you on the entrance exams for those programs!) and in your careers. It may not make you glad *while* you're learning it, but it's one of those things you'll be glad you did *after* it's done.

Methods for Long-term Memorization

Different methods work for different people. Some of my students have made flash cards out of index cards. Some have taken the Top 100 Words and taped them on a bedroom or bathroom wall (with parental permission) or a refrigerator. Some have put the words on their computers or audio players and listened to them incessantly. Others have drawn cartoons or put the words into sentences or made jokes incorporating the words or even color-coded them (some colors represented anger or happiness or relaxation). Whatever works for you is a good method, but do *something*. The only bad method is doing nothing!

For myself, when I was in high school trying to raise my Verbal score by developing my vocabulary (the best method for doing so, as it turns out), I wrote down words and definitions and would look at them, then cover up the definitions and see if I could say what the words meant. At first, I usually failed miserably and had no clue what the words meant. Then I'd look at the definitions again and . . . I *still* had no clue! This would go on for a while, and then I would *sort of* have a clue. And if I went two days without looking at the material, it would seem as though everything had fallen out of my brain. But eventually, after enough repetition, I knew the definitions, and didn't forget them from day to day or week to week. That's the goal. And it's tedious, but it does work.

[My impetus for trying to raise my scores was that my best friend in high school had received a perfect Verbal score and I felt really stupid next to her. I decided to try to raise the scores and did go up about 200 points. I didn't know I was going to make a career out of SATs, but that's another story! Only then, after my scores increased, did my friend tell me that my initial math score had been about 200 points higher than hers. Had I known that, I probably would have said, "Well, you're good at verbal and I'm good at math" and quit right there. But I'm glad I worked on this, because I went into college with far stronger skills and more confidence.]

I've never seen a student whose scores didn't improve significantly by studying these materials. The only time I've seen someone fail to go up is when the student simply didn't do the work. It's just like joining a gym: it isn't enough to pay your dues; you actually have to show up and work out! If paying the gym were enough, we'd all be gorgeous! As I said, this material is Boot Camp for Your Brain™. If you work hard at learning it, you will most likely come out not only with significantly higher scores but with a better level of preparation for college. The myth is that the SAT is irrelevant. Not so! For many-if not most-people, it contains a lot of material that you can use both academically and in your career.

In working on memorization, one thing that helps is humor. For some reason, it helps if you try to think of some silly way to memorize definitions. One of my students used to incorporate the vocabulary into jokes and she was quite successful in memorizing words. Humor helps us get through a lot of things in life, and the SAT can be one of them.

It also helps if you try to connect material to something that's already in your brain. For instance, if you look at the root *nav-*, meaning *ship* or *sail*, it will help if you think of *navy.* You know a navy has ships in it and they sail around. So when you see the root in a word like *circumnavigation,* it helps you define the word without a dictionary if you know that *circum*—means *around* (think if it being like a circle that goes around). You can reason out that *circumnavigation* means *sailing around the world* (circling back to where you started, in a ship).

Another technique is to create mnemonics (aids to memory). For instance, suppose you wanted to help yourself recall the spelling of the word *embarrass.* You might create the sentence *"Two Rats* were embarrassed by their *Sing-Song* voices." The two rats symbolize the two Rs in the word, and *sing-song* symbolizes the double S. That way, people can remember to put the double R and the double S in the word *embarrass* and spell it correctly. It's a silly little sentence, but after you memorize it, you won't ever again misspell the word.

It doesn't matter if the mnemonic is something that won't make sense to anyone else; if it works for you and you remember what you need to remember, that's great. For instance, sometimes when I'm memorizing phone numbers, I group three numbers like 506 and think *May 6* since that's almost how you'd write that date numerically. Because I do this, I no longer am memorizing random number sequences, but am able to recall 7 to 10 numbers at a time, by thinking of 506 - 0893 as two dates (the first being *May 6* and the second being *August of '93*), and it works. If it doesn't work for someone else, that's okay. All you need to do is come up with a method that works for you.

Throughout this book, there are suggestions on how to handle the SAT. If the suggestions help you, great! But sometimes you'll give something a fair try (that's important) and it won't work for you, so be prepared to throw out that advice. But do remember that it's possible to take a test on a day when you're tired or sick or distracted and not have things work. That can happen to anyone, so please don't decide on the basis of one test to toss out the advice.

Measuring Your Progress

Now, suppose you study this material a ton. After you've done some studying, it's time to take the second test in the College Board's book. Score and grade it and see how you've improved. If you've truly studied, you're probably going to see improvement unless you're sick, tired and/or distracted, in which case you will see improvement the next time. In my course, students generally take 5 - 6 tests total, with intensive studying in between. Simply taking tests without studying will not help you. Occasionally students will, without learning anything new, continue to make the same kinds of errors over and over, and their scores will not budge. Not you, though! You, of course, are going to study like crazy, right?!

After you've graded each test, your job is to go look up the methods for math problems you've missed and the definitions of vocabulary words you don't know (many of which are conveniently in this book), and work on them. SATs are not identical from administration to administration, but they are very similar in content. So when you learn the material you didn't know on the last test (say, averages and totals), you get all those problems right on the next test, and *voila!* your scores go up. There is really no magic to it, just work.

If you plug away at learning the material in this text, you should see a major change in what you know how to do on the test. Since there are actual SATs in the College Board's book, what you achieve on them is a very good indicator of how you'll do when you go into that room and take the dreaded test for college entrance purposes. Only now it won't be so dreaded, because you'll know what's there.

Do take time to familiarize yourself with the test directions and math reference information in the College Board's book. When you take the actual test, you can merely glance at the directions and the reference information to make sure it's identical to what you've already seen. Then you'll have more time during the test to check your work, complete the problems and questions, etc.

Demystification is the name of the game. I don't have the actual test you're going to take to get into Harvard or the University of Nebraska or wherever, but I do know the specific subjects that get covered over and over on the SAT and they are here in this book. All you have to do is get them from these pages and into your brain. Alas, I don't have a magic wand to wave over you. That would be nice, but it doesn't exist.

But if you are interested in seeing your scores increase, seeing what your brain can do, learning some things that will help you in college and the rest of your life, the requisite material is here.

A Pep Talk

Having worked with tons of students since 1989, I have seen many students utterly improve their options for college. I'd like you to do so too. If you have questions or comments, please feel free to email me at info@bestprep.com or check out www.bestprep.com. Some of you may even decide to take the entire program. Wherever you are, we can work with you.

But whether you take the course or merely read and study this material, you can end up with much, much better SAT scores if you try. And please tell us how much your scores go up-we love to hear from students!

Note: sometimes students who start out with relatively high scores on the SAT are understandably not as interested in raising their scores. Be aware that the closer you are to the top score, the harder it is to go up. There may be more productive uses of time than increasing your score once you are already at that level.

Perspective

In general, please remember that the SAT is not the most important thing in life. It is an important test for college entrance purposes, but don't drive yourself crazy trying to get top scores. It's important to find time to volunteer in your community, take challenging courses and do well at them, spend time with family and friends, exercise, take part in activities in your school, think, sleep, have fun, help others, etc., etc. It's important to have a perspective on what good SAT scores can and cannot do, and to realize they are just one small part of who you are.

In all the time I've run this course, I've only had one student who did not get into college (he didn't work and didn't show up for class, apparently hoping I'd have that magic wand). Everyone worries about being the second one! But unless you absolutely don't *try* to learn this stuff, you *can* develop your skills. Scientists used to think human brain capacity was fixed at age 3, but recent research points to an 8- to 10-year window between ages 13 and the early 20s when the brain develops a lot. So this is your second chance to become a genius! I say this only half-facetiously; you don't know what your intellectual capacity is until you try: You're Smarter Than You Think™.

The One-Hour-A-Day Theory

And now my One-Hour-A-Day Theory: anything you practice for an hour a day, you will get better at, in spite of yourself! An hour is just a suggestion; you may be able to get by with less.

I learned this when our son wanted me to play tennis with him when he was much younger. I said, "Okay, but I'm terrible at it. I'll play with you, but you can't make fun of me." I couldn't serve, couldn't volley, and didn't have a clue about strategy. But we played regularly (amidst a lot of laughter at how much I truly stank) and the amazing thing was that I began to be able to serve and hit the ball, and to notice simple things like the fact that I could aim the ball where my son wasn't standing or watch where he was hitting it and run to that spot and actually have a chance of hitting it back. These are laughably obvious to those of you who play tennis, but to me, the World's Worst Tennis Player, they were revelations!

If this could happen to me in tennis, it could work anywhere. If you put in time and practice, you will get better, in spite of yourself. What most people do, however, when they're bad at something (or think they are), is avoid the activity like the plague. Thus they never get the practice that would make them improve, and they continue to stink at it! But if you decide to practice something anyhow, while suspending any expectation of failure or success, you can make substantial progress.

Sometimes we just have to make ourselves do stuff. It's not fun or exciting, but it's good for us. So we do stomach crunches, brush our teeth, take out the garbage and all that, knowing that we simply have to do these things because they benefit us. SAT studying is like that. But it can have a big payoff. I've seen lots of students over the years become more competitive in applying to college and in getting scholarship money as a result of the effort they expended. Here's hoping your prospects will improve greatly as a result of studying this material.

Good luck to you!

Study Skills

You've studied for ages. It feels like millennia! And everyone hands you a study skills guide. We hereby do our bit!

Yes, we know. Everybody always hands out a thing about study skills, and it is traditionally boring, pedantic and not even necessarily useful in terms of bottom-line effectiveness. Will we manage to be different? Will you learn some skills that actually help you perform better academically? Gee, we hope so!

Lots of these study skill edicts say to find a quiet place with no distractions. The only remaining quiet place with no distractions is in Nepal, and at last check they were putting a highway right smack in the middle of it. Seriously, what I'm trying to say is that you may have to study under non-ideal conditions, so it makes a certain amount of sense to accept that it is indeed possible to derive great benefits from studying in the midst of a certain amount of chaos (*i.e.*, Life). It turns out that among graduate students, the highest grades are generally earned by older students, who have families, jobs, etc. They are often quite motivated to learn even in the midst of interruptions by small and large offspring, errands and jobs, and the many detailed tasks that are part of running complicated households.

It is often suggested that students refrain from studying with the TV or stereo turned on, and this may in fact be a good idea for most students. A quiet place to get organized and get one's thoughts in order is also a good idea. Certainly there is much to be said for the etiquette of families trying to respect each other's need for peace and quiet. Yet we recognize that in many households there is neither the space nor the privacy for a study niche. The watchwords are: do your best, and accept the rest.

Reading and Rereading

When you confront unfamiliar material, there is often a tendency to be overwhelmed by a sense that it will never be mastered, or even-if it is wholly abstract to you-understood. Please be aware that this is a very common phenomenon, but that the best (read: most successful) students take unfamiliarity and discouragement with a grain of salt.

A second reading of the material will generally cause the reader to feel, "Hey, some of these ideas are my friends!" or to put it differently, that some of the ideas do look a bit more familiar and less threatening. A third reading may create more of that sense. It may help you to realize that even some of the top students we've known have reported this phenomenon. One student was a whiz at biology, math, physiology and foreign languages, but found physics and computer technology to be very daunting. It took many readings and rereadings of material for it to be comprehensible, and additional efforts at outlining and studying for the material to sink in.

Outlining

One student we knew in graduate school maintained a 4-point average even when taking courses that were quite difficult for her. What was the secret? Well, we could say something vapid like "hard work," but you'd be left knowing nothing about how to effect great results yourself unless we dissected it:

One of the key things the student did was that she outlined all the material covered in textbooks and class lectures and put all the key facts, diagrams, relationships, etc., into this form. Something about writing down material helps the brain remember it better (no doubt there will be research documenting this someday if there hasn't already been some). Also, writing down the material separates the wheat from the chaff and gives students less material to review prior to tests. It is important to number each side of each sheet of paper as you go so that you can put sheets into logical order (obviously, this is unnecessary if you are not using loose sheets of paper).

Frequent Review and
Spare Change Amounts of Studying

For some reason, students tend to think (1) that they should study in huge chunks of time, and (2) that they should seldom or never review material. But the most effective use of your time will often be five- to fifteen-minute periods during which you can study a few vocabulary words or a couple pages of reading. If you carry your study materials with you during your day, you will often have the opportunity to learn a little bit here, a little bit there. And the little bits add up. Obviously, it's also important to have extended sessions in order to digest more complicated material and to work on problems in a meaningful way, but you will benefit greatly from having numerous shorter sessions that reinforce the learning in the longer sessions.

You can take a page of your Latin words and see in ten minutes if you can remember their meanings. You can test yourself on whether you remember the rules about angles in about five minutes. You can read a page of the assigned materials or do two or three problems in five minutes. Each investment you make will reinforce the learning and help make it a permanent part of your repertoire.

Many kinds of learning require repetition. It is important for you to understand this so you won't expect to learn something from reading it once. Even the students labeled "brains" usually know the material only because they have gone over it enough times to make it theirs.

Testing Yourself

Sometimes people will read and reread material many times and therefore assume they could take a test on the material and do quite well. This is often a false assumption. It's a good idea to test yourself frequently on all material you are covering so you can see whether you actually know it.

Please don't feel discouraged if you have pockets of ignorance. It's better to find out now that you need more studying than to realize it awkwardly during a test, when there isn't a lot you can do about it.

Writing It Down

We mentioned that outlining material is useful. So is any other writing down of material you're trying to learn, since writing involves motor and visual reinforcement of learning. If you write down vocabulary words or math theorems, you will aid the learning process. For some reason, seeing things in your own writing helps learning.

Working With Others

Misery loves company, so perhaps you can study with friends. We strongly recommend that you do at least 75% of your studying solo since it is easy to find that a group has neglected to cover essential material; also, because groups have particular strengths and weaknesses in the material that may not be the same as your own, you may find yourself spending valuable time on things you already know and not focusing on material in which you need lots of work.

Groups can boost morale, counteract boredom, and provide a social aspect to studying; and group members can balance each other's strengths and weaknesses and thus help one another. You just need to be careful to provide yourself with enough individual study time so that you can counteract the potential group shortcomings listed above.

Organizing Time and Prioritizing

At the college level, students often will be given a lot of assignments in a clump; it's important for students to get used to figuring out where best to spend their time and energy, since they may not have enough of either to do everything.

It's common in college and graduate school to be given a course syllabus, which lists daily class assignments and/or deadlines for major projects. For instance, a student might have a two-page lab report due at the end of Week 2, an oral presentation in Week 6, a midterm in Week 8, a fifteen- to twenty-page term paper due in Week 14, and a final exam in Week 16. It is up to the student to organize his or her time in order to meet the deadlines. It's a good idea to combine all course schedules into a master calendar or schedule, so that you don't have a bunch of fragmented lists floating around that have no relationship to one another. Also, if you discover when you put all your various deadlines into a master list that Week 7 is horrendous, you may need to do some things to adjust as early as Week 3 or 4 in order to avoid a pile-up.

Suppose your syllabus tells you that your midterm is worth twenty points, your final is worth thirty points, your term paper is worth thirty points, class participation is worth ten points, and lab reports and the oral presentation are together worth ten points. This breakdown will help you decide to focus relatively less time on your lab reports than on your term paper, though it's probably not a good idea to do a sloppy job on the first assignment; first impressions are hard to overcome, and you don't want to give your professor a bad first impression even if it's only worth three points. But those percentages do give you an indication of where to put your time, and they very commonly show up on a course syllabus.

Time Constraints and Conflicts

Few people have the luxury of focusing all their attention on any one endeavor. Most of us lead multi-faceted lives and need to put our energy, time and attention in a variety of places. Students studying this material also attend high school, do homework, participate in after school sports and other activities, have part- or full-time jobs, enjoy friendships, and live in families where there are chores and other family obligations and involvements to consider.

It would be pointless to focus 100% of your time on studying for the SAT if to do so would mean that your grades plummeted. Furthermore, I feel that there is more to life than applying to colleges, however all-consuming that process may seem. I recognize that you are busy people and that you have many involvements which of necessity create time constraints that affect your ability to study for the SAT.

Obviously, as in the rest of life, what you get out of this material is proportional to what you put into it, but time is only one of the potential inputs. Your energy, enthusiasm and willingness to learn are at least equally important in determining what you will gain from this program. All things being equal (which, of course, they rarely are), the student who spends fifteen minutes a day for six weeks will not get as much out of this material as the one who starts at the end of his or her sophomore year of high school and puts in forty-five minutes a day for eighteen months before the November SAT of his or her senior year. There is a lot of material that can be covered herein, and students who can give more time to it stand a better chance of having a more dramatic effect on their scores.

Most people can find quite a bit of extra time if they consider studying while they're standing in line, waiting at the orthodontist's office, riding on the subway or on a bus, etc. But suppose you simply don't have forty-five minutes a day, even in five-minute dribs and drabs throughout the day. Don't despair. You should do what you can do and not sweat it; there's no point tormenting yourself if you are already doing the best you can and there simply isn't any more time available. Just try to prioritize and determine where your time will most valuably be spent. Perhaps this advice sounds esoteric or abstract, but you will find that with practice, it gets easier to see where you should put your time and energy in order to get optimal results.

Relaxing

Relaxing?! Am I kidding?! How can you relax when you have to worry about getting into the college of your choice (or even into *any* college)? Don't I understand how critical this whole business is? Don't I know how hard it is to relax when you're this tense?!

Yep. I do. It's just that I also know that people can become needlessly overwrought and make themselves thoroughly miserable over things that are not fully within their control. Give it your best shot to get into a particular school and work hard to bring your application portfolio up to a certain level, but please understand that some of the admissions officers at top schools acknowledge that up to 60% or even 80% of those rejected are capable of being successful students at their schools. There is a certain luck of the draw even after you've done everything you can. So you have to recognize that what happens in terms of college rejections and acceptances is not fully a function of what you do.

It is well and good to work hard, to have goals, and to strive for those goals, but it is important to develop a sense of balance and perspective. Believe it or not, you may find that relaxing and pacing yourself sensibly yields better results than driving yourself relentlessly and pushing yourself past reasonable limits. Certainly, part of having balance and perspective is managing to create islands of calm for yourself in the middle of chaos, a skill which will be invaluable as your life progresses. The ability to say, "It is now time to relax, to play, to laugh," will help you keep up your spirits. Having a sense of humor helps; sometimes you can tell yourself that an unpleasant event will make a funny story someday. But whatever your goals in life, all work and no play does make both Jack and Jill rather dull. Try to balance your life and keep up your mental, emotional and physical health, for even the attainment of goals for which you have worked hard can feel remarkably empty when you're physically or emotionally drained from the effort.

Since part of the goal of The World's Best Prep Course, Inc. is to enhance students' college admissions prospects at least insofar as SAT scores are concerned, we dislike mentioning the possibility of college rejections, but there is one final point we think should be stated: sometimes, a rejection may seem like the end of the world. It's not. It is at most a temporary setback. People who don't get into the colleges of their choice often find great happiness later in life (and often not very far in the future from the rejection letter's arrival). We have known many outstanding people who have received rejection letters and who felt disappointed, but who ultimately have looked at those setbacks as a temporary blip on the screen, so to speak, something that counts not at all in the long run. Sometimes we think it is lamentable that the college applications procedure has become Ulcer City. While it is my job to do what I can to beef up the SAT portion of students' applications, I hate to see so many unhappy people or at least people who are setting themselves up to be wholly miserable if they do not get into a specific college or university.

The Long Run

If you look at the study skills you use herein as a long-run venture, rather than mere attempts to cram enough material into your brains to survive the SAT, you will take something out of this curriculum that can be invaluable not only in academia but in other parts of your life. It is important to learn to manage your time, maintain a master list of things to do, prioritize, set goals, make use of dribs and drabs of time, relax and have a sense of balance and humor. Did the other study guides tell you to have a sense of humor? I didn't think so!

Overview of the New SAT

The SAT changes prove the old saying, "The more things change, the more they stay the same."

Yes, there are changes, but not to key curricular material. Students still need to have a command of how to problem-solve in math; they still must show reading skills and analyze passages; and they still need to know how to write—all areas covered extensively in this book.

Having weathered a number of changes to the SAT in the past, I will tell you that my experience is that skills are often relabeled, but not really changed at base. For instance, The Test of Standard Written English was eliminated at one point and essentially resurrected years later in the Writing section: both essentially tested grammar, syntax, punctuation, and so forth. By some reports, changes in one go-round took five years and cost $30 million. What changed? Well, they eliminated analogies, made reading passages a larger percentage of the Reading sections, added an essay and the aforementioned Writing questions to test grammar, and in Math added the median, the mode and slope of a line. They added functional notation at one point, supposedly to reflect Algebra II courses in high school, but really they had tested functions for decades with funky little symbols that defined those functions, symbols like & or * or #, always defined within each problem so people could solve the functions.

So, why am I telling you this?

Because I want you to relax. If you think you are entering uncharted territory, you might panic, right? But if you know that the SAT is still based on regular skills which you can acquire if you have not already done so, you can rest assured that this is all a doable task. You don't have to panic or give up sleep or stop going to school or give up on your college dreams. Chances are, you've covered much of this in school. If you have forgotten material, or if you never really learned it, or if you haven't yet had it in school, you can nonetheless beef up your skill set and do well on the current version of the SAT.

So what has changed? For all the talk, as I said, not as much as one might imagine. But here are a few areas:

A concept called "Command of Evidence" by the College Board expects you to focus on clear analysis of ideas in the Reading Test, of sentences and passages in the Writing and Language Test, and of a passage you'll read before doing your SAT Essay. Of course, the SAT has always expected you to analyze clearly!

Word definitions will be tested in context, but knowing the meanings of words is still important. Without a command of vocabulary, context doesn't help as much as one might wish. But for years, vocabulary has been taking an increasingly smaller seat on the test, and that trend merely continues. So students are not encouraged to spend the bulk of their studying time on vocabulary development.

You'll have texts and informational graphics to analyze in Reading sections and there will be some contextual material in science, social studies and historical ideas, as well as United States founding documents like the Bill of Rights, the Declaration of Independence or perhaps the Federalist Papers, and sources world-wide on issues like liberty, human rights and dignity, and concepts in justice. You might read a passage written by Martin Luther King, Jr. or Nelson Mandela or Gandhi. While I salute the College Board for including such critical topics on the SAT, on a curricular level one still must rely on the ability to read, analyze and understand, and those abilities must be nourished whatever the reading selection topic.

The essay topic involves reading a passage and showing how the writer constructs the argument. It is now a 50-minute essay instead of a 25-minute essay, and it's more analytical now. Students still have to know how to construct sentences and paragraphs and build cohesive essays; they still must know rules of grammar, punctuation, syntax and usage. Because these rules are still important, some exercises in this book use slightly different formats than questions on the current test to build your skills. While the essay is optional, some schools require or highly recommend doing it, so it is not necessarily actually optional for any given student.

On multiple choice questions, there are four answer choices rather than five. Students are no longer penalized for wrong answers. But it is still important to maximize the number of correct answers one gets, so one mustn't be too, too excited about the lack of penalties for wrong answers!

Math is divided into two parts, one which allows calculator use and another which does not. Please do not be intimidated by setting aside your calculator, but do practice going without it so you get more secure during those questions. For the record, I have never found the use of a calculator to be needed on any SAT, nor have I ever used one on an SAT (though I do know how to use one!) and I have taken way, way more of these tests over a number of decades than any student will ever have to take. The Math questions will include algebra, data analysis, some complex equations, geometry and some trigonometry, so basically if you practice and learn the material herein, you'll be fine.

A little over 20% of the math questions will be gridding-in your answers, not doing multiple choice.

Once again, practicing on real sample SATs put out by the source, The College Board, is far and away the best way to prep, along with materials like this book you are reading and Strunk and White's *The Elements of Style*.

My feeling is that the test has supposedly been redesigned to focus on skills needed for college, but the SAT has always focused on those skills. Those who have mastered the material covered herein will do well, and those who haven't done so will do less well.

Despite the wishful thinking of those who want quick gimmicks or ready tricks to outsmart the test, the reality is what it always has been: there is no substitute for knowing the curricular material that comprises the test.

A quick comparison of old and new SATs:

The old one lasted 3 hours, 45 minutes. The new one lasts 3 hours, with an additional 50 minutes for that "optional" essay. I suggest you do the essay, because if you need it for a particular school, you'll have it under your belt already and not have to scramble to retake the test.

Old components were called Critical Reading, Writing, Mathematics and Essay. Here's a case where labels on the new test are really just reconfigured: Evidenced-Based Reading and Writing is composed of Reading questions and Writing and Language questions. There's Math. And there's that optional Essay.

I could list the important feature differences, but to me, as someone who feels things have been renamed rather than really changed so much, I'll pass on doing so, because only real changes need to be listed. Old scores ranged from a low of 600 on the test to a high total score of 2400, with lows of 200 and highs of 800 on each of 3 areas: Critical Reading, Mathematics, and Essay and Writing. New scores range from 400 to 1600 total, with lows of 200 and highs of 800 on Evidence-Based Reading and Writing, and on Math. and 2 to 8 on each of 3 aspects of the Essay. Essay outcomes are reported separately from the rest of the test.

There was no sub-score report on the old test, and there is one on the new test.

On the old test, the essay was given first thing, in Section 1. The essay is given at the end of the new test.

Old test: Critical Reading was allotted 70 minutes for 67 questions. Writing allowed 60 minutes for 49 questions. Essay took 25 minutes for 1 essay. Math allowed 70 minutes for 54 questions, for a total of 225 minutes for 171 questions or tasks.

New test: Reading allots 65 minutes, Writing and Language 35 minutes, Essay 50 minutes, Math 80 minutes for a total of 180 questions or tasks without the essay and 230 with the Essay.

That's it in a nutshell.

So now, all you have to do is learn the stuff herein and you'll be fine. You might supplement with a few readings of founding documents and, say, Nelson Mandela's writings or a tract of Gandhi's and you'll be ready.

MathFacts™

Seven invaluable modules on algebra, geometry and arithmetic

The first thing to know about the math on the SAT is that it's algebra 1 and 2, geometry, and arithmetic—no pre-calculus, no calculus, no post-calculus. (One time, a student said during class, "Can't you do this problem using integral calculus?" and everyone else in the room got visibly pale and nervous-looking. "Yes, you could," I answered, "but it isn't necessary to know calculus. It doesn't even save time to use it on this problem." An audible sigh of relief swept the room as people realized they were still in the running for college).

And there isn't any of that really fancy stuff you see in the typical algebra or geometry class. There are no proofs. The same kinds of problems show up over and over again, so it is actually possible to learn the skills necessary to solve them. Many problems just involve setting up equations correctly (maybe translating English into "equation language") and manipulating both sides of the equation equally, *e.g.*, if you have $x + 3 = 4y$, and you want to solve the equation in terms of x, you just subtract 3 from both sides of the equal sign and get $x = 4y - 3$.

Sound familiar? You *can* do this stuff. Please don't worry if you've always hated math or thought you stank at it. Sometimes people think of themselves a certain way, as being clumsy or bad at math or shy, and then they avoid any experience that would prove otherwise. But I've seen people go up enormously on the SAT, and you can be one of them.

These modules aren't *that* big or hairy. You can memorize everything herein, and you should truly know it well enough that if you were to close the book, you could teach it to someone else and visualize what's on every page. This requires more than one reading, obviously, unless you are one of those lucky people with a photographic memory, in which case you probably aced your SATs the first time around. For the rest of us, we need to go over and over things.

That's not so terrible, though. It doesn't mean we're not smart enough, and there isn't a bigger prize if you learn something after two repetitions rather than twelve repetitions. The main thing is: did you eventually put this stuff into your brain? I hope the answer will be a resounding *"Yes!"*

MathFacts™ 1

Everything You Always Wanted to Know About Triangles

The Bermuda Triangle has nothing on the rest of the triangles in the world. Just as ships have allegedly disappeared into its watery jaws, so have many students allegedly disappeared in the three angles and three sides of garden-variety triangles, and they have been heard to moan in agony at the very words *isosceles* and *equilateral*.

Relax, mates. You are about to learn all you need to know about triangles.

First off, a plane-geometry triangle-the only kind on the SAT-is a two-dimensional (flat) figure with three angles and three sides (the *tri*-prefix is your tip-off; it means *three* just as in *tricycle*). Since it's two-dimensional, we can compute area:

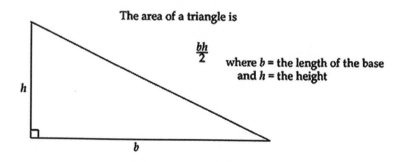

The area of a triangle is

$$\frac{bh}{2}$$

where *b* = the length of the base and *h* = the height

h

b

This formula works for any kind of triangle, as you may see by the examples below:

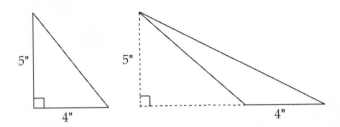

These 2 triangles have identical area: 10 square inches.

The three angles of a triangle always add up to 180 degrees. This is true even if one of those angles has 170 degrees in it, in which case the remaining two have 10 degrees to share, and we have a very skinny elongated triangle.

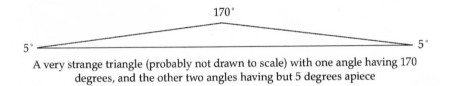

A very strange triangle (probably not drawn to scale) with one angle having 170 degrees, and the other two angles having but 5 degrees apiece

Now, suppose you want to compute the lengths of the sides of a right triangle (and I guarantee there will be a point during the SAT when this desire will befall you). Let's take an example which has a shortcut that can save you precious minutes during the exam. The Pythagorean Theorem says that the sum of the squares of the lengths of the two shortest sides of a right triangle is equal to the square of the length of the hypotenuse, which is the side opposite the right-or 90 degree-angle:

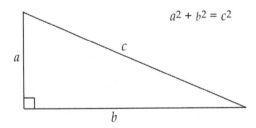

$$a^2 + b^2 = c^2$$

What this means is, if you add together the squares of the two shorter side lengths, you get the square of the hypotenuse. (Pythagoras was a philosopher in the sixth century B.C., so you can see that students have been dealing with his theorem for well over 2000 years, and many of them wish he had stuck to the normal philosophical questions of "Why are we here?" and "What is the essence of life?" rather than messing around with mathematics. But I guarantee: if you just learn it once and for all, this part of the SAT will forever be easier for you to grasp and master.)

Now comes the fancy part that saves you time on the SAT! Suppose the test tells you $a = 3$ and $b = 4$. Do you have to use the formula above to compute the answer? No! You get to pass GO and collect $200 because you've learned this shortcut:

> If $a = 3$ and $b = 4$, then $c = 5$.
> If $a = 6$ and $b = 8$, then $c = 10$.
> If $a = 9$ and $b = 12$, then $c = 15$.

Do you see a pattern?

This works for every right triangle with every multiple of 3, 4 and 5. So, if $a = 30{,}639$, and $b = 40{,}852$, then $c = 51{,}065$. You don't need to calculate squares and square roots, and thus you save time for tough questions.

What about equilateral triangles? If you know your Word Building and Discovery™ stuff, you see that *equi*—means *equal* and *lateral* is Latin for *side*. So an equilateral triangle is one where all three sides are the same length. This also means that all three angles are the same size. Now, since there are *always* (in every plane-geometry triangle everywhere on the face of planet Earth) 180 degrees total for all three angles, there must be 60 degrees in each angle in an equilateral triangle (180 divided by 3 = 60).

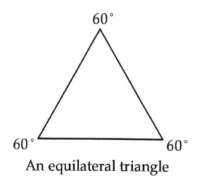

An equilateral triangle

Now, if you are told the length of any side of an equilateral triangle, you therefore know the length of each other side, and you can figure out the perimeter of the triangle (three times the length of any one side). Also, there is a particular kind of triangle which results when you make a line from the top of the "pyramid" that an equilateral triangle resembles, and make that line perpendicular to the base of the triangle.

Since a perpendicular line in math is one which forms or intersects at right angles, we are back to right triangles.

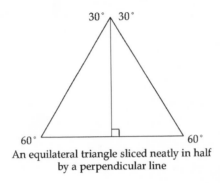

An equilateral triangle sliced neatly in half
by a perpendicular line

Well, let's take either one of these two resulting right triangles. It has one 90 degree angle, and one sixty degree angle, so the remaining angle is a 30 degree angle (30 + 60 + 90 = 180). We go back to the Pythagorean Theorem. If the side opposite the 30 degree angle has a length of 1, the hypotenuse will have a length of 2 and the third side (the one opposite the 60 degree angle) will have a length of "the square root of 3." This relationship also works for multiples of 1, 2, and the square root of 3 (For instance, if the hypotenuse length is 4, then the side opposite the 30 degree angle is 2 (it's always half the length of the hypotenuse in a 30 - 60 - 90 triangle), and the remaining side length is two times the square root of 3.

An isosceles triangle has two equal sides, which means that two of the three angles are also equal. The SAT often contains problems that use a special form called a right isosceles triangle, where one angle is 90 degrees and the two equal angles are each 45 degrees. Because it's a right triangle, the hypotenuse length can be computed by the Pythagorean Theorem.

If each of the equal sides of a right isosceles triangle is 1 in length, then the hypotenuse length will be the square root of 2. Once again, this works for multiples, so that if the equal sides' lengths are 2, the hypotenuse measures "2 times the square root of 2." Etc., etc., etc.

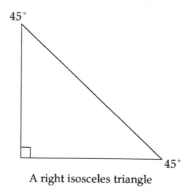

A right isosceles triangle

There is one more Pythagorean triangle configuration, in which if one side measures 5, and another side measures 12, the hypotenuse measures 13. This also works for all multiples: if one side is 10, and another side is 24, then the hypotenuse is 26. So we have the "3 - 4 - 5" triangle, the "5 - 12 - 13" triangle, the "1 - 2-square root of 3" triangle, and the "1 - 1-square root of 2" triangle, where multiples of these relationships hold true too, as long as they are the same multiple for each side in the triangle.

We covered perimeter of an equilateral triangle, but it's just as easy to find perimeter of any triangle, for the perimeter is the total of all three side lengths added together, just as if you were taking a walk all the way around a triangle and ending up back where you started.

Now, from the information in this MathFacts™ unit, you should have no difficulty finding area, perimeter and angle measures in most situations. Other helpful facts will appear in other MathFacts™ units.

You have earned a break, and the right to enjoy it heartily.

MathFacts™ 2

Angles and Parallel Lines and the Slope of a Line

Everybody's got to have an angle on the SAT, and you are no exception. If you want to do well on those questions regarding angles, you should study well the material below.

When two straight lines intersect (cross each other), vertical angles are equal.

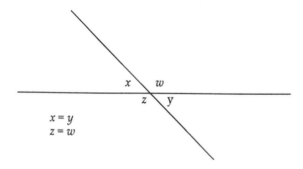

$x = y$
$z = w$

Two straight lines intersecting, and the resulting angle relationships

Since all three angles in a triangle add up to 180 degrees, and since there are 180 degrees in a straight angle (which looks remarkably like a straight line to most of us, because it is), there are some nifty things you can figure out about angle measurements if you combine the above facts.

You can figure out that if one angle in the figure below measures 40 degrees, and another one measures 80 degrees, the remaining interior angle measures 60 degrees (and so does its vertical angle outside the triangle).

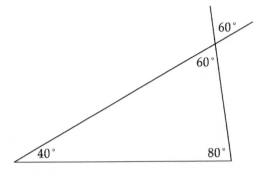

In the case below, if you know that one interior angle has 60 degrees, and the exterior angle has 140 degrees, you can figure out the other two interior angles; since 140 + ? = 180 degrees, one angle has 40 degrees. And since 60 + 40 + ? = 180 degrees, there are 80 degrees in the remaining angle.

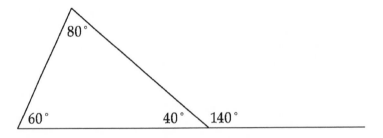

Suppose that you have two parallel lines which you intersect with a third straight line:

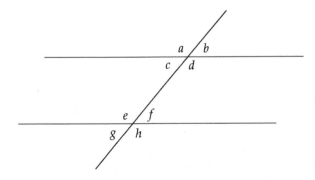

In the above drawing, we have labeled the angles a, b, c, d, e, f, g, and h. The following things are true: $a = d = e = h$; and $b = c = f = g$. Now, since $a + b = 180$ degrees, we can substitute, say, d for a and c for b, and the statement will remain equally true.

Another interesting angle fact is this: If you have a four-sided polygon, the sum of its angles will be 360 degrees, since it can be divided into two 180-degree triangles. Similarly, a five-sided polygon (see below) will have 540 degrees worth of total angles. A six-sided polygon will have 720 degrees in total angles. If you forget this, you can just draw subdivisions into triangles, count how many triangles you get and multiply that number by 180 degrees, and you will have the correct number that is the sum of all the angles in the polygon.

A shortcut is to take the number of sides of the polygon and subtract 2, then multiply the resulting number by 180. For instance, a pentagon has 5 sides. Five minus two is three. Three times 180 is 540, the correct number of degrees for a pentagon.

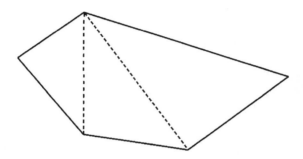

The slope of a line is a simple concept if you envision a corporate chart showing profits. If the line slopes from the lower left-hand corner to the upper right-hand corner, the slope is positive (*i.e.*, the company's profits are growing); if it slopes from the upper left-hand corner to the lower right-hand corner, the slope is negative (the company's profits are shrinking).

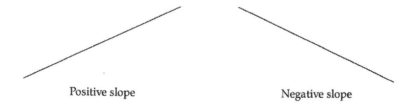

Positive slope   Negative slope

Anytime you have a problem involving slope, think of this diagram in deciding whether the slope is positive or negative.

The computation of the slope of a line is also easy: just take the "rise" over the "run". For example, if the line runs from 3 to 6 on the x-axis, and rises from 4 to 8 on the y-axis, the "rise" is 4 (which is 8 minus 4) and the "run" is 3 (which is 6 minus 3), so the slope is 4/3. If the line runs from 3 to 6 on the x - axis and from 8 to 4 (downward) on the y - axis, the slope is -4/3. For *any* two points (a,b) and (c,d), the slope will be $(d - b)/(c - a)$, where b and d are y-coordinates and a and c are x-coordinates.

End of module; this is a short one, so you can afford to go over it twice, unless it's already crystal-clear to you. Be honest with yourself when you cover material: if you know it already, fine; but if you need work in this area, make the time for it. You'll thank yourself for your own diligence during the SAT.

MathFacts™ 3

Area, Perimeter, Volume and Circumference

Area, perimeter and volume often seem like the kind of thing someone else should figure out. For instance, when you have carpeting installed, the carpet people measure the area of your house. When you buy a carton of milk, someone else has already figured out how much milk it can hold. Few of us will have to figure out the perimeters of our housing lots or the Louvre or anything else, but on the SAT, this stuff shows its face and the carpet guy is nowhere around. You are alone in a room full of test-takers. But you will carry in your brain the information below, so there's no reason to panic, or merely guess the answer, or cancel your college plans. You are *ready*.

The area of a triangle is covered in MathFacts™ 1. But to recap, the area of a triangle is base times height, divided by two.

The area of a rectangle equals length times width, and the perimeter is $2(L + W)$, where L is the length and W is the width.

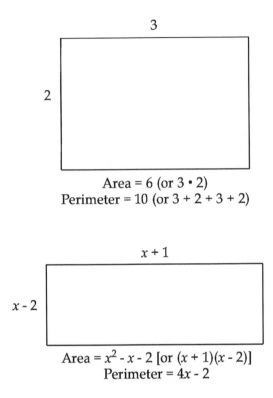

Area = 6 (or 3 • 2)
Perimeter = 10 (or 3 + 2 + 3 + 2)

Area = $x^2 - x - 2$ [or $(x + 1)(x - 2)$]
Perimeter = $4x - 2$

Circles often cause people to panic, because they see a weird little symbol for *pi* (π), the 16th letter of the Greek alphabet. People feel aggrieved enough having to learn math without having π thrown in, but really you should be glad when you see the symbol for π; it is a lot easier than seeing the number 3.14159, which is a rounded-off approximation of the value of π. The decimal places of the computation have been carried out to billions of positions and it never *ever* repeats itself. This makes the symbol for *pi* seem like a piece of cake (no pun intended).

The area of a circle = πr^2, with *r* standing for the radius. The radius is half the diameter of a circle (the diameter *d* being a straight line going through the center of the circle and touching the periphery of the circle on both sides). The circumference of a circle = $2\pi r$, or, since $d = 2r$, the circumference of a circle = πd.

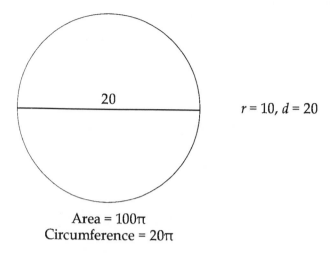

$r = 10, d = 20$

Area = 100π
Circumference = 20π

The volume questions on the SAT do not seem as fancy as many covered in the typical high school geometry course, but you should know how to compute the volume of a box, also known as a rectangular solid.

The volume of a rectangular solid = *LWH*, or length times width times height.

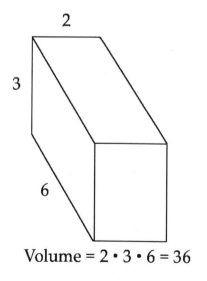

Volume = 2 • 3 • 6 = 36

This solid has variables given for the side lengths, but the formula *LWH* still applies:

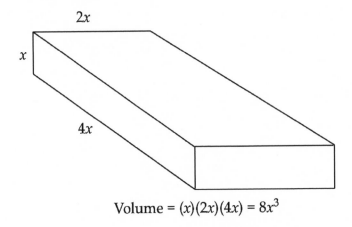

Volume $= (x)(2x)(4x) = 8x^3$

In a cube (imagine dice), in which each of the six faces is a square, the volume may be computed by using the length of one edge (length, width or height, since all are the same) and cubing it: if length is 2 inches, volume will be 8 cubic inches.

That's it for area, perimeter and volume. It's not a great amount of info relative to the much fancier info you've covered about the volume of cones and cylinders and such, so consider yourself as getting off easy and feel grateful as you memorize it!

MathFacts™ 4

Integers, Positive and Negative Numbers, Odd and Even Numbers, and Percentages, Ratios and Fractions (a Toughie)

There are a lot of things that show up on the SAT which you started acquiring years ago, as far back as first grade or even earlier. For instance, simple addition, such as "1 + 1 = 2" is a necessary concept. So is subtraction: "4 - 2 = 2." Multiplication ("3 • 2 = 6") and division ("4 ÷ 2 = 2") show up also.

Most of these concepts are second nature to you by now, and your main concern with them is that you check your answers and avoid careless mistakes. Most people hate to check their answers, because they didn't particularly enjoy doing the problem the first time around, and they sure as heck don't feel like doing it a second time. But make yourself a promise that you *will* double-check your answers if you have time left over on the SAT, and also verify every time that you've put your pencil mark neatly as directed in the correct answer space and erased any changed answers or stray marks thoroughly. There are in fact people who don't know the answer to question #3 in a section and then go on to question #4 and put its answer inadvertently into one of the ovals in answer #3, and thus throw off the rest of their answers for the whole section. Try to eyeball where you should be on your answer sheet and be sure you're putting your answers in the correct spaces.

Odd and even numbers are a simple concept. All even numbers are divisible by 2 with nothing left over. Thus 0, 2, 4, 6, 8, 10, 100, and 412 are all even numbers. These numbers may be positive (greater than 0) or negative (less than 0). Odd numbers (also positive or negative) are not evenly divisible by 2. Thus, 1, 3, 5, 7, 9, 11, 49, 613, 717, and 819 are all odd numbers.

There are rules you should learn about even and odd numbers: If you add two even numbers together, the result is an even number. Just try a sample like "2 + 2 = 4" if you forget this rule (one of the great things to remember is that if you are sitting in a room taking the SAT and, horror of horrors, you have forgotten a rule, you can usually reconstruct it by taking a very simple example that takes just a few seconds to compute).

An odd number added to an odd number also gives an even number (*e.g.,* "1 + 3 = 4").

An even number added to an odd number creates an odd number (*e.g.,* "1 + 2 = 3").

When you multiply an even number by an even number, you get an even number (*e.g.,* "2 • 2 = 4").

When you multiply an even number by an odd number, you get an even number (*e.g.,* "3 • 2 = 6").

And, lastly, when you multiply an odd number by an odd number, you get an odd number as a result (*e.g.,* "3 • 3 = 9").

Because people often get somewhat confused on these even-odd questions, it's a good idea to do simple computations such as we've done here. The extra few seconds will help you assure yourself of the right answer.

Another concept you should know is "What's an integer?" An integer is a member of the set of whole numbers (either positive or negative) and zero. The word *integer* comes direct from Latin, where it means *whole, complete* and also *perfect* and *virtuous.* (it may be easier for you to remember the meaning of it if you think of the word *integrity,* which is a kind of wholeness or completeness of character). So positive integers would be whole numbers starting with 1 and going up (*e.g.,* 1, 2, 3, 4, 5, 6, 7, 8, 9, 10, etc.). Negative integers would be whole numbers starting with -1 and "going down," as they say in the elevator business (*e.g.,* -1, -2, -3, -4, -5, -6, -7, -8, -9, -10, etc.). Zero, of course, is not positive or negative, but it's an integer nonetheless. If we form a list of plain old integers (not just positive or negative), we get something like the following: -6, -5, -4, -3, -2, -1, 0, 1, 2, 3, 4, 5, 6, 7, 8 . . . .

Negative numbers sometimes throw people off. Was it humorist-author Fran Lebowitz who said that in real life there's no such thing as algebra? But in real life, we *can* actually come up with examples of negative numbers. A federal deficit is a negative number compared to a federal budget surplus (a positive number). If someone has one hundred dollars and spends one hundred ten dollars on his credit card, that's a negative ten that the person has (and we won't cloud up the issue by talking about debt forgiveness and bankruptcy).

Negative number and positive number examples were shown above in the section on positive and negative integers. But non-integers can also be positive or negative.

The following non-integer numbers are negative: -0.32; -1.6; -109.1. The following non-integer numbers are positive: 0.54678; 76.1; 432.54. It's important to understand how to manipulate positive and negative numbers.

A positive number times a positive number equals a positive number (*e.g.*, 3 • 2 = 6).

A negative number multiplied by a negative number is a positive number (*e.g.*, -3 • -4 = 12; perhaps this aspect of negative numbers and positive numbers *does* seem a little surreal).

A negative number times a positive number results in a negative number (*e.g.*, 2 • -4 = -8).

A negative sign before parentheses requires that it apply to all items within the parentheses; for example, -(3 - 1) = 1 - 3 = -2. You can verify this by noting that (3 - 1) = 2, and the negative sign before the parentheses makes that -2. Thus -(3 - 1) = -3 - (-1), which is the same as -3 + 1, which equals 1 - 3, or -2.

On a number line like the one below, it will be true (unless indicated otherwise on the SAT) that a number on the right is always higher than a number on the left, and vice versa.

| -3 | -2 | -1 | 0 | 1 | 2 |

Where there is a grid formation (*e.g.*, x- and y-axes), numbers on the right side of the y-axis are positive, and numbers to the left of it are negative; similarly, numbers above the x-axis are positive, while numbers below it are negative. The grid is often called the Cartesian coordinate system, after René Descartes, the philosopher and mathematician born in 1596. He introduced the use of coordinates in 1637 in *La geometrie* (Geometry), so this has been confusing students for many years! Descartes also is famous for the 1637 phrase *Cogito ergo sum*, which means "I think, therefore I am." You can alter this phrase slightly to "I learn all the stuff in this book, therefore I get into college." He also wisely said in the same year (obviously a good year!), "It is not enough to have a good mind; the main thing is to use it well." Words to take to heart. Widely credited with having developed analytical geometry (which fuses algebra and geometry to create a method of visualizing functions), Descartes is rumored never to have gotten out of bed before 11AM (though he did much of his best work then, it's said). So much for "the early bird gets the worm!"

In the case of a positive fraction between 0 and 1, the square of that fraction is less than the fraction itself (*e.g.*, the square of $^1/_4$ is $^1/_{16}$, which is less than $1/4$). For a negative fraction, this would not be true (*e.g.*, the square of $-1/4$ is also $1/16$, but $1/16$ is greater than $-1/4$). It is important on the SAT to do simple and quick computations in order to avoid silly mistakes; for instance, a person may quickly look at a problem and think that the square of (-3) is less than $1/10$, because -3 is clearly less than $1/10$, but in fact, the square of (-3) is 9, and 9 is more than $1/10$.

A few paragraphs up we were talking about integers. The last example in that paragraph is also an example of consecutive integers, which are next-door integers or successive integers that follow without interruption; *e.g.*, 4 is the next integer after 3, so it's the consecutive integer, because it's 3 + 1. For any n which is an integer, consecutive integers are formed in this way: n, $n + 1$, $n + 2$, $n + 3$, and so on.

The square of an integer is equal to the integer multiplied times itself. The square of a negative integer is a positive integer; for example, the square of -1 is 1, and the square of 1 is also 1. The squares of -2 and 2 are both 4. There is no such thing as a square that is a negative number (except in an esoteric branch of mathematics-not covered on the SAT, fortunately!-where the square of the imaginary number i is -1). Nine is the square of both 3 and -3. Sixteen is the square of -4 and also the square of 4.

Divisibility is a concept you need to know, and if a number is divisible by another number, we are saying that it can be divided by it with no remainder. For instance, 16 is divisible by 4 with no remainder, but not by 3 or 5. A number which divides evenly into another is called a *factor* of that number.

A prime number is one that has only itself and the number 1 as its factors. For example, 6 is not a prime number, because its factors are 1, 2, 3, and 6. But 7 is a prime number because only 1 and 7 are its factors. Examples of prime numbers are 2, 3, 5, 7, 11, 13, 17, 19, 23, 29, ... No even number above 2 is a prime number, since all even numbers are divisible by 2, in addition to any other numbers by which they may be divisible.

Sometimes on the SAT they will expect you to know, in one form or another, that 3, 5, and 7 are the three prime numbers that have the form "n", "$n + 2$", and "$n + 4$."

Percentage computations and questions give many students headaches, but this needn't be the case. *Per cent* comes from the Latin *per centum*, meaning *by the hundred*. A percentage is a ratio or fraction understood to have 100 as denominator; *e.g.*, "50%" means "50 out of 100." To find what 50% of 6 would be, then, is to say: "50 is to 100 as ? is to 6." This translates into the equation $50/100 = x/6$. The answer is 3, since $50/100 = 3/6$.

If you want to change a percent to a fraction or decimal, divide by 100. To go the other way, from fraction or decimal to percent, multiply by 100. So the following expressions are true:

$$12\% = 0.12 = {}^{12}/_{100} = {}^{3}/_{25}$$

$$34\% = 0.34 = {}^{34}/_{100} = {}^{17}/_{50}$$

$$30\% = 0.3 = {}^{3}/_{10}$$

$$100\% = 1.0 = {}^{1}/_{1}$$

$$350\% = 3.5 = {}^{35}/_{10} = {}^{7}/_{2}$$

For any fraction ${}^{x}/_{y}$, one converts it to a percent as follows:

$$x = ?$$
$$y = 100$$

Multiply both sides of the equation by 100: ? = 100 times ${}^{x}/_{y}$. For instance, $1/4 = {}^{?}/_{100}$, so ? = 100 $(1/4)$ = 25. Thus, $1/4$ is the same as ${}^{25}/_{100}$, which is 25%.

In some of the examples given above, the percent is more than 100 (*e.g.*, 350%).

Sometimes on the SAT, there are problems such as the following:

Q: 62 is what percent of 10?
A: Now we know that 10 is all of 10, and therefore 10 is 100% of 10. 62 is 6.2 times 10, so 62 is 6.2 times 100% of 10, or 620%.

Another way of looking at this is to use the formula above for converting fractions to percents. Thus, ${}^{62}/_{10}$ is equal to ${}^{?}/_{100}$; ? = 100 times ${}^{62}/_{10}$, which is ${}^{6200}/_{10}$, or 620. Thus, the answer is 620%.

Let's try another:

Q: 65 is what percent of 13?
A: ${}^{65}/_{13} = {}^{?}/_{100}$, so ? = 100 • ${}^{65}/_{13}$ = 100 • 5 = 500. So the answer is 500%. After you get used to this sort of problem, you'll find that you look at the question and notice that 65 is 5 times 13 and just

multiply 5 by 100 to get the answer of 500%. But it doesn't hurt to check your work.

Don't let money or labels throw you off. Story problems strike fear into the hearts of most students, but math is the same whether you're dealing with dollars or apples or iguanas. If Bill earns 10% more than Andrew, and Andrew earns $7.00/hour, then Bill earns $^{110}/_{100}$ times $7.00/ hour, or $7.70/hour. If Alice eats 50% of exactly what Claire eats, and Claire eats 10 potato chips and a Bartlett pear, then Alice eats 5 potato chips and half a Bartlett pear. (What would be a more likely problem, though, is speaking of 50% of the calories and not of the exact item consumption.)

Percents less than one are not really any trickier. For instance let's take the following problem:

Q: 6 is what percent of 1000?

A: $^6/_{1000}$ = .006 = 0.6%, which is equal to $^6/_{10}$ of 1%, which is equal to $^3/_5$ of 1%.

Again, please don't let a story problem format throw you off. Let's try one:

Q: Nick can buy one shirt for $15.00, or four shirts for $59.70. If he buys 4 shirts, his savings will be what percent of the total cost at the single-shirt rate?

A: Well, Nick isn't going to save great hunks of money. You can eyeball that 4 shirts at the single rate will cost $60.00. At the 4-shirt rate, the savings is only $0.30. What percent of $60.00 is $0.30? Using our formula, $^{0.30}/_{60}$ = $^?/_{100}$; ? = 100 • $^{0.30}/_{60}$ = $^{30}/_{60}$, which is $^1/_2$. Thus, the savings is $^1/_2$ of one percent or 0.5%.

There is a wonderful method for dealing with ratios on the SAT and elsewhere, and it works for both algebra and geometry. Bear with us since it is well worth memorizing. Many people either skip the ratio problems on the SAT, or guess, or do some really convoluted method, but you will have a foolproof method if you memorize this one.

First, let's try a problem. Suppose you have three people (Ed, Julie and Pam) running a business. They all put in money in the following ratios, respectively (*i.e.*, in the same order as the names appear): 1:2:5. When a profit of $12,000 is made, they will split the profit in the same ratio as the original investment (*i.e.*, 1:2:5).

How to do this? Step one is to add up all the numbers in the ratio (1 + 2 + 5 = 8). Then take the total (in this case, $12,000), and divide it by the number you got when you added up the numbers in the ratio (8). Your resulting number is $1500. If you then take that number $1500 and multiply it by each of the numbers in the ratio (1, 2 and 5), you'll get the profits each person receives. $1500 times 1 is $1500. $1500 times 2 is $3000. $1500 times 5 is $7500. If you want to check your work, add the $1500, $3000 and $7500, and you'll get $12,000, which is the total profit figure mentioned originally.

This works for geometry too. Suppose we tell you that the degree measures of a triangle have the ratio 1:2:9. Your total degrees in a plane-geometry triangle-which is the only kind appearing on the SAT-are 180 degrees. So add up the numbers in the ratio (1 + 2 + 9) and get 12. Take 180 and divide by 12, and you get 15. If you then multiply 15 by the numbers in the ratio, you'll have the degree measures of each angle of the triangle. 15 times 1 is 15. 15 times 2 is 30. 15 times 9 is 135. Do 15, 30 and 135 add up to 180? Absolutely, so you know you didn't make a stupid computational error.

OK, now a few words about fractions. If you have two fractions with the number 1 as the numerator of both of them, adding them is a breeze. An example: add $1/2$ and $1/3$. What you do is add together the denominators of the original fractions (2 + 3) and make that your new numerator. Then multiply the original denominators (2 • 3) and that becomes your new denominator. So your answer for the sum of the two fractions is $5/6$. If you are subtracting these fractions with one as the numerator, (i.e., $1/2 - 1/3$), you subtract 2 from 3 and that's your new numerator, and (again) multiply the denominators to create your new denominator. So your answer for the difference is $1/6$. This only works if 1 is the numerator of *both* fractions.

More on fractions. Suppose you are dividing by a fraction. Please remember that dividing by $2/3$, for instance, is the same as multiplying by the reciprocal or inverse of $2/3$, which is $3/2$. If you are dividing by $7/12$, that's the same as multiplying by $12/7$.

That brings to a close this module (and you need not stifle your feelings of celebration; this has been a tough one, full of abstractions and x, y, a and b). Some footwork you need to do in order to excel on the SAT is just plain demanding, and we think you owe yourself some pats on the back.

MathFacts™ 5

Averages

This is your average MathFacts™ module, and we mean that literally: we discuss dealing with averages on the SAT.

There are many kinds of averages, but probably the most-utilized average, and the one to which we usually refer, is called the *arithmetic mean*. To find this average or mean, we add together all numbers in a set of n numbers and divide the sum by n. Thus, we can take three SAT scores and find their mean in the following manner:

$$\frac{670 \text{ Math} + 600 \text{ Math} + 530 \text{ Math}}{3} = \frac{1800 \text{ Math}}{3}$$

= 600-point mean Math score for the three people (or perhaps these are three scores from the same person on three different occasions).

It is no different to find the average where algebraic expressions are used:

Q: Compute the average of $(2a - 6)$, $(a + 14)$ and $(3a + 1)$.

A: $\dfrac{(2a - 6) + (a + 14) + (3a + 1)}{3} = \dfrac{(6a + 9)}{3} = 2a + 3$

Sometimes, the SAT will request that you find a weighted average:

Q: The average of 20 numbers is 8. If one number is taken from the set, the average of the remaining numbers is 6. What number was removed?

A: The sum of the numbers originally is 20 • 8 = 160. The sum of the 19 numbers is 6 • 19 = 114. By subtracting 114 from 160, we get 46, which is the value of the number that was removed.

Realize that the average could go up when a number is removed if that number was smaller than the previous average:

Q: The average of a set of 6 numbers is 16. When one number is removed, the average of the remaining 5 numbers is 19. What number was removed?

A: The sum of the original numbers was 6 • 16 = 96. The sum of the five remaining numbers is 5 • 19 = 95. The value of the number removed is therefore 1.

You may have to calculate a weighted average on the SAT:

Q: In a set of dishes, it was necessary to replace four that had broken. Thus, there are eight dishes that are 18 years old and four dishes that are 2 years old. What is the average age of the twelve dishes?

A: The tendency for someone who wants a quick answer is to do something that gets the wrong answer: to average 18 and 2 and get 10. But the real solution is a little (only a little) trickier.

$$\frac{8(18) + 4(2)}{12} = \frac{(144 + 8)}{12} = 12\,^2/_3 \text{ years.}$$

The idea of a weighted average is that we don't have the same number of items that are 18 years old and 2 years old; if we did, then 10 would in fact be the correct answer. But we have two times as many 18-year-old dishes as we have dishes that are 2 years old, so we have to give the 18 twice as much weight. 18 has to get a weight of 8 and 2 has to get a weight of 4.

Another kind of average problem shows up fairly often:

Q: Ira walked one hour at a rate of 3 m.p.h. and two more hours at a rate of 2 m.p.h. What was his average speed for the 3-hour trek at Yosemite National Park?

A: This is another sort of weighted average problem, if you think about it. We have the following:

$$\frac{1(3) + 2(2)}{3} = \frac{7}{3} = 2\ ^1/_3 \text{ miles per hour.}$$

Two other averages show up: the mode and the median.

The mode is the most frequently occurring number in a set of numbers. For example., if we have the set {4, 7, 8, 8, 3, 2, 8, 9, 8, 10, 4, 8, 1}, we first put the numbers in the set in ascending order: {1, 2, 3, 4, 4, 7, 8, 8, 8, 8, 8, 9, 10}; the mode is 8, because it occurs the most times. It is possible to have more than one mode if two or more numbers occur an equal number of times: *e.g.*, for the set {4, 5, 6, 4, 7, 6, 9, 2, 1, 4, 6}, we first put the members of the set in ascending order: {1, 2, 4, 4, 4, 5, 6, 6, 6, 7, 9} In this case, 4 and 6 are both modes because they occur three times each and three times is the most that any number occurs.

The median of a set is the number with an equal amount of bigger numbers above it and of smaller numbers below it. For instance, if five people have five different amounts of money {$5.00, $8.20, $9.00, $52.00, and $120.00}, the median is $9.00, since half the numbers in the set are bigger than $9.00 and half are smaller. You always put the values in order from smallest to largest in order to determine the median. If you have an even number of values, you find the two middle ones and take their arithmetic mean to get the median: *e.g.*, for the set {1, 2, 7, 19, 56, 95}, the median is the average of the two middle values 7 and 19, so the median is 26 divided by 2, or 13. Even if the two middle values are really far apart (e.g., $1.00 and $1,000,000.00), you would still add them together and divide by two to get the median, in this case $500,000.50!

That's it for averages. A lot of this material is straightforward and logical if you think carefully what you are being asked to do and if you follow methods in this module. You will find that practicing will make it almost second nature, and it helps to have that level of understanding when you get into a situation like the SAT where you have limited time to do problems.

Please try to drill yourself on this and other modules after we have covered them and look at them periodically. Your best chance for learning the material comes not from going over something once and then ditching it forever; instead, you are most likely to retain material that you look over periodically so that you can reinforce the learning process. Try to look at this as an opportunity to develop a grasp of a great deal of material which will most certainly be useful to you on the SAT and which will also help you in further course work you may have at the college level. If there is material that you never quite grasped when you had it in school, this is a golden opportunity to play "catch-up" and seize some control over the material. It's not nearly as difficult (once you really grasp it) as it seems at first blush, and it is our sincere hope that you will benefit not only in terms of the SAT, but in terms of your education, your future occupation and your confidence in your own ability.

At the end of every module, stop to congratulate yourself for having completed it. It shows a very good attitude on your part that you are working this hard to master the material.

MathFacts™ 6

Algebra: Quadratic Equations, Exponents, Inequalities, Roots, Linear Equations and Simplifying Algebraic Expressions

Algebra uses symbols (generally alphabet letters) to represent at least some elements in mathematical expressions; these symbols, along with possibly some numbers, are connected by arithmetic operations symbols (*e.g.*, +, -, etc., denoting addition, subtraction, multiplication, division, root extraction, exponentiation, or combinations of the above). For example, $a + b$ is an algebraic expression. If $a = 6$ and $b = 9$, then $a + b = 15$. If $a = 4$ and $b = 10$, then $a + b = 14$. Symbols like a and b are also called literal numbers, because they are letters of the alphabet.

The word *algebra* comes to us from the Arabic *al-jebr* or *al-gabr*, which means *reunification* or *bone-setting*.

We have already covered some algebra in other modules, so you may consider yourself to have a leg up on this material (not a broken leg, even though we are covering *bone-setting*).

First, we need to cover linear equations, or equations in which the highest-degree term in any variable is of the first degree (*i.e.*, there are no terms like x^2 or a^3). An example would be $b + ay = 6$, where y is an unknown quantity but b and a are known. A linear equation may be shown on a graph as a line (hence the name; you see, mathematics does have logic to it!).

In a linear equation, it is possible to solve for the unknown quantity by manipulating both sides of the equation until one gets the correct answer. If we take an equation like $2x + 14 = 20$, we can solve for x by subtracting 14 from both sides of the equation (this is very important: if you perform a function on one side of the equation, you must do the same thing on the other side of the equal sign, or you will have destroyed the equation). After subtracting 14 from both sides, our new equation is $2x = 6$. To find x, we must divide $2x$ by 2 (which means we have to divide

6 by 2 also). Our resulting equation, "$x = 3$," also gives us our answer: x equals 3.

Let's try another. We'll solve the following equation for x:

$$6x - 9 = 4x + 15$$
$$2x = 24 \quad x = 12$$

If given a linear equation with all variables, you can still solve for x:

$$a - b = c + dx$$
$$a - b - c = dx$$

$$x = \frac{(a - b - c)}{d}$$

So, in this case, x is equal to the expression "$a - b - c$" divided by d. We don't know the numerical values of a, b, c, or d, but we have solved for x, just the same.

Now, sometimes you may get a rather complicated algebraic expression that may be simplified by combining like parts. For instance, let's look at the expression below:

$$4a + 20ab + 16b = 2a - 2b - 16ab$$

If we combine all like parts (terms that have the same letters, like $4a$ and $2a$), we simplify things. We take $4a$ and subtract $2a$, and get $2a$. We add $20ab$ to $16ab$ and get $36ab$. We take $16b$ and add $2b$ and get $18b$. Our expression therefore simplifies to:

$$2a + 36ab + 18b = 0$$

This may also be written as:

$$2(a + 18ab + 9b) = 0$$

It is a good idea on the SAT to simplify algebraic expressions before you solve them; not only does it save time, but it avoids the possibility that you will forget to include some part of the expression and throw yourself off-track to a hopeless degree, arriving at an answer which is totally wrong. Some of the answers on the test may be the ones you would mistakenly get if you neglected to include, say, the $16b$ part of the expression when you solve for a particular variable.

Do not make the mistake of simplifying an expression in the following way, however: if you take the expression "$16b - b$" you do not get "16" as the answer, as some people wrongly assume. You are subtracting $1b$ from $16b$ and therefore will get $15b$. You are not able to get rid of the "b" part of the "$16b$" in such a fashion. To avoid this sort of error in your thinking, it helps to put a 1 before the b to remind you of what you are really trying to do. Thus, $16b - 1b = 15b$, and you avoid a mistake which will cost you points on the SAT.

Sometimes you may confront an inequality on the SAT. An inequality is a statement whose form is as follows:

$$a > b \ (a \text{ is greater than } b)$$
OR
$$a < b \ (a \text{ is less than } b)$$

An equation is a statement in which the equal sign appears, meaning that two mathematical expressions have the same value., *e.g.*,

$$a = b$$

It is possible for a to be greater than or equal to b:

$$a \geq b$$

Another possibility: a is less than or equal to b:

$$a \leq b$$

It is possible to manipulate inequalities. For instance, if we take the following inequality:

$$3a < 6$$

we can divide each side of the inequality by 3 and get:

$$a < 2$$

You will also be expected to know how to factor. Factoring is a method by which you take an expression and change it into a product of two or more simpler expressions which are called factors. You will recall that a number like 4 may be divided by 1, 2, and 4 with no remainders; thus,

1, 2, and 4 are all factors of the number 4. Similarly, we are able to factor algebraic expressions. Let's look at the following expression:

$$x^3 - 2x^2 + x$$

We see that we can "factor out" the x, and get

$$x (x^2 - 2x + 1)$$

It happens that the parenthetic expression can be factored:

$$x^2 - 2x + 1 = (x - 1)(x - 1) = (x - 1)^2$$

So our answer is: $x (x - 1)^2$.

You have to remember that when you see an expression like

$$(x - 1)(x - 1)$$

you must multiply four parts in order to get the correct result.

You multiply the following:

$$x \text{ times } x$$
$$-1 \text{ times } x$$
$$-1 \text{ times } x$$
$$-1 \text{ times } -1$$

(recall that -1 times -1 = 1.) Then you add all four quantities to get your answer.

This brings us to quadratic equations.

A quadratic equation is one which has the following form:

$$ax^2 + bx + c = 0$$

To solve a quadratic equation, you need to think of two numbers which when added together equal b and when multiplied by one another equal c. This sounds tricky, but you will get the hang of it. Let's take an example:

$$x^2 + 3x + 2 = 0$$

What two numbers add up to 3 and when multiplied by one another equal 2? The answer is 1 and 2; they add up to 3 and multiply out to 2. So, to solve this quadratic equation in x, we create the following:

$$(x + 2)(x + 1) = 0$$

If either parenthetic expression equals zero, the whole expression equals zero, so we have two answers for x: 2 or -1.

If there are any subtractions in the quadratic equation, there will be at least one parenthetical expression that has a subtraction in it. For instance,

$$x^2 - 3x - 4 = 0$$

What two numbers add up to -3 and when multiplied by one another equal -4? The answer is -4 and 1. Thus, when we factor out this quadratic equation, we get the following:

$$(x - 4)(x + 1) = 0. \text{ Thus, } x = 4 \text{ and } x = -1$$

Now, in "x^2" the "2" indicates that we should multiply x by itself. If we had x^3, that would indicate that we multiply x times x times x. Exponents are numbers that tell us to multiply repeatedly a number or expression by itself. Thus,

$$10^3 = 10 \times 10 \times 10 = 100$$
$$x^4 = x \text{ times } x \text{ times } x \text{ times } x$$
$$a^{99} = \text{Oh, well, forget this one; you get the idea } \ldots$$

We can do an operation that is the *reverse*, so to speak, of finding the nth power of a number. Just as 10 cubed is 1000, so we can ask "What is the cube root of 1000?"; the answer is 10.

10 squared is 100. Conversely, the square root of 100 is 10. So finding a root is the opposite of raising a number to a power.

A couple of square root values that you should know are the square root of 2, which is equal to approximately 1.4, and the square root of 3, which is equal to approximately 1.7.

Ah, algebra. I know you are having so much fun that you wish this module went on forever. Sorry to disappoint you, but we are going to have to stop at this point and you are going to have to find something else to do. Doubtless, it will not be nearly as fun as solving quadratic equations, but such is life . . . .

MathFacts™ 7

To Scale or Not to Scale, That is the Question: You May or May Not Assume From Drawings on the SAT

(With Profound Apologies to Hamlet and Shakespeare)
Also: Calculator Use and Grid-in Answers

There will be a number of geometric figures that show up on the SAT, and there is no polite way to refuse these guests; they will brashly demand that you work with them, and some of them will not even be drawn to scale, but they will at least tip you off about not being drawn to scale when such is the case.

When you are asked to interpret a figure, you need to be careful not to make assumptions that cannot be substantiated. For instance, you should not guess the number of degrees in an angle or decide that two line segments are the same length even if they appear to be equal in length. You should use the theorems you know about vertical angles and side relationships in right triangles and so forth, and use them to the fullest extent possible. But when you reach a point at which you have to make up or assume information that is not given and cannot be derived mathematically, you need to stop yourself. This is not the time or place for an excess of enthusiasm!

Let's look at the following figure for an example of what you can say with certainty, and what you must *not* assume if you see the words "Note: figure not drawn to scale":

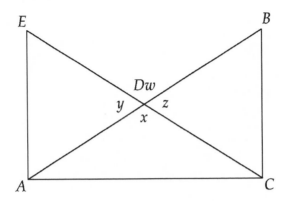

Now, you can assume safely that:

a) *ADE, ACD,* and *BCD* are triangles.
b) *D* is between *A* and *B.*
c) *D* is between *C* and *E.*
d) $x = w.$
e) $y = z.$
f) The measure of angle *BCE* < the measure of angle *ACB.*
g) The measure of angle *BAE* < the measure of angle *CAE.*
h) The length of segment *AD* < the length of segment *AB.*
i) The length of segment *CD* < the length of segment *CE.*
j) $x + z = w + y.$

But you'd better *not* assume the following:

a) The length of segment *AE* = the length of segment *BC.*
b) Angle *ACB* is a right angle.
c) Angle *CAE* is a right angle.
d) The measure of angle *BAC* = the measure of angle *ACE.*
e) The length of segment *AE* < the length of segment *BC.*
f) $x = 110.$
g) The length of segment *AC* is 1.3 times the length of segment *AE.*
h) $x > y.$

In short, if you scrutinize the lists above, you will see that the first set contains only facts and deductions and information that you are given or that you have derived from mathematical rules. But the second set includes things you cannot know, even if the figure has been drawn to scale. There may be an 89 degree angle in a triangle that you assume is a 90 degree angle, but the Pythagorean Theorem doesn't apply to 89 degree angles. If you are not told it's a 90 degree angle either directly or through other signs (such as that the other two angles are each 45 degree angles), then you must refrain from jumping to conclusions.

The people who put out the SAT will designate when a drawing is not done according to scale, a warning that signifies that the lengths of line segments and the measures of angle degrees are not necessarily accurately shown. But if points appear to lie on the same line, it may be assumed that they are in fact on the line. Also, relative positions may be assumed; for instance, in the drawing below:

you may assume that D is between C and E and that E is between D and F. If two straight lines intersect, you may apply what you know from other modules about angle relationships and assume that the vertical angles are equal.

You have to ask yourself what you know and how you know it. If the answer is, "Well, it *looks* like a 45 degree angle," you are on very shaky ground. Demand proof of a fact; don't make unsubstantiated assumptions during the test.

Calculator use is allowed on the SAT. Some people are supposing that this allowance means that the math questions have become super-difficult and that they require more complicated or time-consuming computations. The latter supposition is not generally true. Calculators are being allowed, at least in part, because they have been such standard tools in the classroom curriculum, and the SAT reflects that usage.

The SAT also contains "grid-in" answers, where you write in an answer and then darken corresponding ovals in columns below your answer. Again, this does not really constitute a greater challenge, for if you know how to do a problem, it isn't really terribly tricky to write down your answer and fill in the ovals below, rather than picking it out of a multiple-choice list. And if you have mastered the techniques in MathFacts™ 1 - 7, you really shouldn't worry that the grid-in answers will present any special challenges. Sometimes, you will even have greater leeway in picking a correct answer on the grid-ins than you do on the multiple-choice problems; *i.e.,* sometimes the answer can be any value in a range from, say, 1.2 to 3.7, which gives you the freedom to choose a number of correct answers.

Congratulations on completing Module 7. You're doing a great job. And remember: even if your brain feels tired, you are exercising it and increasing your ability to do well on this important test.

Math Worksheet I

The following pages contain 60 highly representative math problems for you to practice using what you've learned in MathFacts™ 1 - 7. Try to see if you can do them without help. Then, if you don't know how, use the materials in the text to help you solve them, and then *learn* the methods. You will see material very much like this when you take your exam.

If you go over and over these problems, you will eventually put them into your brain. You will not see these exact problems on the SAT, but you will see problems very similar to them and you'll be so glad you did your homework! (Later, that is, not while you're doing it!)

Use separate sheets of paper to work on these and do them at least 5 - 6 times. Remember: repetition is critical to long-term learning, which is what's tested on the SAT. Good luck!

1. Eighteen percent of $90 is what percent of $270?

2. Paragon CDs is having a sale. The first CD is full-price and each CD after that of equal or lesser value is half price. Elise bought three CDs: their full prices were $20, $15, and $15. What did Elise pay for the CDs, and what percent discount did she get on the whole purchase?

3. Rich has made an average of 18 points per basketball game for the last 12 games. The season has 3 games remaining and he would like to average 21 points a game for the season. How many points must he score in the remaining 3 games to do so? How many points average is this for each of the remaining games?

4. Andi runs a total of 50 miles a week. On Tuesdays and Thursdays, she can only do 2 miles a day, since she works all day. On Monday,

Wednesday and Friday, she manages 6 miles each. How many miles must she average each day on Saturday and Sunday?

5. If the average number of objects in 9 groups is $8x$, what is the total?

6. B is the midpoint of line segment AC. $AB = x + 7$ and $BC = 3x - 6$. What is the total length of AC?

7. B is the midpoint of line segment AC. If $AB = 9y - 16$, and $AC = 14y + 3$, what is the length of BC?

8. Which is greater: y or $-y$?

9. Which is greater: y or $1/y$?

10. The diagonal of a square measures 3 times the square root of 2. What is the area of the square? What is the perimeter of the square?

11. Name the percentage equivalents of these numbers: $1/2$, $1/3$, $4/5$, 2, 16, $1/10$.

12. A square has the same perimeter and area. What is the length of a side of the square?

13. A circle is circumscribed inside a square. The radius of the circle is 3. What is the area of the square?

14. An equilateral triangle has one side in common with a square. The perimeter of the square is 20 centimeters. What is the perimeter of the triangle?

15. A bag is filled with black, red and yellow golf tees. There are 96 tees in the bag. If the probability of picking a black tee is 50%, and the probability of picking a red tee is 25%, how many yellow tees are in the bag?

16. A rectangle's diagonal measures 8. It creates two triangles, and the shortest side of each triangle is 4. What does the remaining side measure?

17. Molly and Jim have set up a lemonade stand. It takes them $1/2$ cup of concentrate and 6 cups water to make lemonade for 8 people. They decide to set up a stand at the county fair and serve 200 people. How much concentrate and how much water will they need?

18. Lisette wants to lose 30 pounds in a year (3500 calories equal a pound). Assume that this is not a leap year and that the current calories maintain her weight. How many calories must she cut out from her diet per day in order to accomplish this goal? Round to the nearest hundred calories.

19. Bob, Al and Kathy are running a business. Because of their various investments they split the profits in a ratio of 2:3:5 respectively. Their total profits are $100,000. How much does each of them receive?

20. Two numbers total 144 and have a ratio of 2:7. What are the two numbers?

21. Alice wants to build a 3-level house. She wants to perimeter to be 100 feet. What is the biggest-area rectangular house she can build?

22. A triangle has degree measures in the following ratio: 1:2:6. What are the degree measures of the three angles of the triangle?

23. Stephanie has 15 CDs and gives $1/3$ of them to Al and $1/5$ of them to Pete. Al gives 40% of the CDs he got from Stephanie to Pete. Assuming that Pete started out with 10 CDs, how many does he end up with?

24. A circle has an area of 9π. What is the circumference of the same circle?

25. Will and Alice are doing a project together. If Will spends 2 hours a night for 7 nights, and Alice spends 1 hour a night for 21 nights on the project, what percentage of total time was contributed by each?

26. There are 100 juniors taking American History during first semester. If 30% of these students are absent on Tuesday and

80% of those present go on a field trip to a museum, how many students go on the trip? What percent of the entire 100 juniors taking American history that semester go on the field trip?

27. A triangle measures 6 on each of two sides and 6 times the square root of 2 on the third side. What are the degree measures of the angles of the triangle?

28. A terrarium is 20 inches long, 10 inches deep and 15 inches high. Dirt is put on the bottom and it comes from bags each holding 500 cubic inches of dirt. How many bags are needed to fill the terrarium $1/3$ of the way up?

29. Wanda is painting her house. She can get 300 square feet out of every can of paint, and her house has 4600 square feet of surface area. How many cans of paint must she buy? Assume she can only buy full cans of paint.

30. Five students got their algebra tests back. Bob and Theresa each got a 92. Doug got a 70. Mitch got a 65. And Dan got a 97. What is the average (arithmetic mean) test grade? What's the mode?

31. Thirty students in room 6 gave an average of $5 apiece to a charity. What was the total amount collected? If 10 of them gave an average of $10 apiece, what was the average amount given by the remaining students?

32. A machine produces 150 widgets per hour. A faster machine produces 250 widgets per hour. How many more widgets will the faster machine produce in a week? Assume the machines operate 24 hours a day, 7 days a week.

33. What angles do the hands of a clock create when the clock says 4:00?

34. A bus gets 15 miles per gallon in city driving and 20 miles per gallon in highway driving. It needs to go from City A to City B and back again, and one-way distance is 300 miles. 80% of the trip is highway driving. How many gallons of gas are needed?

35. Which is greater, the number of factors of prime number A or the number of factors of prime number B?

36. Joe and John are walking the same distance to school. Joe walks at a rate of 6 km per hour and John walks at a rate of 4 km per hour. Which is greater, the time it takes Joe to get to school, or the time it takes John to get to school?

37. A movie grosses $300,000,000. If 15% percent of each ticket sold goes to the theater owners, and $100,000,000 was spent on production, and another 35% of the ticket price goes for promotion and miscellaneous expenses, how much profit is there after expenses? What percentage of the gross receipts is this?

38. A cube has an area of 36 square inches on a side. What is the volume of the cube?

39. The volume of a cube is 125 cubic inches. What is the total surface area of all the faces of the cube?

40. The average weight of 3 people is 150 pounds. If one of the people weighs 200 pounds, what is the average weight of the remaining two people?

41. Fifteen percent of 700 is less than forty percent of some integer b. Determine what b could be.

42. Ten people shoot baskets. In 60 seconds, they get the following scores: 12, 16, 18, 24, 28, 28, 36, 40, 42, and 48. What are the arithmetic mean, median and mode?

43. The average caloric intake of 5 people is 2300 calories per day. Rob is training for a marathon and takes in 4500 calories a day. Kate does aerobics and takes in 2000 calories, even though she's not very big. What is the average caloric intake of the remaining people? Round to the nearest integer.

44. Two squares share one side to make a rectangle. The area of each square is 49 square inches. What is the perimeter of the rectangle?

45. Bob lives in Scarborough. He travels 15 miles due north, then 20 miles due east to Mitchellsville. How far is it from Scarborough to Mitchellsville as the crow flies? Assume the crow flies straight!

46. Alice buys 3 apples and 3 pears for $1.25. Stacy buys 2 apples and 3 pears of the same kind in the same place for $1.05. What is the cost of a pear?

47. Two workers each make $30,000 a year. Mike gets a raise of 3% every six months, and Rick gets one annual raise of 6%. At the end of a year, are they making the same amount of money?

48. Alfonso and Luis each has a 3.0 grade point average. Alfonso is at the end of freshman year and Luis is at the end of junior year. Compute the highest GPAs that Alfonso and Luis can achieve by the end of senior year. Assume 4.0 is the value of the highest grade earned and that they are both taking the same number of credits each of the four years.

49. A farmer arranges with some people to harvest the apples in his orchard. He agrees to give them 20% of his crop in exchange for their labor. If the farmer ends up with 2 tons of apples after paying the apple pickers their share, how much did the farmer originally have?

50. Ellie has a stock portfolio. Her first stock is bought for $15 a share and goes up to $25 a share, and she has 100 shares. Her second stock is bought for $10 a share and goes down to $5 a share and she has 200 shares. How much money does Ellie make? Forget about commissions and taxes for the purpose of the problem.

51. Rafi ran a race is 27.2 seconds. Yesterday it took him 29.3 seconds. By how much did his time improve?

52. A formula reads: $4x + 2y = 200$. Solve for x.

53. A formula reads $4x + 8y = 100$. What is $x + 2y$?

54. One square has a side length of the square root of 2. Another square has a side length of the square root of 3. What is the difference between the areas of the two squares?

55. Compare these two quantities:

    1) The number of distinct factors of x^4 where x is a prime number.

2) The number of distinct factors of y^2 where y is a prime number.

56. The probability of it raining today is 38%. What is the probability of it *not* raining today?

57. Which costs more, a coat bought at full price for $120 or a coat whose full price is $200 bought for a 35% discount?

58. Sue invests $100 a week. Ignoring taxes, assume that she makes an actual annual return of 15%. How much money will she have at the end of the first year? How much money will she have at the end of two years?

59. $3x + 4y + 10z = 72$. $2x + 5y + 10z = 36$. What is $x - y$?

60. If the width of a rectangle is $^1/_4$ its length, and the total perimeter is 20 decimeters, what is the width?

Math Worksheet I Answers

1. This translates to the following: $^{18}/_{100}$ times $90 = ^{x}/_{100}$ times $270. To solve for x, multiply both sides of the equation by 100 and divide both sides by $270. $x = 100$ times $^{18}/_{100}$ times $90 divided by $270. Thus, $x = ^{1}/_{3}$ (from $90 divided by $270) times 18%, which equals 6%.

2. $20 + $7.50 + $7.50 = $35 out of $50 (full price). $15 divided by $50 equals x divided by 100, so the answer is 30%.

3. $18 \cdot 12 = 216$ points total so far. To end up with 21 points average for 15 games total, 315 is the total that must exist. So he has to score 99 points (315 minus 216) in the next 3 games, or 33 points average per remaining game.

4. $2 \cdot 2 = 4$.
    $6 \cdot 3 = 18$.
    $4 + 18 = 22$.
    $50 - 22 = 28$.
    So 28 miles divided by 2 = 14 miles average on each day of the weekend.

5. $8x$ times $9 = 72x$.

6. $(x + 7) = (3x - 6)$, so $2x = 13$, so $x = 6.5$. Plugging 6.5 into $x + 7$, we get a length of 13.5, which is half the length of AC, so $2 \cdot 13.5 = 27$.

7. Since AB is half of AC, we can double AB and set that doubled amount equal to AC. $18y - 32 = 14y + 3$, so $4y = 35$, so $y = 8.75$. Since $BC = AB$, $BC = 62.75$ by substituting 8.75 for y in $9y - 16$.

8. It can't be determined from the information given, since it makes a difference whether y is positive or negative.

9. It can't be determined from the information given, since it makes a difference whether y is a fraction or an integer.

10. The length of each side of the square is 3 (The diagonal of a square creates two equal isosceles right triangles and that diagonal is the hypotenuse of each triangle, so the rules for isosceles right triangles help solve this). So the area is 9 and the perimeter is 12.

11. 50%, 33.33%, 80%, 200%, 1600%, 10%

12. In other words, $x^2 = 4x$. So $x = 4$.

13. If the radius is 3, the diameter is 6. And that's also the length of a side of the square, so its area is 36.

14. A side of the square is 5 centimeters. So 3 times 5 centimeters = 15 centimeters.

15. 100% = the total. 75% are black and red. So 25% times 96 are yellow. There are 24 yellow tees.

16. These are 30 - 60 - 90 degree triangles, so the remaining side measures 4 times the square root of 3.

17. 200 ÷ 8 = 25. So 25 times ¹/₂ cup concentrate is 12.5 cups. And 6 cups of water times 25 is 150 cups of water.

18. 3500 times 30 = 105,000 calories. Divide 105,000 by 365 to get average number of calories per day Lisette needs to cut out. Rounded to the nearest hundred, it's 300.

19. 2 + 3 + 5 = 10. $100,000 divided by 10 = $10,000. $10K times 2 = $20K for Bob, $10K times 3 = $30K for Al, and $10K times 5 is $50K for Kathy. To check work, add $20K, $30K, and $50K to get the total of $100K.

20. 2 + 7 = 9. 144 ÷ 9 = 16. 16 • 2 = 32. 16 • 7 is 112. To check, 32 + 112 = 144.

21. $100 \div 4$ is 25; a square will maximize the area for a given perimeter of a rectangle. $25 \cdot 25$ is 625 sq. ft. per floor, and there are 3 floors, so 1875 sq. ft.

22. $1 + 2 + 6 = 9$. 180 degrees total divided by 9 is 20. $20 \cdot 1$ is 20, 20 $\cdot 2$ is 40, and $20 \cdot 6$ is 120. To check, $20 + 40 + 120 = 180$ degrees.

23. $1/3$ of 15 is 5. $1/5$ of 15 is 3. 40% of 5 is 2. So Al gets $3 + 2$ more CDs. 10 that he started with and 5 more = 15 CDs total.

24. Area = πr^2. So $r = 3$. Since the formula for circumference is $2\pi r$, the circumference is 6π.

25. $2 \cdot 7 = 14$ hours total for Will. $1 \cdot 21 = 21$ hours total for Alice. $14 + 21 = 35$ hours. $^{14}/_{35} = {}^x/_{100}$ or 40% for Will, and $^{21}/_{35} = {}^x/_{100}$ or 60% for Alice.

26. $^{30}/_{100}$ times 100 are absent, so $^{70}/_{100}$ times 100 are present. Thus 70 are the number who are at school. Of these $^{80}/_{100}$ times 70 go on the trip. Thus 56 go on the field trip. This is $^{56}/_{100}$ or 56% of the juniors taking American History that semester.

27. 45, 45, and 90 degrees.

28. $20 \cdot 10 \cdot 15 = 3000$ cubic inches. Since height is 15 inches, and we want to fill it $1/3$ of the way up, we have to use $1/3$ of the cubic inches, or 1000 cubic inches. Each bag holds 500 cubic inches, so we need 1000 divided by 500, or 2 bags.

29. 4600 divided by 300 is more than 15, so round up to 16 cans.

30. $92 \cdot 2 = 184$. $184 + 70 + 65 + 97 = 416$ total. Divide that by 5, and get 83.2 average. The mode is the most frequent value, so it's 92, since it occurs twice.

31. 30 times $5 is $150 total collected. $10 times 10 is $100. $150 minus $100 is $50. $50 divided by 20 (which we get by subtracting 30 minus 10) = $2.50 apiece for the remaining students' average.

32. $250 - 150 = 100$ more per hour. $100 \cdot 24$ is 2400 more per day. $2400 \cdot 7$ is 16,800 more per week.

33. A circle has 360 degrees, so this setup creates a 120 degree angle and a 240 degree angle ($^1/_3$ times 360 is 120, and $^2/_3$ times 360 is 240).

34. 300 • 2 = 600 miles round trip. $^4/_5$ (or 80%) times 600 miles is 480 miles of highway driving at a rate of 20 mpg. So 480 divided by 20 is 24 gallons for the highway driving. $^1/_5$ (or 20%) is city driving. $^1/_5$ times 600 miles is 120 miles of city driving. 120 divided by 15 is 8 gallons. So 24 gallons + 8 gallons is 32 gallons total.

35. Neither. They're equal, since all prime numbers have, by definition, two factors each.

36. John is walking more slowly, so it's going to take John a greater time to get there.

37. $300 million minus $100 million = $200 million. 15% + 35% = 50% for non-production expenses times $300 million, so it's $150 million for costs other than production. So $50 million is profit, and this is $^1/_6$ or $16^2/_3$% of the gross revenues.

38. The square root of 36 is 6. 6^3 is 216 cubic inches.

39. The cube root of 125 is 5. 5^2 is 25; multiply 25 times 6 (the number of faces of a cube) to get 150 square inches.

40. 3 times 150 lb. is 450 lb. Subtract 200 lb. and get 250 lb. for the remaining two people, so their average is 125 lb. per person.

41. $^{15}/_{100}$ times $700 < {}^{40}/_{100}$ times b. Multiply both sides of the inequation by $^{100}/_{40}$ (which is the reciprocal of $^{40}/_{100}$).
$^{100}/_{40}$ • $^{15}/_{100}$ times $700 < b$.
$^{15}/_{40}$ • $700 < b$.
$15 • 17.5 < b$.
$262.5 < b$.
So 263 or above could be b.

42. The total is 292 points; divided by 10, that's an arithmetic mean of 29.2. The median score is the average of the two middle scores, both of which are 28, so 28 is the median. The mode is also 28, since it's the most frequent value.

43. 2300 • 5 = 11,500 total calories. Subtract 4500 for Rob and 2000 for Kate, and you are left with 5000 calories, divided by 3 people, so 1666.67 calories per day per person rounds up to 1667 per person.

44. The square root of 49 is 7. Since the squares share one side, 6 times 7 is the perimeter = 42 inches.

45. This is a 3 - 4 - 5 triangle problem from MathFacts™ 1.
    15 = 5 • 3.
    20 = 5 • 4.
    So 5 • 5 is our answer = 25 miles. The Pythagorean formula can also be used.

46. Subtract Stacy's purchases from Alice's and the value of 1 apple is $0.20. So 3 apples cost $0.60. $1.25 minus $0.60 is $0.65 for 3 pears, so each costs $21^2/_3$ cents.

47. At the end of the year, Rick is making $31,800. Mike is making slightly more than that, since his first raise of $900 brings him to $30,900, and then the second raise of 3% on that amount brings him to $31,827.

48. This is a weighted average problem. Alfonso has 3.0 times 1 year. If he gets straight A's for the next three years, he'll have 4.0 times 3 years. So 3 times 1 plus 4 times 3 = 15. Divide 15 by 4 (for the 4 years of high school) and it's a 3.75 GPA. Luis is starting later and has 3.0 times 3 years. If Luis gets a 4.0 the final year, 3 times 3 is 9 plus 4 times 1 is 4, for a total of 13. Divide 13 by 4 and get a 3.25 GPA.

49. Two tons represent 80% of the original weight of apples (100% - 20% = 80%). So we say 80% of some number x is 2 tons. To solve for x, we create this equation, $(^{80}/_{100})x = 2$ tons. We multiply both sides of the equation by the reciprocal of $^{80}/_{100}$ and get $x = 2.5$ tons as the original amount of apples.

50. Nothing. She makes 100 times $10 profit on the first stock, or $1000. But she loses 200 times $5 on the second stock, or $1000. $1000 minus $1000 is zero.

51. 2.1 seconds (the difference between the two numbers).

52. This cannot be done. We don't know what x and y are separately, only what they add up to together.

53. That's $1/4$ as much of each quantity on the left side of the equal sign, so take $1/4$ of 100 and get 25.

54. One square has an area of 2. The second has an area of 3. The difference is 1.

55. The number of factors are identical, since one gets no new factors by squaring, taking to the fourth power, etc.

56. It's 100% - 38%, or 62%.

57. $35/100 \cdot \$200 = \$70$. $\$200 - \$70 = \$130$, which is still more than the full-price coat at $120.

58. She totals $5200 a year. Adding $15/100 \cdot \$5200$ (or $780) to that, we get a total of $5980. In the second year, she'll get that $5980 again, but also have the first year's amount, *plus* $15/100 \cdot \$5980$ (or $897), for a total of $12,857.

59. Subtract the second equation from the first one. $x - y = 36$.

60. $W = 1/4L$. So $L = 4W$. Perimeter $= 2L + 2W$. Substituting, we get, $8W + 2W = 10W = 20$ decimeters. So $W = 2$ decimeters.

New Math To Know

Please remember that all the math in MathFacts™ 1–7 and on the Math Worksheet I is needed for the new and SAT.

The SAT has 80 minutes of math: a 55-minute calculator section, and a shorter (be grateful for small things!) no calculator section that's 25 minutes long. As before, it includes algebra, geometry and arithmetic, *i.e.*, the material in MathFacts™ 1–7. It's mostly multiple-choice questions (4 choices apiece) and some student-produced responses. The latter are not harder or easier to do; if you know how to do a problem, it doesn't matter if you're given answer choices. Your final score ranges, as before, from 200 to 800 (preferably closer to the latter if you study hard!). This section will discuss the new topics covered on the SAT, but MathFacts™ 1–7 must be learned also.

What new material is tested? There are questions on absolute value, functions, exponents, exponential growth, geometric probability, data analysis, scatter plots, etc. You can master the added material if you study.

Calculators are allowed on the longer, 55-minute section. You can use a scientific, graphing or four-function calculator, with the College Board recommending a scientific one, even though it is still feasible to get every answer with no calculator at all.

Interpretation of Data, Matrices and Scatter Plots

A *scatter plot* is a visual way of finding and comprehending patterns in numerical data set on an *x* - *y* axis, of seeing how two variables relate to each other. On the SAT, students will have to figure out the line of best fit for the scatter plot (which will be a series of dots that create a strong or weak pattern or no pattern at all; in the latter case, there would be *no* relationship between the variables). No formal methods will be required; just eyeballing the chart will be enough. Scatter plots are constructed when there are two variables (called "bivariate observation") and one is trying to figure out the relationship between the two variables.

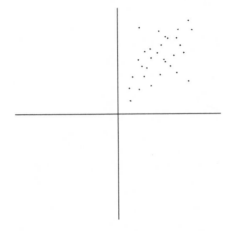

An example might be to put cumulative grade point averages in high school on the *x* axis, and put salaries on the *y* axis, to see what, if any, correlation there is between the two. Or you might have two students list their favorite hobbies (one on the *x* axis, the other on the *y* axis) and analyze the data in the scatter plot to predict whether the people might enjoy spending time together. There might be a positive relationship between the two variables or a negative one; the relationship may be strong or weak. You'll be expected on the test to interpret data in charts, graphs and tables, and also to tell whether the slope of a line is positive or negative, less than 1, greater than 1, etc. General information on slope of a line is in MathFacts™ 2.

Probability

Probability has existed on the SAT for some time, but now students may be asked about *geometric probability*. There might be a figure with part of it shaded and you'll be asked what the odds are that a point selected would be in the shaded area. An example might be that you have a square with sides of length 5. A diagonal is drawn, creating two isosceles right triangles which must be equal in area. One half of the square is shaded and the other is not, so the probability that a point randomly chosen will lie in the shaded region will therefore be .5, $1/2$, or 50%.

Remember that probability always varies between zero and one. Zero means it's not going to happen; one means it's definitely going to happen. Partial probabilities are fractions or decimals between zero and one or percentages between 0% and 100%. You might have a cookie jar holding 2 kinds of cookies: 20 chocolate chip cookies and 15 lemon cookies. What is the probability at random (no fair peeking or feeling around for chocolate chips!) of pulling out a chocolate chip cookie? It's 20 divided by 35 (the total cookies, chocolate chip and lemon combined), which reduces to $4/7$ or which can be expressed as a decimal or percentage. What is the probability at random of pulling out a lemon cookie? It's 15 divided by 35, which is $3/7$. The partial probabilities in such a situation add up to 1.

Exponential Growth

Exponential growth and *geometric sequences* are one and the same. In them, one has a constant ratio between terms; 5, 15, 45, 135, 405 is a geometric sequence. Each term is 3 times the previous term. Such questions have shown up in slightly different form on previous SATs, when students were expected to identify patterns and predict new members in the sequence. A member in the above sequence might be described as $5 \cdot 3^n$ where n is the power of 3. So 5 times 3^2 is 45, since 5 times 9 is 45.

Students on the test might be asked to deal with real-world uses of this concept. For example, one might be told that sales double every 3 years and one would have to find out the sales projected if this pattern continues for x years.

Set Theory

Whether or not you've had set theory in school, the concepts are straightforward and easy to master. A *set* is just a bunch of things. Think of a tea set composed of cups, saucers and teapot. Or think of the set of all positive numbers; each positive number is a *member* or *element* of the set. You might have the set of all positive even integers (2, 4, 6, 8, 10, 12, 14, 16, 18 . . .), or the set of all squares of integers (1, 4, 9, 16, 25, 36, 49 . . .) or the set of all powers of positive 3 (3, 9, 27, 81, 243, 729 . . .).

The new test will want you to look at two concepts:

(1) The *intersection* of two or more sets (or the common elements, the members that are shared by both or all sets).

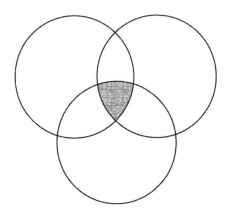

(2) The *union* of two or more sets (which consists of all those members or elements that are in any or all sets).

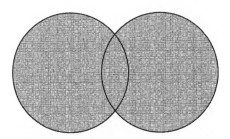

In the sets mentioned above, if you find the intersection of the set of even integers and the set of powers of 3, you'd say there were no members in common, since the one set contains only even numbers, and the other set contains only odd numbers.

The union of those two sets would be the numbers in both sets: 2, 3, 4, 6, 8, 9, 10, 12, 14, 16, 18, 20, 22, 24, 26, 27, 28 . . . .

If you were told that set A is the set of all positive integers and set B is the set of all negative integers, the intersection would be the empty (or null) set, and the union would be the set of all positive and negative integers combined.

Functions and Algebra

There is much functional and algebraic material in MathFacts™, so make sure you master that material. Additional material appears below:

Radical equations will be on the test. These are simple equations having the radical or square root sign in them

$$3\sqrt{y} + 10 = 20.$$

Rational expressions are equations displayed as a ratio or fraction. An example might be

$$\frac{3y - 2}{y + 1}$$

On the SAT, you must use such expressions in equations or inequalities. Thus, you might have to say that the above expression is equal to 4 and solve for y, or that it's greater than (>) or less than (<) or perhaps greater than or equal to (≧) or less than or equal to (≦) 4. Then, performing the same operation(s) on both sides of the sign, you manipulate the equation or inequation to produce an answer.

Absolute value simply refers to the distance a number is from the origin or zero on the number line. The absolute value of -3 and +3 is identical: 3. The symbol used for absolute value is the number flanked by two vertical lines: e.g., $|-3|$ or $|x|$. You will be expected to know the concept well enough to use it in equations, functions, etc.

Exponents, new wrinkles: While the old SAT had exponents, they were limited to positive integers. Hold onto your hats, because the SAT now has negative exponents and fractional or rational exponents too (remember that *rational* just denotes having a numerator and denominator). You know what 5^2 is; well, 5^{-2} is just 1 divided by 5^2. Don't sweat this. As for rational (fractional) exponents, look at some examples. The square root of 3 is written as $3^{1/2}$, and the square root of 9 is written as $9^{1/2}$. The cube root is the $1/3$ power. The fourth root is the $1/4$ power, etc. You might be asked the fourth root of 16, which is 2.

Direct and inverse proportions will be on your exam. You'll have quantities a and b that are directly proportional, *i.e.*, as a increases, so does b. This is expressed as an equation by

$$b = ka$$

with k being a constant. An example of a direct proportion would be that when you increase the length of the sides of a square, the area increases.

But you might also have an inverse relationship between two quantities, where as a increases, b decreases, expressed as

$$ab = k$$

(k again is a constant). An example of an inverse proportion might be that if you have two people sending out a mailing, it takes 6 hours. If you have 4 people, it only takes 3 hours. In the equation above a is the number of people working, and b is the number of hours required. The constant k is 12, so 2 times 6 is 12, and 4 times 3 is 12.

Functions have long been on the SAT, often in the form of weird symbols. Now functional notation is used. If a function f has the definition

$$f(x) = x - 3^x,$$

we can substitute numbers and solve. If x is 3, $f(3) = 3 - 3^3$, or 3 - 27, or -24. (By the way, $f(x)$ is pronounced "f of x").

Domain and range sound odd until you realize they're just fancy words for, respectively, x values and y values. Suppose we have two sets A and B. A function f defined on A looks at each member of set A and assigns it a single, unique member of set B. The set A is the *domain* of function f, and the set B is the *range* of function f.

Another way of looking at it is that the first set (the domain), includes all the values you put into the function. The second set (the range), is all the values you get out of it.

If you want a mnemonic for remembering which is x and which is y, take the letters DXRY and say "**DeX**ter likes **RY**e bread." That will pair the D for *domain* with the x values, and the R for *range* with the y values.

You will be expected to solve problems concerning values of x outside the domain (ones for which the function given isn't defined), or values of y outside the range, in other words, that $f(x)$ can't possibly equal.

Real-life scenarios using functions: Functions can be used to model situations such as population growth, sales figure projections, etc. For instance, you might get info on the SAT that deals with anticipated population at various levels of food production and be asked to come up with a graph or equation showing different population levels as a function of food production levels. (Extra credit: would you expect such a graph to show a *direct* relationship between food production and population levels or an *inverse* relationship?)

Equations and graphs that express linear functions: A linear function is one in which x is the input variable and x is only to the power of one, *i.e.*, there are no linear equations in which you have x squared or cubed or higher. Linear functions create graphs that are straight lines, hence the name *linear*. **If you see a graph that's a curve, it's not describing a linear function.** Period. No fancy calculations, just the sweet knowledge that you can eliminate that drawing as a graph of a linear function!

You will be given questions using linear equations, *e.g.*,

$$y = mx + b$$

or

$$f(x) = mx + b$$

where m and b are constants; you might see how changes in values of m and b affect a graph of the function, or look at a graph and see if it matches the linear equation where m and b are constants. Some questions may involve identifying graphs of linear functions.

Sometimes you may be asked to compute slope of a line for a linear function. Please see MathFacts™ 2.

Equations and graphs that express quadratic functions: Questions of this type involve squaring a quantity in the equation (quadratic equations are also explained quite a bit in MathFacts™ 6, so please look there for further clarification).

The quadratic formula is:

$$ax^2 + bx + c = 0$$

Remember that, in solving a quadratic equation, you are always solving for x. And because x is squared, you will *always* have two solutions. A good way to remember this is to recall that the square of a positive number is the same as the square of its corresponding negative number, *e.g.*, the square of both +2 and -2 is 4.

It is critical, in working with quadratic equations, to remember that a positive number times a positive number is (drum roll, please) . . . positive. And a negative number times a positive will always be . . . negative. Negative times negative will always be . . . positive .

Let's say you have $x^2 - 3x + 2 = 0$. When you solve it, you get two solutions (as always): 2 and 1. If you substitute either of those numbers for x in the equation, you will in fact get zero for your answer.

Now, *how* do you solve this? Look at the first term x^2; the fact that there's no coefficient (multiplier) in front of it tells you that you can write something having the following format:

$$(x + \text{fill-in-the-blank\#1})(x + \text{fill-in-the-blank\#2}) = 0$$

(note that the fill-in-the-blank quantities #1 and #2 can and often *will* be different from one another.

Next you need to find two numbers that add up to -3 and that multiply out to 2. Well, there are two sets of integers that provide a product of 2, and they are 2 times 1 and -2 times -1. Then you look at those two choices and pick the two numbers that add up to -3. That choice is -2 and -1.

Now you take those numbers and fill them into

$$(x + \text{fill-in-the-blank\#1})(x + \text{fill-in-the-blank\#2}) = 0$$

and get

$$(x + (-2))(x + (-1)) = 0$$

or, more simply,

$$(x - 2)(x - 1) = 0$$

Once you get to this point, if either of the two parenthetic expressions equals zero, the whole equation equals zero. So x can be 2 or it can be 1.

Let's take another example:

$$x^2 + 6x + 5 = 0.$$

Using $ax^2 + bx + c = 0$, $a = 1$ (since there's no number before the x), $b = 6$, and $c = 5$. By figuring out what two numbers have a product of 5 and sum of 6, you can express this quadratic equation in the following way:

$$(x + 5)(x + 1) = 0.$$

So x could equal -5 or x could equal -1. If either expression in parentheses equals 0, the whole left side of the equation equals 0.

The name *quadratic* has *quad*–in it as in *quad*rilateral, a *four*-sided figure (*quad*–of course means *four*). An equilateral quadrilateral is a square, so that's a connection you can make between the *quad*–and the square or squared quantity in the quadratic equation.

Quadratic functions on an *x* - *y* axis are parabolas.

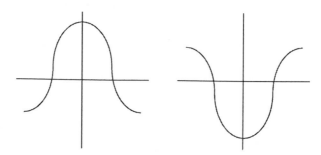

These parabolas will look sort of like a "U" or an upside-down "U". If you see a parabola, think of a quadratic equation!

On the SAT, you'll deal with quadratic equations or their graphs or both, and also compare the graphs of two quadratic equations. You might take the two equations, $y = 3(x + 2)^2$ and $y = 4x^2$, and compare their graphs. Or you might compare the graphs of $y = 2x^2$ and $y = 2(x - 1)^2$.

Once again I remind you that you can get the hang of this stuff. It may not be fun (ok, it won't be fun!), but you can do it. And you can get a good score on the SAT without mastering every single thing on the test.

Factoring will be important for solving quadratic equations. Let's try one more: this one a little tougher because x^2 is multiplied by 4, but you can still do it:

$$4x^2 - 5x - 6 = 0$$

This factors to

$$(4x + 3)(x - 2) = 0$$

so the answers for *x* are $-3/4$ and 2.

On tough quadratic equations (which may or may not appear on the SAT), you can use the quadratic formula, which is

$$x = \frac{-b \pm \sqrt{(b^2 - 4ac)}}{2a}$$

Geometry, Trig, Graphs, More Functions, Measurement

Geometric Notation: People have always had to deal with some of these concepts in geometry on the SAT, but now they will expect you to know common notation for concepts used in high school math courses. For instance,

$\overleftrightarrow{AB}$ represents the line going through points *A* and *B*.

$\overrightarrow{AB}$ represents a ray starting at *A* and going through *B*.

$\overline{AB}$ represents the line segment with *A* and *B* as endpoints.

$|\overline{AB}|$ is the length of *AB*

You are expected to know that, if two lines are congruent, they are equal in length. The symbol for the congruence is a tilde or squiggly line over an equal sign ($\cong$).

The Big Trig Gig

To Trig or Not to Trig, That is the Question (apologies to Hamlet and Shakespeare!) The test does not currently include trig. There was, I think, some speculation ahead of time that trig might be on the new SAT, but when the revised test finally came out, it wasn't there. However, it was a real pain to write this section, so I'm leaving it in the book in case the testmakers add trig to a later version! If it helps you today in a trig class, all the better! But for the purposes of the SAT, you may quite reasonably skip this section and any problems pertaining to trig in Math Worksheet II. *Trig*onometry, of course, has to do with the relationships between different sides and angles of *tri*angles (hence the same start to both words). You will have more questions on 30 - 60 - 90 triangles and isosceles right triangles, *i.e.*, 45 - 45 - 90 triangles. MathFacts™ 1 deals heavily with those. In fact, there will be questions answerable via trig or other methods, the latter sometimes being simpler than dealing with sines, cosines, etc. I *strongly* recommend that you study those extra hard and memorize that material.

Let's take an example: say you have a 30 - 60 - 90 triangle, and the hypotenuse measures 10. You can say that the sine of a 30 degree angle is always .5, or you can simply know that the side opposite the 30 degree angle in a 30 - 60 - 90 triangle is half the length of the hypotenuse, and just say 10 times $^1/_2$ is 5. If you memorize the relationships in 30 - 60 - 90 triangles and 45 - 45 - 90 triangles, you will be *waaaay* ahead of the game.

But for some people (not for most!), trig is easier than geometry. If that's the case for you, the following info can be useful. When you have 30 - 60 - 90 triangles, the side measures have the ratio 1, 2, √3, as you know from MathFacts™. Of course, multiples of those numbers work as long as you keep the same ratio; *e.g.*, 2, 4, 2√3, or 3, 6, 3√3. In trig, the following information summarizes those relationships in slightly different terms:

$$\sin 30° = {}^1/_2 \text{ or } .5; \cos 30° = \sqrt{3}/2$$
$$\sin 60° = \sqrt{3}/2; \cos 60° = {}^1/_2 \text{ or } .5.$$

Note that the sines and cosines are reversed for the 30 and 60 degree angles in 30 - 60 - 90 triangles.

In your 45 - 45 - 90 triangles, the side measures have the ratio of 1, 1, √2 (so obviously, multiples of those three numbers work too, as long as the basic ratio remains the same: e.g., 2, 2, 2√2, or 3, 3, 3√2). Thus, sin 45°= 1/√2 (OR, if you multiply both numerator and denominator by the square root of two, you get: √2/2). The next formula yields the same results: cos 45° = 1/√2 OR, again (if you multiply numerator and denominator by the square root of two), the √2/2. Handy hint: in an isosceles right triangle, the sines and cosines are equal, because the two 45 degree angles are equal.

A common item on the SAT is material that draws on 30 - 60 - 90 triangles or isosceles right triangles but with an additional wrinkle. Remember that all squares divide along the diagonal into two 45 - 45 - 90 triangles, so you can use the 45 - 45 - 90 information to solve such a problem. If a problem states that the diagonal of a rectangle creates either a 30° or a 60° angle with one side of the rectangle, you are dealing with two 30 - 60 - 90 triangles, so the 30 - 60 - 90 geometry or trig relationships kick in. Sometimes the square or rectangle is circumscribed within a circle, and then you can use the side length information on the two kinds of triangles to figure out area or circumference of the circle, using the formulas for those.

It's not a bad idea to memorize the definitions of sine, cosine and tangent, which apply to right triangles:

Sine (or sin) is defined as the opposite side from an angle divided by the hypotenuse, *i.e.*,

$$\sin = \text{opposite/hypotenuse}$$

Cosine (or cos) is defined as the non-hypotenuse side adjacent to an angle divided by the hypotenuse., *i.e.,*

$$cos = adjacent/hypotenuse$$

Tangent (or tan) is defined as the side opposite an angle divided by the non-hypotenuse side adjacent to the angle, *i.e.,*

$$tan = opposite/adjacent$$

Here's a mnemonic (memory aid) for each formula:

> *Sin*ead is the *opposite* of *hyp*er.
> *Cosmo adj*usts to having *hyp*ertension (high blood pressure).
> *Tan*zania *oppos*es *adj*ustments to the trade balance.

Or just use the classic SOHCAHTOA (sounds like a friend of Pocahontas, doesn't it?):

> **S**ine is **O**pposite over **H**ypotenuse, **C**osine is **A**djacent over **H**ypotenuse, and **T**angent is **O**pposite over **A**djacent.

Or make up your own mnemonic, *e.g.,*

> **S**ome **O**ld **H**angars **C**ould **A**wkwardly **H**old **T**wenty **O**bsolete **A**irplanes.

It's unlikely that you will have to know all the complexities of trig on the test. And keep in mind that most calculators have trig functions on them; it may be worth your while to spend a little time acquainting yourself with those functions on your particular calculator so you don't stumble around during the test trying to find the right keys.

I doubt that you will need to know *all* of the following material, but I'm putting it in, just in case.

> tangent (tan) = sin/cos
> cotangent (cot) = cos/sin OR 1/tan
> secant (sec)= 1/cos
> cosecant (csc)= 1/sin

So tangent and cotangent are reciprocal functions. Secant and cosine: ditto. Cosecant and sine: ditto. *Reciprocal* of course means you take a quantity and reverse the numerator and denominator.

In the four quadrants created by the x - y axis, you start in the upper right quadrant, and that's quadrant I. Going *counterclockwise*, you have quadrants II, III and IV.

All 6 trig functions must be positive in quadrant I. In quadrant II, both sin and csc are positive. In quadrant III, both tan and cot are positive. In quadrant IV, both cos and sec are positive.

Mnemonic time:

All 6 of us were *positive* the meeting was at 1 o'clock (all 6 trig functions positive in quadrant I).

*Sin*ead works at *CSC* (Computer Service Corp.) 2 times a week. (SIN, CSC, quadrant II).

I wore my *tan coat* 3 times. (TAN, COT, quadrant III)

The *cost* per *second* of running this machine is $4. (COS, SEC, quadrant IV).

Radians: There are 2π radians in a circle. Thus 2π radians is equal to 360 degrees. This means, of course, that 1 radian = $180/\pi$ degrees, and

1 degree = $\pi/180$ radians or $(1/180)\pi$ radians. Your 90 degree angle is $\pi/2$ radians or $(^1/_2)\pi$ radians.

Maybe you will have to work with the *cosine rule* for determining lengths of sides:

$a^2 = b^2 + c^2 - 2bc \cos A$ or $\cos A = \dfrac{b^2 + c^2 - a^2}{2bc}$

$b^2 = a^2 + c^2 - 2ac \cos B$ or $\cos B = \dfrac{a^2 + c^2 - b^2}{2ac}$

$c^2 = a^2 + b^2 - 2ab \cos C$ or $\cos C = \dfrac{a^2 + b^2 - c^2}{2ab}$

Some of the above may be beyond the scope of what you'll need for the test, but I've included it just in case.

Your calculator will be a major help in the sine-cosine-tangent department! Ditto for a lot of the graphing and scatter plot problems as long as you have a scientific or graphing calculator.

Geometry on the x - y axis: When you have lines on an x - y axis, you are dealing with *coordinate geometry*. Make sure you review all info on slope in MathFacts™; also, you need to know properties of the slopes of parallel or perpendicular lines. Parallel lines have the same slope, and the slopes of perpendicular lines are negative reciprocals of each other, *i.e.,* if one line has a slope of 3, a line perpendicular to it will have a slope of $-^1/_3$ (this is covered in detail below).

You will also be asked to describe lines by equations, calculate distance between two points on the x - y axis (*i.e.,* calculate line length) and find midpoints of line segments. If the x coordinates of 2 points are the same, find the difference between the y coordinates and that's the length of the line segment; if the y coordinates of 2 points are the same, find the difference between the x coordinates and that's the length of the line segment. That's the easiest way, but what if there are no common x and y coordinates? Then you use the following method: add together the two x coordinates and divide by 2, and that will be your midpoint's x coordinate; add together the two y coordinates and divide by 2, and that will be your midpoint's y coordinate.

If you have a line, you can use the distance formula to determine the length. Say PQ is the line. If P's coordinates are (x_1, y_1) and Q's coordinates are (x_2, y_2), your formula is as follows:

$$\sqrt{(x_1 - x_2)^2 + (y_1 - y_2)^2}$$

Example: If P's coordinates are (3, 2) and Q's coordinates are (7, 4), then the midpoint of that line segment is (5, 3). The length of that line segment is $\sqrt{20}$ or $2\sqrt{5}$.

Line equations are a little trickier, but not much. To create an equation of a line, you need two things:

1. the slope of a line, and
2. any point on the line.

Let's take an example: Suppose you have a line that passes through the point (2,6) and has a slope of 3. If a line goes through (x_1, y_1) and has a slope of m, you'd use this equation:

$$y - y_1 = m(x - x_1)$$

So let's go back to that line with a slope of 3 and the point (2,6). We take that equation above and plug in the numbers we have, and we get

$$y - 6 = 3(x - 2).$$

Now we play with that equation to get the slope/intercept form of the line. So we multiply the stuff inside and outside of the equation and get

$$y - 6 = 3x - 6$$

which simplifies to $y = 3x$. This is the equation for a line passing through point (2,6) and having a slope of 3.

What happens if we're given two points and no slope? Easy! You can figure out the slope from knowing the 2 points, and then use one point and the slope and the equation above to solve. Suppose with have the points (5,2) and (-1,-1). To find the slope, we use the slope formula:

$$m = \frac{(y_2 - y_1)}{(x_2 - x_1)}$$

The slope of the line including the points (5, 2) and (-1, -1) is $-3/-6$, or positive $1/2$.

Now we can take the point (5, 2) and the slope $1/2$ and use the equation $y - y_1 = m(x - x_1)$:

$$y - 2 = 1/2(x - 5)$$

which simplifies to:

$$y - 2 = (1/2) x - 2.5$$

and further,

$$y = (1/2)x - .5$$

As a function, this could be written several ways:

$f(x) = .5x - .5$
$f(x) = (1/2)x - 1/2$
$f(x) = .5(x - 1)$

So the line that goes through points (5,2) and (-1,-1) could be expressed in functional notation as $f(x) = 1/2x - 1/2$. Parallel lines will have the same slope, but each line will have a different point/slope equation.

What about perpendicular lines? Their slopes are *negative reciprocals* of each other. You know positive reciprocals multiply out to one; *e.g.*, 2 times $1/2$ equals 1, so 2 and $1/2$ are positive reciprocals, usually just called reciprocals. But negative reciprocals multiply out to -1. Thus 2 and $-1/2$ are negative reciprocals. So if the slope of one line is $-1/2$, the line perpendicular to that line has a slope of 2.

What about vertical and horizontal lines? A horizontal line always has the form $y = c$, since the y coordinate is constant, *e.g.*, $y = 7$. Likewise, a vertical line always has the form $x = c$, since the x coordinate is constant.

Remember: a positive slope resembles that of a stock you bought for $3 which is now worth $84. A negative slope resembles that of a stock you bought for $15 which is now worth $1.

Tangent Line Properties

Take a circle and draw a radius line from its center to the edge of the circumference. Now draw a line perpendicular to the radius line, intersecting the circle at the same point (and only that point). You have a tangent line.

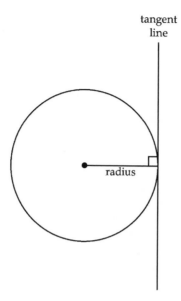

You are expected to know that the line perpendicular to the radius is *tangent to the circle*. A corollary is that if you draw a line perpendicular to the tangent line at the point at which it contacts the circle, that line passes through the center of the circle.

Transformations' Effects on Graphs of Functions

This kind of question has been on the SAT before, but in slightly different form. You would be given an expression like

$$y = 2x \text{ [which is now } f(x) = 2x]$$

and be asked what would happen if you added 4 to x. So your new equation would be

$$y = 2(x + 4) \text{ [or } f(x) = 2(x + 4)]$$

All you do is put the x in parentheses, and apply the transformation (change) asked. If they say x is tripled, you write

$$y = 2(3x)$$

and then simplify to

$$y = 6x.$$

The SAT expects you to figure out what such a transformation will do to the function's graph, *e.g.,* they might ask you to compare the graphs of the functions $f(x) = 2x$ and $f(x) = 2(x + 4)$.

Functions and Graphs, And Their Qualitative Behavior

You might look at a function's graph and determine how many values there are of x for which $f(x) = -2$. You look at the graph portion shown and see how many times y equals -2 and that's your answer. In the drawing below, the answer is 4, since there are 4 distinct or different points where $y = -2$.

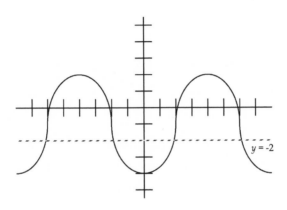

Math Worksheet II

Here are 60 more math problems for you to practice using the math skills in MathFacts™ 1 - 7 and the information in the previous chapter.

Use separate sheets of paper to work on these and
do them at least 5 - 6 times. Remember: repetition is critical
to long-term learning, which is what's tested on
the PSAT and the SAT. Good luck!

1. A square has side length 2 and is circumscribed within a circle so that all four vertexes of the square are on the circumference of the circle. What is the area of the circle? What is the circumference?

2. Bob and Leeza train for a marathon (a little over 26 miles). On Day 1, they run 1 mile. On Day 2, they run 2 miles, on Day 3, they run 3 miles, and so on until on Day 26, they run 26 miles. What is the difference between the average (arithmetic mean) and the median of the distances they run in each one of all 26 days?

3. There are two seats in the front of a car and two more seats in the back of the same car. If 2 people, Abby and Beth, can drive, and if there are two more people, Candyce and Dana, who don't drive, and if all four people will be simultaneously seated in the four seats of the car any time they go somewhere, how many seating possibilities are there for these four people?

4. In a certain country, if food production doubles, population triples. All other factors staying the same, what happens if food production quadruples?

5. What is the midpoint of a line with the following coordinates: (6,2) and (12,2)?

6. What can you say about a line (drawn in two of the four quadrants created by an x - y axis) that has the form $y = 6$?

7. What can you say about a line (drawn in two of the four quadrants created by an x - y axis) that has the form $x = 6$?

8. What can you say about two lines (drawn in any of the four quadrants created by an x - y axis) that have, respectively, the forms $y = 6$ and $x = 6$?

9. If a line passes through the points (4, -3) and (12, -3), and another line passes through the points (6, -1) and (6, -35), what is the largest degree measure created where the lines cross each other?

10. If line AB is 6 and line BC is 4, and B is considered to be the same point in this problem, what is the longest length possible for line AC? The shortest?

11. Taking the points in the previous problem, keep all things the same except for one detail: C cannot be on the same line as the one containing A and B. What are the longest and shortest lengths possible for line AC?

12. Picture a parallelogram (four-sided figure with 2 sets of equal parallel sides). The degree measures of two angles are 30 apiece, and the degree measures of the other two angles are 150 each. If side lengths are 10 and 5, what is the area of the parallelogram? (Area is base times height, with height being a perpendicular line drawn to the base or an extension of the base.)

13. Picture another parallelogram with two angles measuring 45 degrees each and two other angles measuring 135 degrees each. If the side lengths are $5\sqrt{2}$ and 22, what's the area?

14. Four business owners share profits of $200,000 in the following ratio: 1:2:3:4. What are the shares?

15. There are x students in a class with an average grade of 94. There are y students in a class with an average grade of 90. There are z

students in a class with an average grade of 54. When the classes are combined, the average score is 70. What is the value of z in terms of x and y?

16. What is 16 to the $^1/_4$ power plus 32 to the $^1/_5$ power?

17. What is 9 to the $^1/_2$ power plus 16 to the $^1/_2$ power plus 25 to the $^1/_2$ power?

18. Six people do a mailing of 1200 packets in 4 hours. If each one brings a friend and there are no other factors affecting the mailing, how long will it take the new set of people to do the same-size mailing?

19. If the domain of the function $f(x) = 4 + x$ is the set A, consisting of (1, 2, 3, 5, 7, 9), what is a possible value in the range of this function?

20. AB is a line segment on an x - y grid. If the endpoints A and B are the points (-6, 0) and (4, 0), what value is the midpoint?

21. If the hypotenuse of a 30 - 60 - 90 triangle measures 4, what is the measure of the shortest side? What is the measure of the side opposite the 60 degree angle?

22. What is the length of a line having the following 2 endpoints on an x - y grid: (6,7), (4,3)?

23. Create the equation of a line passing through the point (1,5) and having a slope of 2.

24. Create the equation of a line passing through the points (1, 7) and (2, 10).

25. If line AB has a slope of 3 and line CD has a slope of $-^1/_3$), what can you say about these two lines?

26. What happens to $f(x)$ in the following function when x is doubled? The function is $f(x) = x^2/_2$.

27. If the radius of a circle is 3, what happens to the area of the circle if you triple the radius?

28. Paul has 10 blue socks, 12 brown socks, and y gray socks. If the probability at random of picking a gray sock is .45, how many gray socks does Paul have?

29. If the ratio of the four degree measures of a quadrilateral is 2:3:5:8, what are the four angles' degree measures?

30. What are the two solutions for the equation $x^2 + 2x - 24 = 0$?

31. What are the two solutions for the equation $6x^2 + 5x + 1 = 0$?

32. What are the two solutions for the equation $4x^2 + 16x - 20 = 0$?

33. Evaluate the following statement: There can be only one solution to a quadratic equation.

34. What is the absolute value of -3? What is $|-3| + |6| + |-2|$?

35. What is the probability at random of tossing two ones with a pair of fair dice, each side of which has a different number of dots (1, 2, 3, 4, 5, or 6)?

36. Marvin's sales commissions in 1998 were $3000. If his sales commissions doubled every year after that, what were his sales commissions in 2003?

37. How might Marvin's sales commissions be described as a geometric sequence formula?

38. What is the intersection of the set of all positive even integers and the set of all positive odd integers?

39. What is the union of the two sets above?

40. Solve for z in the following radical equations:

$$4\sqrt{z} + 16 = 20.$$
$$4\sqrt{z} - 16 = 20.$$

41. Simplify this expression: $(6y - 4)/(3y - 2)$.

42. Solve for y: $(6y - 4)/(y + 1) = 2$.

43. What is $5^{-2} + 3^{-2}$?

44. A square is circumscribed in a circle. The square is shaded in. What is the probability at random that a point within the circle will be in the shaded region?

45. Set A is the set of numbers of the form $3x$. Set B is the set of numbers of the form y^2. And set C is the set of numbers of the form 3^z, where x, y and z are all integers. Which two of the following numbers are in the intersection of the three sets: 7, 9, 27, 81, 99?

46. A metal tube is a hollow cylinder. If the radius of the circle formed by the opening at either end is 2.5, and if the length of the tube is 12, what is the greatest distance that can be traced in a straight line from a point on the circumference of one opening to a point on the circumference of the other opening?

47. AB is a ray starting at A, passing through B. AC is a ray starting at A and passing through C. If the two rays create a right angle at A, and if $AC = 8$ and $AB = 6$, C is the midpoint of a line measuring AE, and B is the midpoint of a line with measure AD, what is the value of DE?

48. True or false: A curved line can portray a linear equation.

49. True or false: Parallel lines have the same slope.

50. True or false: Each line in a set of parallel lines has the same point/slope equation.

51. True or false: In a 30 - 60 - 90 triangle, the sine of the 30-degree angle is the cosine of the 60 degree angle.

52. If x is the set of all positive integers and y is the set of all squares of positive integers, how many members between 1 and 100 are in the intersection of sets x and y?

53. One company lost $2.5 million last year. Another gained $2.25 million. What is the difference between the absolute values of those numbers?

54. What is the sum of $2^{-2} + 3^{-2}$?

55. If $b = ka$, what happens to a when b triples?

56. If $b = 1/ka$, what happens to a when b triples?

57. If $ab = k$, there is an inverse relationship between a and b. What happens to b if a doubles and k doubles?

58. The domain of the function $f(x) = (3x + 2)/x^2$ is the set (-1, 2). What is the range?

59. For the following function $f(x) = 3x + 4$, what is the range if the domain consists of the integers 5, 6, 7, and 8?

60. The mode is the most frequent value. Five people have the following amounts of money: y, $y + 2$, $2y - 6$, $3y - 8$, and $y - 1$. The arithmetic mean of those numbers is \$10.20. What is the mode? (Disregard the dollar sign when working this out.).

Math Worksheet II Answers

1. The diagonal of the square is $2\sqrt{2}$, so that's also the diameter of the circle. The radius is $\sqrt{2}$. The formula πr^2 gives us the area of the circle, so the area is 2π. The circumference formula is πd or $2\pi r$, so the circumference is $(2\sqrt{2})\pi$.

2. The answer is zero. When you have consecutive integers (or even just identical intervals between numbers, *e.g.*, .1, .2, .3, .4., .5 etc.), the arithmetic mean and the median are identical, so the difference is always 0.

3. If Abby drives, Beth can be in the passenger seat in front, and Candyce and Dana can sit in the back seats in two ways (Candyce on the left and Dana on the right, or vice versa). Or Candyce can be in the front passenger seat, and Beth and Dana will have two positions in back. Or Dana can be in the front passenger seat, making two more positions for Beth and Candyce in back. So there are 6 possibilities when Abby drives. When Beth drives, there are 6 more possibilities, since Abby is substituting for Beth in the above 6 positions. So the answer is 12.

4. Population becomes 9 times as big. *i.e.*, you're squaring the original factors of doubling (multiplying by 2) and tripling (multiplying by 3). So instead of multiplying by 2 to the first power and 3 to the first power, you're multiplying by 2 squared and 3 squared.

5. (9,2). Since the y coordinates are the same, you just add the x coordinates and divide the sum by 2.

6. When the y coordinate is constant, the line is horizontal.

7. When the x coordinate is constant, the line is vertical.

8. They're perpendicular to each other. If one line is horizontal and the other is vertical, they are perpendicular.

9. All four angles are 90, since one line is horizontal and one line is vertical, and therefore the two lines are perpendicular to each other. Thus, the answer is 90.

10. Six plus 4 is 10, so 10 is the answer for longest. Six minus 4 is 2, so 2 is the answer for shortest. This is a situation that can happen with two roads laid out in a straight line back to back, so that, e.g., 6 miles plus 4 miles is 10 miles. Or the road BC can backtrack onto AB; in the latter case, you are driving 6 miles forward, for instance, and then backtracking 4 miles on the same road, and now you are 2 miles from where you started. Once you know the two outside limits (i.e., 10 and 2), all numbers between those work too since a road can branch off at all kinds of different angles from the other one.

11. Both this and the previous problem are common on the test. The actual longest and shortest lengths cannot be determined but we can figure out what those lengths are greater than or less than. The figure described is a triangle, and unless you are given the angle between lines AB and BC you can't settle on one value; however, anything between 10 and 2, but not including 10 and 2, will work. Where two sides of a triangle are given, the third side's length must be less than the other two side lengths added together, and more than the difference between the two given side lengths.

12. 25. Why? 5 is the measure of the hypotenuse of a 30 - 60 - 90 triangle created when one draws the line that is the height. So 2.5 is the measure of the height, since it's the side opposite the 30 degree angle. Sin 30 is .5, and also the side opposite the smallest angle in a 30 - 60 - 90 triangle is half the length of the hypotenuse. So 2.5 times 10 is 25.

13. The line that's the height has to measure 5, since it's a shorter side in an isosceles triangle created by the height. 5 times 22 is 110, which is the answer.

14. Add 1, 2, 3, and 4; get 10. Divide $200,000 by 10; get $20,000. Multiply the latter number by 1, 2, 3, and 4, and get, respectively, $20,000, $40,000, $60,000, and $80,000, which add up to $200,000, the total profit.

15. Multiply the number of students in each class by the average score to get the total score for each class, and then add those 3 numbers and divide by $x + y + z$. When you have a non-fractional number like 70, you can always put it over the number 1 and then you have two fractions equal to each other and you can cross-multiply.

$$\frac{94x + 90y + 54z}{x + y + z} = 70$$

$$94x + 90y + 54z = 70(x + y + z)$$

$$94x + 90y + 54z = 70x + 70y + 70z$$

Subtract $70x$, $70y$ and $70z$ from both sides of the equation:

$$24x + 20y - 16z = 0$$
$$16z = 24x + 20y$$

Dividing both sides of the equation by 4, you get

$$4z = 6x + 5y$$

Dividing both sides of the equation again by 4, you get your final answer:

$$z = \frac{6x + 5y}{4}$$

16. $2 + 2 = 4$. Two is the fourth root of 16 and also the fifth root of 32.

17. This is $3 + 4 + 5 = 12$.

18. Two hours. Twice the number of people means the job takes half as long, since there is an inverse proportion.

19. Plug in any number in set A and see what you get. Possible answers are as follows: 5, 6, 7, 9, 11, and 13.

20. (-1, 0). Since the y coordinates are the same, you add the x coordinates and divide by 2. That becomes your x coordinate, and your y coordinate has to be 0.

21. The shortest side is 2. The side opposite the 60 degree angle is $2\sqrt{3}$. You just have to memorize these relationships.

22. You find the difference between the x coordinates and the difference between the y coordinates, and you square each of those differences and add them together. Then you take the square root of that sum. $(6 - 4)^2 + (7 - 3)^2$ is 20. The square root of 20 is $2\sqrt{5}$.

23. Use the equation, $y - y_1 = m(x - x_1)$. So $(y - 5) = 2(x - 1)$, which simplifies to $y - 5 = 2x - 2$, or even simpler, $y = 2x + 3$.

24. Get the slope by this formula: $m = (y_2 - y_1)$ divided by $(x_2 - x_1)$. The slope is 3 [numerator (10 - 7) over denominator (2 - 1)]. Now use the equation $y - y_1 = m(x - x_1)$ and just one of the two points and the slope. So $y - 10 = 3(x - 2)$. This simplifies to $y - 10 = 3x - 6$, and then $y = 3x + 4$.

25. The slopes are negative reciprocals, so they are perpendicular to each other. Memorize this!

26. Put x in parentheses and multiply inside parentheses by 2. You get $f(x) = (2x)^2/2$; it simplifies to $4x^2/2$ or $2x^2$. In other words, it's 4 times as much as it was.

27. Because of the formula πr^2, area is multiplied by 9.

28. The answer is 18. Add together the 10 blue and 12 brown socks, and get 22 socks. These are .55 times the total number of socks. So the total number of socks is 100/55 times 22, or 40. If you then multiply 40 by .45, you'll get 18.

29. Add up the numbers in the ratio, and get 18. Divide 360 (the total number of degrees in a quadrilateral) by 18, and get 20. Multiply

20 by each of the numbers in the ratio and get 40, 60, 100, and 160.

30. When you factor this out, you get $(x - 4)(x + 6) = 0$. So $x = 4$ or $x = -6$.

31. This factors out to $(2x + 1)(3x + 1) = 0$. Solutions are $-\frac{1}{2}$ and $-\frac{1}{3}$.

32. This factors out to $(4x - 4)(x + 5) = 0$. Solutions are 1 and -5.

33. False. There are always two.

34. $|-3| = 3$
$|-3| + |6| + |-2| = 11$.

35. $\frac{1}{6}$ times $\frac{1}{6}$ equals $\frac{1}{36}$.

36. $6000 in 1999. $12,000 in 2000. $24,000 in 2001. $48,000 in 2002. $96,000 in 2003.

37. $y = \$3000(2^n)$

38. Since the intersection contains only members that are common to both sets, this intersection has no members (it's the null set).

39. Since the union contains all members in either or both sets, the union contains all positive integers.

40. $4\sqrt{z} = 20 - 16$, or 4. Divide both sides by 4, and $\sqrt{z} = 1$, hence $z = 1$. In the second part of the problem, $4\sqrt{z} = 20 + 16$, or 36. Divide both sides by 4, and $\sqrt{z} = 9$, hence $z = 81$.

41. Everything in the numerator is twice everything in the denominator, so the quick and easy answer is 2.

42. $6y - 4 = 2(y + 1)$
$6y - 4 = 2y + 2$
$4y = 6$
$y = \frac{3}{2}$ or 1.5

43. This is $1/5^2 + 1/3^2$, or $1/25 + 1/9$, which is .04 + (approximately) .11, so the answer is approximately .15.

44. Say the square has side of length 1. Thus the diagonal of the square (also the circle's diameter) is $\sqrt{2}$. The area of the square is 1. Using the formula πr^2, and radius of $\sqrt{2}/2$, the circle's area is $\pi/2$. The odds of being in the shaded area is 1 divided by the circle's area, which simplifies to $2/\pi$.

45. 9 and 81 both work, because they remain integers when divided by 3; they're squares of integers, and they are powers of 3. All three constraints must be met.

46. The diameter is 5. The length is 12. This is a 5 - 12 - 13 triangle problem, with the line in question forming the hypotenuse, so you can solve it via the Pythagorean Theorem: $5^2 + 12^2 = 13^2$, or 169.

47. *AE* is 16, *AD* is 12, so *DE* is 20. This is a 3 - 4 - 5 triangle problem, but you can use the Pythagorean Theorem.

48. False.

49. True.

50. False. The slope is the same, but each line has a different point/slope equation.

51. True. The sines and cosines are reversed for 30 and 60 degree angles in a 30 - 60 - 90 triangle.

52. Eight. The numbers: 4, 9, 16, 25, 36, 49, 64, and 81. 1 and 100 don't work, since the problem did not state "between 1 and 100, inclusive."

53. 0.25 million.

54. $1/4$ plus $1/9 = 13/36$.

55. The value of a triples too.

56. The value of a is $1/3$ what it was.

57. The value of b stays the same, since both sides of the equation have been multiplied by 2.

58. Plug the domain values into $f(x)$ and you'll find that the range is also (-1, 2).

59. Plug the numbers into $f(x)$ and you get 19, 22, 25, 28.

60. Add up all the values, and get $(8y - 13)/5 = 10.2$. So $8y - 13 = 51$, so $8y = 64$, and $y = 8$. Plug that value of 8 back into each of the expressions and you'll get values of 8, 10, 10, 16 and 7. Since 10 occurs twice, and nothing else occurs more than once, 10 is the mode.

Word Building and Discovery™

Wherein we learn to break down words into their component parts so that we can figure out what the heck they mean, even if we've never seen the words before.

Words belong to families the same way people do. Often, very different-seeming words have common ancestors and roots. Let's look at an example:

> duct . . . reduce . . . production . . . introduction . . . deduction . . .
> educe induction . . . conductivity . . . transducer . . . ducat . . .
> duchy . . . duke subdue . . . abduction . . . duchess . . . conducive . . .
> traduce . . . seduce ductile . . . adductor . . . inducement . . .
> produce . . . adduce deduce . . . conduit, and many more words.

What do these words have in common? They all come from the Latin root *duco*, meaning *to lead*. They are therefore related but they have different meanings because of their prefixes and suffixes. For example, *de-* means *from*, while *in-* means *in, into or within*. *Pro-* means *before, in front of or for*, while *e-* or *ex-* means *from, away from or out of*.

Now, this may sound complicated at first, but try to imagine the difference between having to remember thousands of distant relatives' names, professions and hometowns, on the one hand, and on the other hand, only having to remember which family they descend from, and a handful of rules about how they are different. This is what etymology (the study of word derivations, families and relationships) does; while it asks you to learn some strange words in an antiquated language, it ultimately simplifies the learning of words enormously and gives you a great deal of vocabulary development for a much smaller amount of memorization.

The Latin dictionary in this book contains a list of common Latin words, their meanings and the English words that have sprung from them over the years. You will find that language is a fascinating and much more logical study than you may have formerly believed. Furthermore, the study of word families is often fun and amusing, in the same way that the study of people's families can be amusing (there are always some rather exotic specimens in any family tree).

For instance, let's take the root *pes, pedis* (these are two Latin forms of the same word, and yes, there are more forms, but this book will not burden you with declining nouns and adjectives or conjugating verbs; we will merely list the different forms so you can see the variety and get a notion of the words derived from them). From *pes, pedis*, which is Latin for *foot* (and from its relative, the Greek *pous* and *pod-*), we get the following:

> pedestal . . . pedestrian . . . pedicure . . . millipede . . . pedigree
> piedmont . . . tripodal . . . expedition . . . impediment . . . pedicel
> tripod . . . octopus . . . podiatrist . . . platypus . . . pedal . . . podium
> pedometer . . . polyp . . . expedite . . . polypod . . . pediform
> antipodes . . . monopodium . . . peduncle, and so forth.

Another example is *lego, legere, legi, lectum,* meaning *to choose, gather, or read,* from which we get the following:

> collection . . . selective . . . predilection . . . recollection lectern . . .
> elective . . . intelligentsia . . . selectivity . . . negligent lectionary . . .
> legendary . . . illegibility . . . legion . . . lecture sacrilege . . .
> neglectful . . . elegance . . . diligently . . . electorate collectanea . . .
> negligible . . . prelecting . . . legionnaire . . . . etc.

The Latin *facio, facere, feci, factum,* meaning *to make or do,* has spawned a wealth of English words:

> . . . fact . . . perfection . . . defective . . . efficacious . . . effect . . .
> sacrifice . . . surfeit . . . fashionable . . . facsimile feasance . . .
> feasibility . . . amplification . . . sufficient . . . vivify featured . . .
> confection . . . affectation . . . benefactor . . . rarefaction
> rectify . . . qualification . . . putrefaction . . . benefit . . . profitable
> modification . . . artificial . . . counterfeit . . . notify . . . forfeiture
> manufacturing . . . deficit . . . nullify . . . ineffectual . . . affection
> faction . . . beatific . . . confetti . . . justification . . . mollification
> feat . . . factorial . . . malefactor . . . defeated . . . discomfit prefect . . .
> misfeasance . . . affair, and dozens and dozens more.

In the worksheets you will practice breaking words into component parts. Spend time going over the most common prefixes, suffixes and roots (the ones in **boldface**) so you become accustomed to seeing words etymologically.

While the list is sizable and intimidating at first, it will seem less so after a while. You will find it opens up a vast vocabulary to you and allows you to figure out the meaning of a word even if you have never seen it before, a skill which presents an obvious advantage during the Evidence-Based Reading part of the SAT.

Note: I am not trying to make a Latin scholar out of you, only to help you have a greater actual and potential English vocabulary. Since it is estimated that 90% to 95% of all English derives directly or indirectly from Latin, you will find this unit establishes an orderly way of developing a large vocabulary.

This section is to be used in conjunction with the section on Latin vocabulary as well as any other vocabulary-building materials available to you.

In this unit I will introduce a method that can help you greatly develop your actual and potential vocabulary by teaching you to break down words into their component parts, into prefixes, roots and suffixes.

You will probably recognize and know the definitions of many of the words shown, and will note that what you see here are not dictionary definitions; rather, they are rough definitions formed from the meanings of the prefixes, roots and suffixes.

You should not be concerned with whether you already know many of the words in this section; in fact, some familiar words have deliberately been employed so that you have an opportunity to see how the method works.

The development of vocabulary is a long-term project, but you can relatively quickly learn to use the methods of Word Building and Discovery™ in ways that will be useful to you during the SAT. The ability to look even at words you have never seen before and figure out pretty much what they mean will prove invaluable to you in the Evidence-Based Reading portions of the exam. Word Building and Discovery™ requires that you learn a finite number of mostly Latin words and become accustomed to dissecting English words.

At first, these endeavors may well seem cumbersome and very tough but they will get easier as you go along. As more and more of the material becomes familiar to you, I think you'll find that the method works.

If you have any foreign language training, it will come in handy during Word Building and Discovery™. If you lack this training, please don't despair; you can still master this unit, though it may initially take some extra effort. French, Spanish, and Italian will all help you grasp the Latin vocabulary a little faster, though in truth you will find that any foreign language background will make it easier for you to digest strange-looking words and connect them with English meanings.

As you look at words in the coming weeks and months and years, try to figure out anything you can about them. For instance, if you see the prefix *neo-*, meaning *new*, you will at least know that the word has to do with a new something; you may not understand anything else about it, but knowing something about the word may be enough to give you a glimmer of what you need to know during the SAT.

We strongly recommend that you keep a log of words as you read and later look them up in the dictionary, but only after you've tried on your own to figure out what they mean. The practice may seem tedious and less than fun, but we believe you'll find the SAT a lot easier if you put the time in now.

Okay. When you get discouraged, give yourself a pep talk or take a break for a bit. This is admittedly dense material, and there's no way around some toughness in preparing for the SAT. I figure it would be unfair to hand you a whole bunch of easy modules now and act like the SAT is a piece of cake, and then have you discover when you take the test that you're not adequately prepared. I think you'd rather work harder now and have an easier time during the actual exam.

Word Dissection

It sounds messy, and it does resemble the process in biology, but it won't ruin your lunch (or the lab specimen's lunch either, for that matter).

Word dissection is merely a matter of breaking it down into logical parts. To do this, you need some familiarity with how those parts look. Let's take as an example the word *perennial*.

If you knew nothing about English or Latin, it might seem reasonable to break the word into sections as follows:

pe•ren•ni•al

In a different universe, perhaps this would make sense; in ours, however, it does nothing for you. In our own universe, the word *perennial* is broken down as noted below:

per•enni•al

The reason for this is that *per* means *through, enni* means *year(s)* and the suffix *al* means *pertaining to or about.* Thus, the approximate meaning you get when you correctly dissect the word *perennial* is *pertaining to (something that lasts) through the years,* which is a pretty good approximation of the meaning of *perennial.* (The *enni* part of the word is a slight variation of *annus, anni,* meaning *year* from the Latin section.)

Let's look at another word (learning the method involves quite simply looking at a lot of examples so that you begin to get a feel for logical breaks in the words):

ex•clude

This word consists of two parts: *ex,* meaning *from, out of,* or *away from;* and *clude,* which comes from the Latin word *claudo* or *cludo,* meaning *to close.* To exclude someone means to shut someone out.

bene•diction

The above word divides into *bene,* meaning *well or properly;* and *diction,* coming from the Latin *dico, dicere, dixi, dictum,* meaning *to say or speak.* So a benediction involves speaking well or properly.

male•diction

This word combines the same root as the last word, but has the prefix *male,* meaning *bad or ill.* So a malediction involves speaking ill (of something).

astro•logy

breaks down into *astro,* meaning *star;* and *ology,* meaning *the study of (something),* so the meaning is *the study of stars.*

audio•phile

divides into *audio,* which pertains to *hearing or listening;* and *phile,* which denotes *one who loves (something).* Thus, an audiophile is someone who loves listening; its more specific meaning is someone who is a connoisseur of stereo systems.

biblio•phile

breaks down into *biblio*, meaning *book*; and *phile* (see directly above). Thus a bibliophile is a lover of books.

inter•cede

divides into *inter*, meaning *between or among*; and *cede*, coming from *cedo*, meaning *to go*. To intercede means to go between.

The above samples give a taste of how this process works. You need to learn the meanings of prefixes, roots and suffixes. Obviously, it doesn't help to break words into parts if you don't know what those parts mean. It is recommended that you study both the Latin section and all the materials that follow.

Word Building and Discovery™ Worksheets

Look at the following worksheets and try to approximate word meanings by the method shown in the previous section. Write your definition in the space marked (T) for TRIAL. After you have completed each page, refer to a dictionary and write a brief dictionary definition in the space marked (D). Try to see how well your definition fits the dictionary definition, but don't be concerned if the latter is much more fleshed-out; it's supposed to be. You are learning to find approximate meanings, an invaluable skill to have on a day when you won't be allowed to bring a dictionary into a certain testing site.

Worksheet #1 for Word Building and Discovery™

rectify:
    (T) _____

    (D) _____

regression:
    (T) _____

    (D) _____

adhesion:
    (T) _____

    (D) _____

projectile:
    (T) _____

    (D) _____

illegibility:
    (T) _____

    (D) _____

introspection:
    (T) _____

    (D) _____

tangibility:
    (T) _____

    (D) _____

preclude:
    (T) _____

    (D) _____

Worksheet #2 for Word Building and Discovery™

convention:

(T) _____

(D) _____

versatility:

(T) _____

(D) _____

impervious:

(T) _____

(D) _____

clairvoyant:

(T) _____

(D) _____

revocation:

(T) _____

(D) _____

benevolence:

(T) _____

(D) _____

circumvolve:

(T) _____

(D) _____

retention:

(T) _____

(D) _____

Worksheet #3 for Word Building and Discovery™

temporal:

(T) _____

(D) _____

extension:

(T) _____

(D) _____

tenable:

(T) _____

(D) _____

abstinence:

(T) _____

(D) _____

cessation:

(T) _____

(D) _____

corporation:

(T) _____

(D) _____

cordiform:

(T) _____

(D) _____

nullify:

(T) _____

(D) _____

Worksheet #4 for Word Building and Discovery™

discredit:

(T) _____

(D) _____

crescendo:

(T) _____

(D) _____

concurrence:

(T) _____

(D) _____

documentary:

(T) _____

(D) _____

reduction:

(T) _____

(D) _____

genuflect:

(T) _____

(D) _____

infinitude:

(T) _____

(D) _____

transgression:

(T) _____

(D) _____

Worksheet #5 for Word Building and Discovery™

collaboration:

    (T) _____

    (D) _____

elapse:

    (T) _____

    (D) _____

levorotation:

    (T) _____

    (D) _____

aquifer:

    (T) _____

    (D) _____

confluence:

    (T) _____

    (D) _____

interrogation:

    (T) _____

    (D) _____

nescient:

    (T) _____

    (D) _____

non-sequitur:

    (T) _____

    (D) _____

Worksheet #6 for Word Building and Discovery™

postscript:

    (T) _____

    (D) _____

legalization:

    (T) _____

    (D) _____

liberalize:

    (T) _____

    (D) _____

loquacious:

    (T) _____

    (D) _____

circumlocution:

    (T) _____

    (D) _____

luciferous:

    (T) _____

    (D) _____

remittance:

    (T) _____

    (D) _____

premonition:

    (T) _____

    (D) _____

Worksheet #7 for Word Building and Discovery™

suspension:

    (T) _____

    (D) _____

pedicure:

    (T) _____

    (D) _____

nascent:

    (T) _____

    (D) _____

importation:

    (T) _____

    (D) _____

pugnacious:

    (T) _____

    (D) _____

plenitude:

    (T) _____

    (D) _____

phonetics:

    (T) _____

    (D) _____

proponent:

    (T) _____

    (D) _____

Worksheet #8 for Word Building and Discovery™

misnomer:

(T) _____

(D) _____

petition:

(T) _____

(D) _____

candescence:

(T) _____

(D) _____

miscreant:

(T) _____

(D) _____

vivification:

(T) _____

(D) _____

fortification:

(T) _____

(D) _____

digression:

(T) _____

(D) _____

concordance:

(T) _____

(D) _____

Worksheet #9 for Word Building and Discovery™

precursor:

    (T) _____

    (D) _____

induction:

    (T) _____

    (D) _____

agriology:

    (T) _____

    (D) _____

introject:

    (T) _____

    (D) _____

multipurpose:

    (T) _____

    (D) _____

novice:

    (T) _____

    (D) _____

cooperation:

    (T) _____

    (D) _____

partition:

    (T) _____

    (D) _____

Worksheet #10 for Word Building and Discovery™

paternity:

(T) _____

(D) _____

maternity:

(T) _____

(D) _____

ambidextrous:

(T) _____

(D) _____

antenatal:

(T) _____

(D) _____

circadian:

(T) _____

(D) _____

contraposition:

(T) _____

(D) _____

geocentric:

(T) _____

(D) _____

infrasonic:

(T) _____

(D) _____

Worksheet #11 for Word Building and Discovery™

subatomic:

(T) _____

(D) _____

omnipresence:

(T) _____

(D) _____

intranuclear:

(T) _____

(D) _____

credibility:

(T) _____

(D) _____

supersonic:

(T) _____

(D) _____

unilateral:

(T) _____

(D) _____

pseudopod:

(T) _____

(D) _____

desist:

(T) _____

(D) _____

Worksheet #12 for Word Building and Discovery™

inanimate:

    (T) _____

    (D) _____

dialogue:

    (T) _____

    (D) _____

euphemism:

    (T) _____

    (D) _____

epidermis:

    (T) _____

    (D) _____

egocentricism:

    (T) _____

    (D) _____

biped:

    (T) _____

    (D) _____

alterable:

    (T) _____

    (D) _____

disparity:

    (T) _____

    (D) _____

Latin Words, Their Meanings in English, English Derivatives

Far from being a dead language, Latin appears daily in most English words. It can pave the way to learning tens of thousands of new English words.

Note: Sample English derivatives appear in parentheses after the Latin words and their definitions. In the case of prefixes, only the first part of the English words will employ the prefix; the remainder of derived words will come from other roots in Latin. E. g., see *a, ab, abs* and *ad* below. Words and roots in **boldface** are especially important to study.

a, ab, abs: from, away from, out of, of (absent, abstain, abdicate).

abdicatio: disowning, renunciation (abdication)

abhorreo: to shrink back from (abhorrence)

abluo: to wash (ablution)

abrado: to scrape off, shave (abrasion)

absorbeo: to swallow, gulp down, carry away, engross (absorbent, absorption, absorbefacient, absorptance)

abundo: to overflow or grow in abundance (abound, abundance)

abusus: wasting (abusive, abuse)

accuso [comes from *ad + causa*]: to blame, find fault with (accusation, accusatory) *acer, acris, acre*: sharp, keen (acrid, acerate)

acerbo: to make bitter, to aggravate (acerbity, acerbate, exacerbate)

acetum: vinegar (acetic acid, acetify, acetous)

acidus: sharp, sour (acidity, acid, acidulous, acidosis, acidophilus)

acus: needle (acumen, acupuncture, acute)

ad-: towards, to, until, at, about (admixture, adventure, adept, adequate).

adamanteus: hard as steel (adamantine, adamant)

adeps, adipis: soft, fat (adipose, adiposity)

administro, administrare: to help, direct (administration)

admissio: audience (admission, admissible)

adolesco: to come to maturity (adolescence)

adopto: to choose for oneself, to adopt (adoptive, adoptable, adoption)

adorno: to prepare, furnish, adorn (adornment)

adulatio: cringing, flattery (adulation)

aemulor, aemulari: to rival, emulate (emulation, emulous)

aenigma: a riddle, mystery (enigma, enigmatic)

aequus: even, level (equality, equate, equanimity, equation)

aerius: the lower air, the atmosphere (aerial, aerate)

aestas: summer (aestival, aestivate)

aestimatio: an appraising in terms of money, assessment of damages (estimation)

aeterno: to make eternal, immortalize (eternal, eternity, eternize) *aether*: the upper air, heaven (ethereal, ether)

ager, agri: land, territory, field (agriculture, agriology, agrestal, agrobiology)

ago, agere, egi, actum: to set in motion, drive, do, discuss, live, or spend (agile, agent, agenda, agitation, actor, action, inactive, cogent)

alacer, alacris, alacre: lively, eager, quick (alacrity)

albus, alba, album: white, pale, bright (albedo, albescent, albinism, albino, albite, album, albumen)

alius, alia, alium: other, another, different (alias, alienate, alien)

alter-: one of two, the one, the other (alternate, alternative, alter ego, alterable, altercation, alternator)

ambitio: canvassing for office, desire for office, popularity or fame (ambitious, ambitiously)

ambulo, ambulare: to walk, march, travel (amble, ambulance, ambulate, ambulatory, perambulate)

amicus, amica, amicum: friendly, well-wishing, favorable (amicable, amicability, amity)

amor: love, fondness (amorous, amoretto, amorist, amour)

amplus: ample (amplify, ample, amplification, amplitude)

amputo, amputare: to cut off, remove (amputation, amputee)

angulus: angle, corner (angling, angular, angularity, angulate)

animal, animalis: a living being, animal (animal, animalism)

animo, animare: to animate, give life to (animation, inanimate)

animus, animi: the spirit, heart, character, soul, mind (animosity, animus)

annus, anni: year (annual, anniversary, superannuated, biennial, perennial)

ante-: before, sooner than, above (antecedent, antechamber, antediluvian, antenatal)

antiquus: coming before, previous, earlier (antiquity, antique, antiquate)

anxius: anxious, uneasy (anxiety, anxious)

apex: the top, highest honor (apex, apices)

apis or *apes*: a bee (apiary, apian, apiarian)

appello, appellare: to address, speak to, name, entitle, pronounce (appellation, appellate, appellative, appellee)

aptus: fitted, fastened, suitable (aptitude, aptness, ineptitude)

aqua: water (aqueous, aquamarine, aquifer, aquatic, aquarium, aquarelle, aquaplane, aquatint, aqueduct, aquaculture)

arbiter: witness, judge, ruler (arbitration, arbitrage, arbiter, arbitrament)

arbor: tree or, by association, any wooden object (arbor, arboreal, arborescent, arboretum)

arcanus: closed, silent, secret (arcane, arcanum)

ardor: flame, burning, heat, eagerness (ardor, ardent)

argentum: silver (argent, argentine, argentite)

arguo, arguere: to put in clear light; to declare or prove; to accuse or blame (arguable, argument, argumentative)

arma, armorum: defensive arms, weapons, thus also war, soldiers, defense, military power (armaments, disarm, armadillo, armed forces, armor)

ars, artis: skill, method, technique (artist, artisan, artistic, artifice, artifact, artificial, artistry, artlessness)

articulus: small joint, division, part (article, articular, articulation)

asper: rough, uneven, sour or harsh (asperity, asperate, asper) *astrum, astri*: star or constellation (astrology, astronomer, astrolabe, astronaut, astronomical, astrophysics)

astutus: adroit, clever, crafty (astute, astuteness)

atrox, atrocis: terrible, cruel, harsh (atrocity, atrocious)

audacia: courage, daring (audacity, audacious)

audio, audire: to hear, listen (audience, audio, audiometer, audiophile, audiovisual, audit, auditorium, auditory)

augeo, augere, auxi, auctum: to enlarge, increase (augment, auctioneer, auction, augmentation)

augustus: consecrated, holy, majestic (augustness, august)

aurum: gold (aureate, aureole, auriferous)

auris: ear (aural, auricle, auricular, auriform)

auxilium: help, aid (auxiliary)

avarus: covetous, greedy (avarice, avariciously)

barbarus: foreign, strange, savage, uncultivated (barbaric, barbarian, barbarity, barbarous)

beatus: happy, blessed, prosperous (beatitude, beatific)

bellum, belli: war, fighting (belligerent, bellicose, antebellum)

bellus, bella, bellum: pretty, handsome (belladonna, belle, belles lettres)

bene-: well, rightly, proper (benefactor, benediction, benefit)

bestia: an animal without reason, a brute (bestial, bestiary, bestiality)

bi-: two (bifurcated, bifocals, biped, bicycle, bimonthly, binary, bireme, bipartite)

biblia: book (bible, bibliographer, bibliophile)

bibo: to drink (bibulous, imbibe)

blandus: flattering, alluring, caressing (blandness, blandish)

bonus, bona, bonum: good (bonus, bonny) *melior* [comparative form]:better (ameliorate) **optimus, optima, optimum** [superlative form]: best (optimist, optimal, optimize)

brevis: short, shallow, concise (brevity, breve, breviary)

caldus: warm, hot, fiery (caldron or cauldron, caldera, scalding)

campus: open field, level space (camp, campus, campground, encampment)

cando, candere: to glow, be white (candescence, incandescence, candid, candidate, candle, candor)

canis: dog, hound (canine, canary islands)

cano, canere, cecini, cantum: to sing or play (cant, cantabile, cantata, incantation, recant) also, *canto, cantare, cantavi, cantatum*: to sing or play

capillus: a hair (capillary)

capio, capere, cepi, captum: to take, seize, (perception, recapture, reception, acceptance, captive, capture, inception, concept, conceive, intercept)

caput, capitis: the head, top, chief, headquarters (capital, capitalization, capitalist)

carbo, carbonis: burning or burnt wood (carbon, carbonation, carbonize, carburetor, carbuncle)

carcer, carceris: prison, cell (incarceration)

carrus, carri: a four-wheeled baggage wagon (car, career, careerism, caricature)

causa: a cause, reason, motive, lawsuit, case, situation (causative, causality) *caveo, cavere, cavi, cautum*: to be on one's guard, to avoid (cautious, precaution, caveat)

cavus: hollow (cave, cave-in, cavernous, cavern, concave, cavity)

cedo, cedere, cessi, cessum: to go, proceed, happen, go away, yield (intercede, cessation, accede, accessible, recession, procession, process, recess, access, concession, concede)

celeber: filled, crowded, famous (celebration, celebrity)

celer, celeris, celere: swift (celerity, accelerate)

cella: a room, especially a storeroom (cell, cellar, cellaret)

censeo, censere, censui, censum: to estimate, form, express an opinion, think (censor, censorship, census)

centum: a hundred (centennial, century, centipede, cent, centigrade, centimeter, centigram)

cera: wax (cerate, cere, cerecloth, cerement)

cerebrum: the brain, understanding (cerebellum, cerebral, cerebrate, cerebrospinal, cerebrum)

certus, certa, certum: certain, resolved, decided (certify, certain, certification, certitude, uncertainty, ascertain)

cesso, cessare: to leave off, cease work, rest (cessation)

ceterus, cetera, ceterum: the other, the rest (etc. or *et cetera*)

charta: paper, letter, anything written on paper (chart, charterage, chartaceous, chartist)

chorda: catgut, usually as the string of a musical instrument (chord, cord, cordage)

chorus: dance in a circle, singers and dancers in the chorus (choral, chorale) *cingo, cingere, cinxi, cinctum*: to surround, gird oneself, escort, accompany (cincture)

circa-: around, near, about (circadian = *circa*, meaning *about* + *dies*, meaning *day*.)

circulus, circlus: circle (circle, circlet, circular, circulate, circulatory)

circum-: roundabout, around, near (circumnavigate, circumstance, circumference, circumlocution, circumscribe, circumspect, circumvolve)

cito, citare: to excite, start up, call forward, appeal to (cite, recite, incite, excitement, recitation)

civis: a citizen (civic, civil, civility, civilization, civvies)

clamo, clamare: to call, shout, declare (clamor, claim, reclaim, clamorous, exclamation, proclamation, exclamatory)

clarus: bright or clear (clarification, clarinet, clarity, claret, declaration)

classis: group, division, class (classification, class, classic, classical, classifiable)

claudo, claudere, clausi, clausum, cludo: to close, shut up, make inaccessible (clause, claustrophobia, cloister, cloisonne, inclusion, conclusion, recluse, preclude, exclusionary, exclusive, exclude)

clemens, clementis: mild, kind (clemency, inclement, clement)

clepo, clepere, clepsi, cleptum: to steal (kleptomania)

cliens, clientis: a client, vassal, or ally (client, clientship, clientele)

clino, clinare: to bend, lean (inclination, inclinometer, decline, declination, declinometer)

cogito, cogitare: to turn over in the mind, think (cogitation)

colo, colere, colui, cultum: to cultivate, till, tend, take care of (cultivation, culture, agriculture, horticulture) *color, coloris*: color, tint, hue (multi-colored, coloration, discolor, colorimeter, colorist)

comicus: comic (comical, comic, comedian, comedienne)

comis: courteous, kind, friendly (comity)

commendo: to commit to the care or protection of anyone (commendation, recommend, commendable)

communis: shared, common, universal, public (community, communal, commune, communicate)

consilium: union, meeting (conciliatory, reconciliation, counsel, council, counselor)

congruo, congruere, congrui: to run together, meet, correspond with, agree (congruent, incongruent, congruity, incongruous)

consulo, consulere, consului, consultum: to reflect, consult, consider (consultation, consultant, consul, consulate)

contra-: against, opposite, on the opposite side (contradiction, contraband, contralto, contravene, contraindication, contradistinguish, contrapuntal, contrary, contrast, contraposition, counterattack, counterbalance, counterpart, countersign, counterfeit, counterintelligence)

contumax, contumacis: stubborn, disobedient (contumacy, contumely, contumaciousness)

copia: plenty, abundance (cornucopia, copious)

cor, cordis: the heart, judgment (accord, accordance, discord, concord, concordance, cordate, cordial, cordiform)

cornu: a horn, strength, courage (cornute, cornucopia, cornu)

corpus, corporis: body, substance, matter, flesh, main mass of a thing (corporeal, corporation, incorporate, corporal, corpulence, corps, corpuscle) *credo, credere, credidi, creditum*: to trust, commit, rely upon, believe, accept as true (credence, creed, credibility, credit, creditor, discredit, incredible, credulous)

creo, creare: to make, create, produce, beget, bear (create, procreative, recreation, creativity, miscreant)

cresco, crescere, crevi, cretum: to come into existence, arise; to grow or grow up, increase in size or power (crescent, crescendo, decrescendo, accretion, accrue, concrete)

crusta: crust: rind, shell, bark, inlaid work, bas relief (crusty, crustacean, crustal, encrusted)

crux, crucis: a cross, hence torment, trouble (cruciform, crucifixion, crucible, crux, crucial, excruciating, crucifix)

cubo, cubare, cubui, cubitum: to lie down, recline (concubine, incubation, succubus, cubicle)

culpa: blame, fault (culpability, *mea culpa*, inculpate)

cum-: with, together (in english, *con-*, *com-*, etc.: convention, compatible, comparison)

cumulo, cumulare: to heap up, overload, bring to perfection (accumulation, cumulus, cumulative)

cuneus: wedge (cuneiform, cuneal, cuneate)

cupio, cupere, cupii, cupitum: to desire (cupid, cupidity)

cura: care, attention, management; worry (curative, cure, curette, cure all, curious, curiosity)

curro, currere, curri, cursum: to run (concur, concurrence, concourse, recur, precursor, cursive, concurrent, current)

curtus, curta, curtum: short (curt, curtail, curtal, curtate)

curvo, curvare: to bend, arch, curve (curvaceous, curve, curvature, curvilinear) *cuspid*: point, especially of a spear (cuspid, bicuspid, cusp, cuspate)

custodio, custodire: to guard, watch, take care of (custodianship)

damno, damnare: to cause loss or injury to, condemn, or punish (damnation, condemn, indemnity, condemnation, damnable, indemnify)

de-: down from, away from, after (desultory, detract, de facto, desist, desert)

debeo, debere, debui, debitum: to owe (debit, indebted, debenture, debtor)

decem-: ten (december, decathlon, decahedron, decade)

defendo: to repel, to protect (defensive, defensible, defensiveness)

delicatus: soft, tender (delicacy, delicate, indelicate, delicatessen)

demo, demere, dempsi, demptum: to take away, subtract (redemption)

dens, dentis: a tooth (dental, indentation, dentist, orthodontist, dentifrice, dentiform, denticulate, dentine, dentition, denture, dentoid)

densus: thick, dense (density, condensation, condensed, densimeter)

derivo, derivare: to turn into another channel, to divert (derivation, derivative, derivable)

destino, destinare: to make fast; to fix, determine, settle, appoint (destined, destination, destiny)

detergeo, detergere, detersi, detersum: to wipe off, clear away, brush off, cleanse by wiping (detergent, deterge, detergency)

detero, deterere, detrivi, detritum: to rub away, wear out, detract from, weaken (deter, detritus, deterrence, detriment, detrition, detrimental)

deus, dei: a god, deity (deification, deity, *deus ex machina*, deific, deism)

devius: off the beaten track, solitary, erroneous, unreasonable; from *de* + *via* (devious, deviated) *dexter, dextera, dextrum*: right, on the right side or hand, dexterous, skillful, favorable (dexter, dexterity, dexterous, dextral, dextrose)

dia-, di-: through, throughout (diagonal, diachronic, dialysis, dialogue, diabetes)

dico, dicere, dixi: to indicate, appoint, speak, mention. Also *dictum*: a word, saying, speech, order, or command. (benediction, indication, dictum, diction, dictaphone, dictation)

dies: daytime, day (diurnal)

digitus: finger (digital, digit, digitation, digitalis, prestidigitation)

digno, dignare: to consider worthy (dignity, indignant, dignify, dignitary)

dirigo, dirigere, direxi, directum: to arrange or direct (direction, indirect, dirigible, directional, directive, directory)

divido, dividere, divisi, divisum: to divide, distinguish, set off, adorn (division, subdivide, divisive, divisor, dividend, divisible, indivisible)

do, dare, dedi, datum: to offer, give, commit, devote; to cause, bring about (dado, dative, dedicate, edition data, date, tradition, perdition)

doceo, docere, docui, doctum: to teach, inform (documentary, doctor, documentation, doctrine, docent, doctorate)

doleo, dolere, dolui: to suffer pain or to grieve (dolor, condolence, indolence, dolorous)

domo, domare, domui, domitum: to tame, conquer or subdue (indomitable)

domus: house (domain, dome, domestic, domesticate, domicile)

dono, donare: to give, bestow (donation, donor)

dormio, dormire: to sleep, rest or be inactive (dormant, dormitory, dormer, dorm, dormouse)

dorsum: the back (dorsal)

draco, draconis: snake or dragon (draconian, dragon, draconic, dragonfly, dragoon)

dubito, dubitare: to doubt or be uncertain (indubitable, dubitation)

duco, ducere, duxi, ductum: to lead, draw, or draw in; to count, reckon, esteem or consider (duct, induction, reduction, product, introduce, reduce, deduce, abduction, introduction, duke, duchess)

dulcis: sweet (dulcet, dulciana, dulcify, dulcimer)

duo-, duae-: two (dual, duality, duo, duet, duplex, duplication, duplicity)

duro, durare: to inure, to harden, to last, continue (endure, duration)

ego-: I, self (egocentricism, egotism, egomaniacal, egoism)

endo-: in (endomorph, endodontics, endogenous, endocrine)

enormis: irregular, unusual, very large (enormity, enormous)

epi- [Greek]: on, upon, over, around, besides [from Greek; it's a common prefix, so here it is] (epicenter, epidermis, epicure, epitome, epinephrine)

equi-: equal [see **aequus, aequi**]

equus, equi: horse (equine, equestrian, equerry)

erro, errare: to wander, stray, rove (errant, error, erratic)

eu-: good, well done (euphoria, eugenics, euphemism)

ex- or **e-**: from, out of, since, away from (extrude, expend, extension, extol)

excido, excidere, excidi, excisum: to cut out, destroy, root out, or banish (excise, excision)

excuso, excusare: to exempt from blame or accusation, to plead (excuse, excusatory, excusably)

expedio, expedire, expedivi, expeditum: to free from a snare, disengage, set straight or get ready for action (expedient, expedite)

exter and *exterus, ext(e)ra, ext(e)rum*: outward, foreign, strange. comparative: exterior, more strange. *extremus* [superlative form]: most strange (exterior, extreme, extremity)

extra-: outside, beyond (extraterrestrial, extraordinary, extrasensory)

fabrico, fabricare: to form, make, or forge (fabrication, fabric, prefabricated)

fabula: conversation, tale, story, myth or drama (fable, fabulous)

facilis: easy to do, convenient (facile, facility)

facio, facere, feci, factum: to make, do, cause, act, be of service, or support (factor, perfection, fact, imperfect, defect, defective, efficacious, effect, ineffectual, sacrifice, surfeit, fashionable, feasance, feasibility, featured, affectation, amplification, artificiality, benefactor, confection, sufficient counterfeit, deficit, efficiency, edification, facsimile, vivify forfeiture, manufacturing, modification, notification, profitable, putrefaction, qualification, rarefaction, rectify)

fallo, fallere, fefelli, falsum: to deceive, lead astray, cause to be mistaken; to disappoint, fail in (infallible, fallibility, falsity, falsehood, falsetto, falsification)

fama: a report, rumor, tradition; public opinion, repute (fame, defamation, famous)

familia: household, family, fraternity; any group or sect (familiar, family, familiarity)

favor, favoris: favor, good will, support, inclination, acclamation (favorite, disfavor)

febris: fever (febrile, febrifacient, febrific, febrifuge)

felix, felicis: fortunate, successful (felicity, felicitous)

fero, ferre, tuli, latum: to bear, bring, carry, or endure; to produce or put in motion; to fetch or carry off; to offer (aquifer, ferry, differential, differentiation, relation, reference, preference, indifferent, differ, prelate, superlative) *ferrum*: iron, hence any iron instrument (ferrous, ferris wheel, ferric, ferriferous)

ferveo, fervere, ferbui or *fervi*: to boil or seethe, to be excited by passion or rage (fervent, fervid, fervor)

fibra: a fiber or filament (fibrous, fiber, fibril, fibriform, fibrillation, fibrinogen, fibroid, fibrosis, fibrovascular)

fidelis: trusty, steadfast, faithful (infidelity, high-fidelity)

figo, figere, fixi, fixum: to fix, fasten, attach, transfix (transfixion, crucifixion, fixation, prefix, suffix)

figura: form, shape, figure, size (figurative, configuration, disfigure)

filia: daughter and filius: son (affiliate, affiliation, filial)

fingo, fingere, finxi, fictum: to shape, fashion, form, mold, touch, devise, fabricate (fiction, fictile)

finis: end, limit, border, aim (finish, finite, infinity, definite, define, definitive)

flagro, flagrare: to blaze, burn, glow, flame (flagrant, conflagration)

flamma: a flame, fire, source of light, star, lightning (flammable, inflammability, inflammatory)

flecto, flectere, flexi, flexum: to bend, twist, curve, change, alter, influence (deflect, reflection, inflect, flexor, flex, flexible, flexion, flexuous, inflection, genuflect, genuflection)

flo, flare, flavi, flatum: to blow (inflate, deflation, efflatus, flatulence)

flora: flower (floral, flora, florescence, floriculture, floribunda, florida, florist)

fluctuo, fluctuare: to be wave-like, move up and down (fluctuation, fluctuant)

fluo, fluere, fluxi, fluxum: to flow, stream, pour, proceed, spread (flux, fluent, effluent, affluent, confluence, afflux) *fons, fontis*: a spring, fountain; origin, source (font, fontanel)

forma: figure, form, shape; beauty, image, likeness, type, species; general notion (formation, deform, reform, reformation, formation, formative, pro forma, informative)

fortis: strong, powerful, robust, steadfast (fortify, fortis, fortissimo, fortitude, fort)

fortuna: chance, fate, luck, fortune (unfortunate, misfortune, fortune)

frango, frangere, fregi, fractum: to break (fracture, fracas, fractional, refracted, fractious, fragile, fragility, fragment, fragmentation)

frater: brother, also comrade, compatriot, ally (fraternal, fraternity, fraternize)

fraudo, fraudare: to cheat, defraud, swindle (fraud, fraudulent, defraud)

frico, fricare, fricui, frictum: to rub (friction)

frigeo, frigere: to be cold, inactive, lifeless or dull (refrigerator, frigid, frigorific)

frio, friare: to rub, crumble (friable, friability)

frons, frondis: leaf, foliage (frond, frondescent, frondose)

frons, frontis: forehead, brow (frontal, front, frontage, frontier, frontispiece, frontlet, front page, frontward)

fugio, fugere, fugi, fugitum: to flee (fugitive, subterfuge, fugacious, vermifuge, refuge, refugee)

fumo, fumare: to smoke, steam, reek (fume, fumigate, fumatory, fumaric acid, fumarole, fumy)

functio, functionis: performance, execution (function, malfunction, disfunctional)

fundus: bottom or base of anything (fundamental, fundament, founder, fund, fundus) *furca*: a two-pronged fork (bifurcated)

furo, furere: to rage, rave, be mad (fury, infuriated, furious)

fusco, fuscare: to darken, blacken (obfuscation)

gaudeo, gaudere: to rejoice, be glad (gaudy, gaudiness)

gelo, gelare: to freeze (gelatin, gelatinous, gelation)

geminus: twin, double; paired; similar (geminate)

genero, generare: to beget, produce, bring to life (generate, unregenerative, generation, progenerative)

gens, gentis: clan, stock, people, tribe, nation (genre, genotype, gens, gentle)

genus: birth, descent, origin, race, stock, family, kind (genus, gender, general, generalization, generate, regenerate, generous)

geo-: earth (geography, geocentric)

gero, gerere, gessi, gestum: to carry, bear, give birth to, carry on, conduct, manage business (gestation, ingest, suggestion)

glacio, glaciare: to freeze (glacier, glaciation, glacial, glaciology)

gloria: fame, renown, glory (glorify, glorification, glory, inglorious)

gluten, glutinis: glue (glutinous, gluten, agglutinate)

gradior, gradi, gressus: to step or walk (gradient, transgression, regress, grade, congressional, digression)

grandio, grandire: to increase (grandiose, aggrandize)

graphium: a stylus, a pointed instrument for writing (phonograph, photography, graph, graphic, graphite, graphology)

gratia: charm, attraction, pleasantness, esteem, regard (ingratiate, graciousness) *gravis*: heavy, important (gravity, grave, gravitate)

gusto, gustare: to taste, partake of, enjoy (gustatory, gusto, gustative)

habeo, habere, habui, habitum: to have, hold (habit, habitual, habitude, habitus)

habilis: easily managed, handy, suitable, convenient (habilitate, homo habilis)

habito, habitare: to inhabit, to dwell (habitation, inhabit, habitat)

haereo, haerere, haesi, haesum: to stick, adhere, come to a standstill or get stuck (adhere, adhesive, inherent, cohesion, adhesion, hesitant)

halo, halare: to breathe out (exhalation, inhalation, halitosis)

harmonia: melody, concord, harmony (harmonious, disharmony, harmonica)

herba: vegetation, green plant (herbivore, herbaceous, herbal, herbarium, herbage)

hiberno, hibernare: to winter, spend the winter (hibernate, hibernal, hibernaculum, hibernation)

hilaro, hilarare: to make joyful, to cheer up (hilarity, exhilaration)

homo, hominis: human being, man, mortal (hominid, hominoid)

homo-: same, like (homocentric, homogeneity, homogenize, homonym)

humanus: human, of human beings (humanity, humaneness, humanoid, inhuman)

humo, humare: to cover with earth, bury (exhume)

iacio, iacere, ieci, iactum: to throw, cast, hurl, scatter, diffuse (adjacent, projectile, eject, injection, introject, rejection, abject, projection, project, objection, objectivity)

ignis: fire (ignition, ignite, igneous)

imago, imaginis: copy, image, likeness, statue, portrait (imagination, image, unimaginable)

in-: into, on to, towards, against, among (intubation, impound, impress)

in-: not, without (indecisive, inanimate, inappropriate)

incumbo, incumbere, incubui, incubitum: to lie upon, put weight on, overhang; to apply oneself to (incumbent)

index, indicis: an informer, a sign, token; the forefinger; a touchstone (indication, index, indices, indicator, indicative)

infans, infantis: speechless, tongue-tied; youthful, fresh, childlike (infantile, infancy)

infra-: below, under in position, size, rank; later than; lower (infrared, infrastructure, infrasonic)

iniuria: injury, injustice, wrong (injurious, uninjured)

insula: island (insular, peninsula, insulation, insulin)

integer, integra, integrum: complete, whole, entire, pure, innocent, renewed (integer, integral, integrity)

inter-: between, among, amid, during (international, interdiction, intercontinental)

interior: inner, interior, remote from the sea, inland, more secret or intimate (interior)

intra-: inside, within (intramural, intranuclear)

intro-: inwards, within (introduction, introvert)

ira: anger (irate, irascible)

iter, itineris: going, way, direction, journey, march, method (iteration, itinerant, reiterate)

iudico, iudicare: to judge (adjudicate, judicious, judicature) *iugum*: yoke, collar, bond, union (conjugal, conjugation)

iungo, iungere, iunxi, iunctum: to join (junction, juncture, adjunct, injunction)

ius, iuris: right, law; court of justice; jurisdiction (injure, adjure, jury, perjury, jurisdiction, jurisprudence)

iustus, iusta, iustum: just, equitable, fair; lawful, proper; justified (justice, unjust, justification, justifiable)

iuvenis: young (juvenile, rejuvenate, juvenal, juvenescent)

iuxta: close by, near (juxtapose, juxtaposition)

j: the letter *j* was unknown in classical Latin; in words like *iuvenis* above, the *i* changes to *j* in English: i.e., rejuvenate.

kalendae [calendae]: the first day of a roman month (calendar)

labor, labi, lapsus: to slide, slip or fall down or away; make a mistake; decline (relapsing, lapse, collapse, elapse, prolapse)

labor, laboris: work, toil, effort, industry; hardship, distress (laborious, elaboration, elaborate, labor, collaboration)

lacer, lacera, lacerum: torn (lacerated)

lacrima: a tear from the eye (lacrimose, lacrimal)

lacto, lactere: to be milky (lactation, prolactin, lactose, lactic acid, lactiferous, lactoprotein, lactase)

laedo, laedere, laesi, laesum: to strike, hurt, damage; to offend: to violate or outrage (lesion)

laevus: left, the left hand or side; unlucky; unpropitious or awkward (left-handed, leftover, left, levorotation, levulose)

languor: faintness, weariness, inactivity (languorous, languish, languid)

lapis, lapidis: a stone (lapidary, lapis lazuli, lapillus) *largus*: abundant, plentiful, numerous, rich in (largess, largely, largo, larghetto, largish)

lassus: weary, tired (lassitude)

latex, laticis: fluid, liquid (latices, latex, laticiferous)

latus, lata, latum: broad, wide, extensive, diffuse, full, rich (latitude, latifundium)

latus, lateris: the side, flank (lateral, collateral)

laudo, laudare: to praise, commend (laudatory, laud, laudable, laudation)

lavo, lavare [or **lavere**], **lavi, lautum** [or **lotum**, or **lavatum**]: to wash, bathe, moisten (lavatory, lavable, lavage, lavabo, lava, lave, lavish, lotion, ablution)

laxo, laxare: to widen, loosen, enlarge; to slacken or relax; to set free (relaxation, laxative, laxity, lax)

lego, legare: to ordain, appoint (delegation, relegate, legation, legacy, legation, allegation, delegate)

lego, legere, legi, lectum: to collect, choose, read (collection, selective, predilection, recollection, elective, intelligentsia, select, negligent, lecture, neglectful, lectern, collectanea, negligee, legendary, illegibility, legion, sacrilegious, elegance, diligently, electorate, prelecting)

lenis, lene: smooth, mild, gentle (lenient, lenis, lenity, lenitive)

lento, lentare: to bend (relent)

levis, leve: light, swift, trifling (levity, levitation)

levo, levare: to raise, make light, lift up; to ease, relieve; to diminish, weaken, impair (elevation, elevator, lever)

lex, legis: law, agreement (legal, legislation, illegal, legitimacy, legalization)

liber, libera, liberum: free, independent (libertarian, liberty, liberal, libertine, liberalize, liberation) *liber, libri*: book, catalogue (library, libretto, librarian)

licet, licere, licuit or *licitum*: it is allowed; one can or may. present participle is *licens, licentis*: free, unrestrained (illicit, licit)

ligo, ligare: to bind, bandage, harness (ligament, ligation, ligature)

linea: line (delineate, linear, line, lineament, lineage)

lingua: tongue, speech, language (bilingual, language, linguiform, linguini, linguistic, lingulate)

linquo, linquere, liqui: to leave, abandon (relinquish, relic, relict, reliquary, delinquent, derelict, dereliction)

liquo, liquare: to make liquid, melt; to clarify (liquefy, liquor, liquidate, liquescent, liquidity)

lis, litis: a legal controversy, action, suit, quarrel (litigation, litigious, *lis pendens*, litigant)

littera [litera]: a letter of the alphabet; epistle; written records, documents, literature; letters; scholarship (literal, literary, illiterate)

loco, locare: to place, put, set (relocate, locale, location)

locus: place, position; a period or moment in time; passage in a book (locus, locomotion)

logos [logus], logi: word, joke, jest; in English, it sometimes means *the study of* (logic, illogical philology, phraseology, paleontology, archeology, logotype, biological, catalogue, logogram, logistics, syllogism, epilogue, analogous, apologetic, prologue)

longus: long, spacious, tedious (longitude, longevity, long-suffering)

loquor, loqui, locutus: to speak, tell, say, talk of (loquacious, elocution, colloquial, grandiloquent, colloquy, soliloquy, loquitur, ventriloquist, circumlocution, locution)

luceo, lucere, luxi: to be bright; to shine; to be clear or evident (elucidation, lucidity, lucid, pellucid, translucent, lucent) *lucror, lucrari*: to gain, profit, win (lucrative)

ludo, ludere, lusi, lusum: to play; to delude; to imitate or banter; to play at or with (ludicrous, illusion, delusion, allusion, collude, interlude, prelude)

lumen, luminis: light, day, insight; eye; opening (illumination, luminous, lumen, luminary, luminescent, luminiferous)

luna: the moon, night; a month; crescent-shaped ornament (lunar, lunacy, lunatic, lunation, lunula, lunate)

lux, lucis: light, day, the eye; illustration; hope (elucidation, deluxe, lustration, luciferous)

luxuria: exuberant growth, excess, extravagance (luxurious, luxury, luxuriant)

lyra: lyre, flute; lyric poetry, song (lyre, lyrical, lyricism, lyricist)

macero, macerare: to soften, weaken, reduce; to torment, tease, vex (macerate)

machina: machine, contrivance; fabric, trick, stratagem (machine, machination, machinery, machinist)

macies: leanness, poverty, barrenness (emaciated)

macula: spot, mark, stain, blemish (maculate, immaculate, macular, macule, maculation)

magister, magistri: master, director (magistrate, magisterial)

magnus, magna, magnum: great, large, loud, high, important (magnificent, magnitude, magnum opus) **maior, maius** [comparative form]: greater (major, majority, major domo, majuscule) **maximus** [superlative form]: greatest (maximal, maximization, maxim)

malus, mala, malum: bad, evil, unfavorable (malady, malediction, malaria) **peior, peius** [comparative form]: worse (pejorative) **pessimus, pessima, pessimum** [superlative form]: worst (pessimist)

mancipo, mancipare: to sell formally, to give up (emancipate) *mando, mandare*: to commit, entrust; to order, command, commission (command, commando, commandment, mandate, demand, remand)

maneo, manere, mansi, mansum: to remain, stay, endure, last (manse, mansion, remain)

manus: hand (manual, manuscript, manufacture)

mare, maris: the sea (marine, submarine, aquamarine, marina, marinate, marsh, mariner)

margo, marginis: a border, edge, boundary (margin, marginal)

mas, maris: the male (masculine)

mater, matris: mother, source, origin (maternal, maternity, matrix, matriarch, matrimony)

materia: matter, material, stuff, timber (material, immaterial)

maturo, maturare: to make ripe, to quicken, hasten, accelerate (maturation, immaturity)

medicus: doctor (medication, medical, medicine, medic)

meditatio, meditationis: contemplation; practice, exercise; preparation (meditation)

medius, media, medium: middle, central (median, medium, mediate, mediation, immediate, mediant)

mel, mellis: honey, sweetness (mellifluous, mellophone, mellow, melliferous)

melior, melius [comparative of *bonus*, good]: better (ameliorate, meliorism, melioration)

melos: tune, melody (melodize, melodic, melodious)

memor, memoris: mindful, remembering (memory, memorable, immemorial, memorabilia)

mens, mentis: mind, understanding, intellect (mental, mentation, mentality, dement)

mensio, mensionis: measuring (dimension)

mensura: measuring, measure, capacity, amount, proportion (commensurate)

mentio, mentionis: mention (mentionable, mentioner)

meo, meare: to go, pass (meatus, permeate)

mercor, mercari: to carry on trade; to traffic, to buy (merchant, merchandise)

mereo, merere, merui, meritum [and *mereor, mereri, meritus*]: to deserve, earn, obtain (merit, demerit)

mergo, mergere, mersi, mersum: to dip, plunge into liquid, immerse, sink, overwhelm (immersion, merge)

meus, mea, meum: my, mine (*mea culpa*)

migro, migrare: to migrate, depart, change, transport (migration, migrant, migratory)

mille: a thousand (millipede, millennium, millionaire)

minuo, minuere, minui, minutum: to make smaller, lessen, diminish (diminutive, minute, diminish)

miror, mirari: to wonder, be astonished, admire (admiration, miracle, mirage, miraculous)

misceo, miscere, miscui, mixtum: to mix, mingle (mixture, admix, promiscuous, miscellaneous, miscible)

miser, misera, miserum: wretched, unhappy, sad (commiserate, miserable, misery, misericord, miser)

mitto, mittere, misi, missum: to send, dispatch (missive, dismiss, remittance, submissive, admit, commitment, emission, intermission, omission, permissible, premises, promised, transmission) *mobilis*: movable, easy to move, flexible (mobile, mobility)

modus, modi: a measure, standard of measurement (mode, modulate, *modus operandi*, accommodation, commodious, model, modern, modicum, modification, commodity)

mollio, mollire: to make soft, pliable, supple, or gentle (mollify, emollient)

moneo, monere: to remind, warn, advise (admonish, monitor, premonition, monition, summon)

mons, montis: mountain (mountainous)

morior, mori, mortuus [or *moriturus*]: to die, wither away (mortuary, moribund, moratorium)

mors, mortis: death, corpse, destruction (immortality, mortician, mortal, immortal)

moveo, movere, movi, motum: to move, stir, remove, dislodge (movable, motion, motive, immotile, motility, promotion, demotion, movie)

multus, multa, multum: much, many, great (multitude, multiply, multipurpose) **plus, pluris** [comparative form]: more numerous (plus, plurality) **plurimus** [superlative form]: most numerous

munero, munerare: to give, present (remuneration, remunerative)

munio, munire: to build, fortify; to secure, defend (munitions, ammunition)

murus: wall, bank; defense (mural, intramural, extramural)

muto, mutare: to move, shift, change (mutation, mutant, immutable)

narro, narrare: to make known, to say, to speak (narrator, narration)

nascor, nascori, natus: to be born, to arise (natal, nativity, nascent, renaissance, native)

natio, nationis: being born, birth, tribe, race, people (international, nationality)

nato, natare: to swim, float (natatorium)

nauta [and *navita*]: sailor (nautical, nautiloid, nautilus)

nebula: vapor, fog, mist, cloud (nebula, nebulous, nebulize, nebular, nebulosity)

necto, nectere, nexui [or **nexi**], **nexum**: to tie, bind, enslave, affix (connect, nexus, disconnection, annex)

nego, negare: to deny or say no (negation, negativity, abnegation, negate, negatron)

nepos, nepotis: grandson, nephew, descendant; a spendthrift (nepotism, nephew)

nihil [and *nil*]: nothing (nihilistic, nihility)

noceo, nocere: to hurt, injure (innocuous, innocence, nocuous)

nodus: knot, tie, bond, connection (node, nodal, nodule, nodus)

nomen, nominis: a name (nominal, nomination, denomination, ignominious, ignominy, nominative, nomenclature, *nom de plume*, nominate, misnomer)

non: not (nonentity, noncommissioned, nonsense, nonplussed, nonrepresentational)

nonus, nona, nonum: ninth (nonuple, nones, nonagon, nonagenarian)

nosco, noscere, novi, notum: to get to know, to recognize, to approve (notion, notorious, notify)

nota: a mark, token, note, sign (notation, note, notarize, notebook, noteworthy)

novus, nova, novum: new, fresh, young (novice, innovative, renovate, nova, novitiate)

nox, noctis: night, sleep, darkness (nocturne, nocturnal)

noxia: fault, offense, crime (obnoxious, noxiously)

nubo, nubere, nupsi, nuptum: to cover, veil; to be married (connubial, nuptial, nubile)

nudo, nudare: to make bare, to uncover (denude, nudity)

nullus, nulla, nullum: no, none (nullify, null, nullifier, nullity, nullification)

numero, numerare: to count, especially to count out money; to reckon, to consider (enumerate, numerical, numeration numerator, innumerable, numerary, numerology, numerous)

nuntio, nuntiare: to announce, give notice (denunciation, annunciation, pronunciation, enunciate)

nutrio [*nutrior*], *nutrire* [*nutriri*]: to nourish, bring up, support, sustain (nutrition, nutrient)

ob-: in front of, before; in return for; because of; on account of (obtuse, obstruction, obfuscation, objection, obstinate)

obscurus: covered, dark, obscure (obscurity)

observo, observare: to watch, attend to; to keep rules; to respect (observation, observatory, observant, observance, observer)

occasio, occasionis: a favorable moment, opportunity (occasional, occasionally)

occulo, occulere, occului, occultum: to hide or cover (occult)

occupo, occupare: to seize, master, attack, take possession of (occupied, occupation)

octo-: eight (octave, octet, octopus, octagonal, october, octant, octennial, octogenarian, octuple)

oculus, oculi: the eye (ocular, binocular, oculist, oculomotor)

odi, odisse, osurus: to hate, dislike (odious, odium)

odor, odoris: a smell, odor, suspicion (malodorous, odoriferous, odorimeter, odorless) *offensa*: injury, displeasure (offense, offensive)

omen, ominis: an omen, sign (ominous)

omnis, omne: all, every, whole (omnipotent, omniscience, omnipresence)

onus, oneris: a burden, weight, load (onus, onerous)

opino, opinare: to suppose (opine, opinionated)

optio, optionis: choice (optional, adoption, opt)

opus, operis: work (opera, opus, operation, opera, cooperation, operative, operand)

orbis: circle, ring (orbital, orbit)

ordino, ordinare: to set in order, arrange (ordination, subordinate, insubordination, coordinate, ordinal, inordinate)

origo, originis: source, beginning; ancestor (original, aborigine, originality)

orior, oriri, ortus [participle is **oriens, orientis**: rising]: to rise, be born (oriental, disorient, reorientation, orient)

orno, ornare: to equip, furnish (adornment, ornament, ornate, ornamentation)

oro, orare: to speak (oration, oracle, oratory)

os, oris: mouth, opening, source (oral, os, osculate)

os, ossis: bone (ossify, ossification, ossicle, ossuary, osteal, ossifrage)

pactio, pactionis: bargain, agreement (pact, impact, compact)

paene: almost (peninsula, penumbra, penultimate)

pagina: a page (pagination, pageant, pageantry, paginal, page)

pan-: all (panacea, panamerican, panhellenic, pangenesis, panegyric, panoply)

par, paris: equal, like (parity, compare, disparity, disparate, par, peer, nonpareil)

para-, par-: near, beside, beyond, similar to (parallel, parallax, parameter, paraphernalia)

parco, parcere, peperci [parci], parsum: to economize; to spare or refrain from (parsimonious)

pareo, parere: to appear (apparition, appearance, apparitor)

pario, parere, peperi, partum [future participle is *pariturus*]: to bear, produce; to create (post partum, parturition, parturient)

paro, parare: to prepare (preparation, reparation, apparatus, separate)

pars, partis: a part, party, region (partition, compartment, partly, particle, parse, partiality)

parum: not enough *minus* [comparative form]: less (minus) *minime* [superlative form]: least, not at all (see *parvus*)

parvus, parva, parvum: small *minor* [comparative form]: smaller, less (minor, minority) *minimus* [superlative form]: smallest, least (minimum, minimization, minimal, minimax. [see *parum*])

pateo, patere: to be open, be disclosed (patent patency, patentee, patentor)

pater, patris: father, founder (paternal, paternity, paterfamilias, patriot, patrimony, patrician, patrilocal, patrilineal, patristic)

patior, pati, passus: to suffer, experience, allow (patience, compassion, impatient, impassioned, passionate, passional, passive, impassive)

paucus: few (paucity, *poco a poco*)

pax, pacis: peace (pacification, pacifier, pacific)

pecco, peccare: to err or sin (impeccable, peccant, peccadillo, peccability)

pecunia: money (impecunious, pecuniary)

pello, pellere, pepuli, pulsum: to strike, move, propel (compel, repulse, compulsion, impulse, propellent, pulsate, repellent, pulsar, impel)

pendo, pendere, pependi, pensum: to hang; to weigh; to consider or judge (appendage, compendium, suspension, pendulum, pendulous, dependent, independence, impending)

penso, pensare: to ponder, consider, pay for (pension, compensate, recompense, pensive, dispense)

per-: through, along, during, because of (perambulate, percolate, permission, persuade, perennial)

percutio, percutere, percussi, percussum: to strike (percussion, percussive)

perdo, perdere, perdidi, perditum: to ruin, lose or waste (perdition)

peregrinor, peregrinari: to travel, wander (peregrination, peregrine)

pereo, perire, perii [and *perivi*], *peritum*: to die or go to waste (perish)

perpes, perpetis: continuous (perpetual, perpetuity)

perspicio, perspicere, perspexi, perspectum: to see through, to examine (perspicacious)

pes, pedis: the foot (pedestal, impediment, pedestrian, pedicure, impede, pedal, pedigree, piedmont, centipede)

pestis: pest, ruin, bane (pest, pesticide, pestilence, pestiferous)

peto, petere, petivi [and *petii*], *petitum*: to seek, ask for; to attack (petition, petulant, compete, repetition, appetite)

philo-: love (philosophy, philology, philodendron, philadelphia, philter)

-phone [Greek]: sound, voice (telephone, phonetics)

photo- [Greek]: light (photograph, photic, photomontage)

physica: natural medicine (physics, physically, physical)

pilo, pilare: to deprive of hair (depilatory)

pingo, pingere, pinxi, pictum: to paint, draw, decorate (depict, picturesque, pictograph, pictorial, pictogram, picture)

pius: dutiful, godly (pious, piety, impious, piosity)

placo, placare: to soothe (placate, complacent, placable, placebo, placid)

planus: flat, level, plain, clear (plain, plane, planarian, planar, planation)

plebs, plebis: common people (plebeian, plebiscite, plebe)

plenus: full (plenipotentiary, plenary, plenitude, plenty, plentiful, plenum)

plico, plicare, plicui [plicavi], plicitum [plicatum]: to fold (complication, implicate, replicate, duplication, supplicant, explicate)

ploro, plorare: to wail, weep (deplore, implore, exploratory)

plumbum: lead, bullet, pipe (plumber, plumb, plumbago, plumbism, plumb line)

poena: penalty, punishment (penalty, penal, penalize)

polluo, polluere, pollui, pollutum: to defile, dishonor or pollute (pollution, pollutant)

poly- [Greek]: many or much (polyglot, polyhedron)

pompa: parade, showiness; a solemn procession (pomp, pomposity)

pondus, ponderis: weight, burden (ponderous, ponderable, preponderance)

pono, ponere, posui [or posivi], positum [or postum]: to put or place (repository, suppose, position, opposition, component, opponent, proponent, proposition, supposition, deposit, disposal, disposition, imposition, positivity, preposition, posit, positron, postpone, postposition, posture)

pons, pontis: bridge (pontiff, pontificate, pontoon)

populus: people (popularity, populace, population, depopulate, popularize, populous) *porto, portare*: to carry, bring (portable, comportment, report, deportation, export, importation, portage, importance, portfolio, support, transportation, portamento, portative, supportive, rapport)

possum, posse, potui: to be able. Participle is *potens, potentis*: able, powerful. (potent, impotent, potentate, potential, potentiality, posse)

post-: behind, afterwards, later (postgraduate, posterior, postern, posthumous, postmortem, postpone, post partum, postdate)

poto, potare: to drink (potion, potable, potation)

prae-: before, in front, on account of (premonition, premature, prescience, preconceived)

praeter-: except, beyond, more than (preternatural)

premo, premere, pressi, pressus: to press (oppression, depress, repression, irrepressible, decompression, compress, express, impressionable, suppress, reprimand)

prex, precis: request, entreaty (imprecation, deprecate, precarious)

primus: see *prior*.

prior, prius, prioris: fore, former, higher in importance; ancestors; previously. Superlative is *primus*: first, foremost (priority, prime, primate, primacy, primeval, primipara, primitive, primogenitor, primrose, primordial, prima donna, prima ballerina, primarily, prioress, priory, primavera, premier)

privo, privare: to strip, deprive, free, release. Participle *privatus*: private, unofficial (privacy, deprivation, private, privation)

pro-: before, in front of; for, in favor of; in place of, like or as good as (promotion, proponent, proposition, pro bono, protagonist, proclamation, process, procedural)

probo, probare: to make good or find good; to approve, recommend, show, demonstrate (approbation, probate, probable, reprobate, improbability, probation, probe) *promo, promere, prompsi, promptum*: to bring out, produce; to disclose or express (prompt, impromptu)

prope: near (propinquity) *propius* [comparative form]: nearer *proxime* [superlative form]: nearest (proximity, proximate, approximately)

proprius, propria, proprium: one's own, special; permanent; peculiar characteristic (appropriate, proper, impropriety, property)

prosus, prosa, prosum: straightforward (prosaic, prose)

publicus [variation of *poplicus*, from *populus*: people]: public (publication, republican, publicize, publicity, public, publisher, publican)

puer: child, boy (puerile, puerperal)

pugil, pugilis: fighter (pugilist)

pugno, pugnare: to fight (pugnacious, impugn, oppugn, repugnant)

pulvis, pulveris: dust, powder; arena, scene of activity (pulverize, pulverulent)

pungo, pungere, pupugi, punctum: to prick, puncture; to touch, move; to sting or annoy. *Punctum* is a short clause, section, or point. (puncture, punctuation, punctual, expunge, pungent, compunction, expunction)

purgo, purgare: to clean, purify, wash off; to excuse, defend (purge, purgatory, purgative)

purus, pura, purum: clean, pure, faultless (purity, purification, impure, puree, puritan)

puto, putare: to think (impute, computation, reputation, dispute, computer, disreputable, putative)

quadru-: four (quadrillion, quadruple, quadricentennial)

quaero, quaerere, quaesii, quaesitum: to seek, search for (inquisitive, inquisition, requirement, inquire, requisite, acquisitive, exquisite, inquest, query, quest, question, perquisite) *qualis, quale*: of what kind, having some quality or other (qualify, quality, qualification, qualifier, qualitative)

quantus, quanta, quantum: how great or how much (quantity, quantify, quantitative, quantum, quantize)

quartus, quarta, quartum: the fourth (quarter, quart, quartet, quarterage, quartic, quartile, quarterly)

quasi: as if, just as (quasar)

quini, quinae: five at a time, five each (quintet, quintain, quintessence, quintessential, quintile, quintuplet, quintillion)

quotus, quota, quotum: how many, of what number (quote, quotation, quota, quotidian, quotient)

rabo, rabere: to rage or be mad; to rave (rabies, rabidity)

radix, radicis: root, foundation, basis, origin (radish, radical, radicand, radicle, eradication)

rapax, rapacis: snatching, greedy (rapacious)

rarus, rara, rarum: loose, thin, scattered, infrequent, extraordinary (rarify, rare, rara avis, rarefaction, rarity)

ratio, rationis: reason, motive; theory, plan; calculation (rational, ratio, irrationality, rationalization)

re-: again, anew, back (reiterate, restart, recede, renovation)

rego, regere, rexi, rectum: to guide, direct, rule, govern (regent, rector, regime, regional, correction, director, regimentation, directional, directorate, dirigible)

requies, requietis: rest, repose (requiem)

res, rei: thing, object (reify, reification)

rideo, ridere, risi, risum: to laugh, look cheerful, smile (derision)

rigeo, rigere: to be stiff (rigidify, rigorous)

ripa: bank, shore (riparian, rivage, river)

rodo, rodere, rosi, rosum: to gnaw, nibble at; to corrode or consume; to disparage, backbite, slander (rodent, corrosive, erode)

rogo, rogare: to ask, request (interrogation, rogatory, rogation, abrogation, derogative, prerogative, subrogation, arrogate)

rosa: rose (roseate, rose, rosette)

rota: a wheel (rotor, rotation, rotary, rotogravure, rote, rotifer, rotiform)

ruber, rubra, rubrum: red, ruddy (rubicund, rubescent, rubefacient, rubella, rubeola, rubidium, rubric, ruby)

rumor, rumoris: a report, rumor, hearsay (rumormonger)

rumpo, rumpere, rupi, ruptum: to break, burst open; to destroy; to interrupt (interruption, rupture, corrupt, abruptly, bankruptcy, disruption, erupt)

rus, ruris: country, farm, estate (rural, rusticate, rusticity)

sacer, sacra, sacrum: sacred, holy (sacrament, consecrate, execration, obsecrate, sacred, sacrifice, sacrilege, sacristan, sacrum, sacroiliac)

saepio, saepire, saepsi, saeptum: to hedge in, enclose, confine. Participle is *saeptum*: barrier (septum)

sal, salis: salt; sea-water (salinity, salify, salimeter, salina, salinometer)

salus, salutis: health, soundness; safety, well-being (salutation, salubrious, salutatorian)

salvus: safe, well, unhurt (salvation, salve, salvage, salver, salvia, salvor, salvo)

sancio, sancire, sanxi, sanctum: to consecrate, make inviolable, confirm, decree; also, to forbid on pain of punishment, provide against (sanctify, inner sanctum, sanctimonious, sanction, sanctuary, sanctity)

sanguis, sanguinis: blood, blood-relationship, race, family, strength (sanguine, consanguinity, sangfroid, sangria, sanguinary, sanguinolent)

sanitas, sanitatis: health, soundness, sanity, correctness (sanitation, insanity, sanitarium, sanitary, sanitize)

sapo: soap (saponify, saponaceous)

sapio, sapere, sapivi or *sapii*: to taste; to discern, be wise, think. Participle is *sapiens, sapientis*: wise, sensible (sapient, homo sapiens, sapid, saporous)

satis or *sat*: enough (satisfaction, insatiable, satisfactory)

scaena or *scena*: stage, theater, publicity (scene, scenery, obscene, scenic)

scalae, scalarum: a flight of stairs, ladder (escalator, scale, escalade, echelon)

scando, scandere: to climb, ascend (ascent, condescension, scansion, descend, transcendental)

scio, scire, scivi or *scii, scitum*: to know. Participle is *sciens, scientis*: knowing, aware (scientific, scion, scientist, conscience, consciousness, omniscient, prescience, nescient)

scribo, scribere, scripsi, scriptum: to write (scribe, scribble, script, prescribe, inscription, description, circumscribe, conscript, manuscript, postscript, subscription, transcribe)

seco, secare: to cut (sector, dissection, insect, sectional, resection, intersection

secundus: second, following; going the same way, attending, favoring (secondary)

sedeo, sedere, sedi, sessum: to sit, stay fixed; to sit in judgment (sedentary, sediment, session, assessment, obsession, preside, residual, subsidy, seance, residency, residue)

sedo, sedare: to settle, calm (sedative, sedate)

semis-: half (semiaquatic, semiconductor)

senex, senis [comparative form is *senior*]: old, aged (seniority, senescence, senility)

sentio, sentire, sensi, sensum: to feel, experience (sentient, sensible, assent, consent, dissenting, resentment)

septem: seven (September, which was the 7th month of the roman year, septenary, septennial, septet)

sequor, sequi, secutus: to follow, accompany (non-sequitur, sequel, consequence, persecution, prosecution, execution, subsequence, obsequious)

serra: a saw (serration)

servo, servare: to watch over; to keep, save (conservation, preserve, reservation, reserve, observe)

sesqui-: one half more, half as much again (sesquicentennial)

sex-: six (sextet, sextant, sextillionth, sextile)

sicco, siccare: to dry, to drain (desiccate, siccative)

sidus, sideris: constellation, star, season (sidereal, siderite, siderostat)

signum: sign, mark, warning, command (designate, signify, signal, assignment, insignia, resignation, consignment)

sileo, silere, silui: to be still, to be silent. Participle is *silens, silentis*: silent; plural means *the dead* (silence)

silva: forest (sylvan, pennsylvania, sylph, silviculture)

simia: ape (simian)

similis: resembling (similarity, dissimilar, verisimilitude, simile, assimilation)

simplex, simplicis: simple, single; pure, plain (simplicity) *simul-*: at once, at the same time (simultaneous, simulcast)

simulo, simulare: to make like (simulate)

sincerus: pure, whole, genuine (sincerity, insincere)

sine-: without (sinecure, *sine qua non*)

singulus: single, separate (singularity)

sinister, sinistra, sinistrum: left, on the left hand; wrong; perverse, unfavorable (sinister, sinistral, sinistrous)

sisto, sistere, stiti, statum: to cause to stand, set, place. Participle is **status, stata, statum**: fixed, determined, regular (station, desist, consist, status, resist, superstition, existence, insistence, persist, subsistence)

sol, solis: the sun, a day (solar, solarium, solstice)

solidus: dense, solid, whole (consolidate, solidity, solidification)

solus: alone (solitude, solitaire, solipsism, soliloquy)

solvo, solvere, solvi, solutum: to loosen, untie, release, weaken (solution, absolute, resolve, dissolve, solubility, solute, resolute)

sono, sonare, sonui, sonitum: to sound, sing of, celebrate; of words, to mean (resonant, sonar, sonic, unison, consonant, dissonance, sonorous)

sophos or **sophus**: wise (sophomore, sophistry, philosophy)

sopor, soporis: deep sleep, laziness (soporific, sopor, soporiferous)

soror, sororis: sister (sorority)

sors, sortis: a lot, the casting of lots; prophecy; share; part; fate (sort, sorcery, consort, assortment)

spatium: space, extent, room; distance, interval, size (spatial, spacious) *specto, spectare*: to look at, watch (spectator, spectacle, respect, inspection, circumspect, introspection, perspective, retrospective, suspect, respectively)

spero, sperare: to look for, expect, hope for (desperation, esperance, prosperity)

spina: thorn, prickle; in plural, anxieties, difficulties (spineless, spinescent, spiniferous, spinose, spinous, spinule, spinifex, spinulose)

spiro, spirare: to breathe, blow; to be alive (inspiration, aspire, respiratory, inspirited, expiration, conspiracy, transpire, perspiration, suspire, inspirational, spiritualism)

spondeo, spondere, spopondi, sponsum: to pledge oneself to, promise, or vow (respond, sponsor, despondent, correspondent)

spuo, spuere, spui, sputum: to spit out (sputum, cuspidor)

statuo, statuere, statui, statutum: to place, set up, establish, settle (statute, statue, stance, circumstance, distance, stay; instantaneous, substance, station, substitute, statuesque, status, statutory, statistic, stationary, standardization, stapes)

stella: star (stellar, constellation, stellate)

sterno, sternere, stravi, stratum: to stretch out, to spread (stratify, consternation, substratum, stratosphere, straticulate, stratification, stratiform, stratigraphy, stratocumulus)

stipo, stipare: to compress, to crowd (constipate)

strenuus: brisk, active, turbulent, restless (strenuous)

strepo, strepere, strepui, strepitum: to clatter, creak, clash (obstreperous)

stringo, stringere, strinxi, strictum: to bind, tie (constrict, stricture, restriction, strictness, stringent, astringent, strait)

struo, struere, struxi, structum: to arrange, build, devise (construction, restructure, destruction, infrastructure, instruction, obstruct)

studeo, studere, studui: to study a subject, be eager, strive after (studious, student, studio)

stupeo, stupere, stupui: to be amazed, to halt or cease (stupendous, stuporous)

suadeo, suadere, suasi, suasum: to advise or recommend (persuade, dissuasion, suasion, assuasive)

suavis: sweet, pleasant (suave)

sub-: under, at the foot of, before (submarine, submerge, substitution, subatomic, subtract, subordinate, subpar)

subter-: beneath, below, underneath (subterfuge)

suffero, suffere: to support, endure, suffer (suffrage, suffering, insufferable)

sugo, sugere, suxi, suctum: to suck (suction, suctorial, succulent)

sum, esse, fui, futurus: to be, exist, be there. Future participle is *futurus, futura, futurum*: future, about to be; as a noun, *the future* (essence, essential, quintessential, future, interest)

sumo, sumere, sumpsi, sumptum: to take, obtain, assume (assumption, presumption, resume, consumption, sumptuous, sumptuary)

suo, suere, sui, sutum: to sew, stitch, join together (suture, couture)

super-: over, above, besides, beyond, moreover; at, concerning, about; besides, beyond; more than (superlative, supersonic, supercilious)

superbus: haughty, exalted, proud, brilliant (superb)

superus: situated above, upper, higher; the gods. **superior, superius** [comparative form]: earlier, former, past, higher, upper (superiority) **supremus** [superlative form]: highest, last, the end; death (supreme) **summus, summa, summum** [used as another superlative]: (*summa cum laude*)

supra-: over, on the top, before, previously, beyond, more than (supralapsarian, supramolecular, supraglottal) *surgo, surgere, surrexi, surrectum*: to rise up, get up, spring up (surging, insurrection, resurrect, insurgent, resurgent)

taceo, tacere, tacui, tacitum: to be silent or still (tacit, taciturn)

tango, tangere, tetigi, tactum: to touch, push, strike; to steal; to affect the feelings; to touch upon a subject (tangible, tango, contact, contiguous, tactile, taction, tactfully, tactual, tangent, intact)

tantus: of such a size, so great, so much, so far (tantamount)

tardo, tardare: to be slow, delay (tardiness, retardation)

techna: trick or artifice (technique, technical). Related to Greek word *tekhne*, meaning *skill or art.*

tego, tegere, texi, tectum: to cover, conceal, protect. Participle is *tectus, tecta, tectum*: covered, close, reserved, cautious. Noun is made from *tectum*: roof or ceiling, a shelter, dwelling (protection, detection, tectrix, tegument, integument)

temno, temnere, tempsi, temptum: to despise (contemptuous)

tempero, temperare: to be moderate, control oneself; mingle, regulate (temperance, temperature, tempera, temperamental)

tempto, temptare: to prove, test, work upon, disturb (attempt, temptation)

tempus, temporis: time; section; of the temples of the head (temporal, temporary, contemporary)

tendo, tendere, tetendi, tentum and *tensum*: to stretch, extend (tendon, extension, tension, ostensible, attend, contend, intentional, distend, pretender, intensify)

teneo, tenere, tenui, tentum: to hold, keep, know, comprise, persist (retention, tenable, tenure, abstinence, container, continuation, detain, pertaining, sustain, tenet, tenancy, entertainment, obtain, lieutenant)

tenuo, tenuare: to make thin, weaken (attenuate, tenuous, extenuating)

ter-: three times, thrice (tertiary)

terminus: limit, boundary (terminal, term, determination, exterminate, terminus)

terra: earth, land, region (terrarium, subterranean, mediterranean, terra firma, terrace, terrigenous, territorial, terrier, terra cotta, terraqueous, terrene, terrestrial, terricolous, tureen, parterre)

terreo, terrere: to frighten, deter (terror, terrify, deter, terrific)

testis: witness (contest, detest, protest, obtest, testament, testimony, testify, intestate, attest)

tetra-: four (tetralogy, tetrahedron, tetragon, tetramerous, tetrapod, tetrarchy, tetrastichous, tetratomic, tetrode)

texo, texere, texui, textum: to weave, build (textile, contextual, text, textuary, textured, pretext)

thema, thematis: topic, subject (thematic, theme)

tingo, tingere, tinxi, tinctum: to wet, to dye or imbue (tinge, tincture, tinctorial, tinct, taint, intinction)

tolero, tolerare: to carry, bear, endure, support (tolerable, intolerance, toleration)

tollo, tollere, sustuli, sublatum: to lift (extol)

tono, tonare, tonui, tonitum: to thunder (detonate, astonished, stunning, tornado)

tonsor, tonsoris: hair-cutter, barber (tonsorial)

torqueo, torquere, torsi, tortum: to twist, distort, test, torture (torture, torsion, distort, torque, retort, tort, torment, tortuous, contortionist, extort)

totus, tota, totum: whole, complete (total, totality)

traho, trahere, traxi, tractum: to drag, pull, trail, breathe, lengthen, contract (tractor, traction, detract, subtraction, distraction, abstraction, attraction, contract, extract, protracted, retraction, trailer, train, trait, tractive, tract) *trans-*: over, across, on [or to] the other side of (transatlantic, translate, transference, transcontinental, transitive, transgression)

tremo, tremere, tremui: to tremble, quake. Gerundive as adjective is *tremendus, tremenda, tremendum*: fearful, terrible (tremendous, tremor, tremulous)

trepido, trepidare: to be agitated, be busy, bustle about (trepidation)

tres, tria: three (trio, triumvirate, triangle, triarchy, triatomic, triassic, triaxial)

tribuo, tribuere, tribui, tributum: to divide out, allot, assign; to give, allow, yield, ascribe, attribute (tribute, contribution, attribution, retribution)

tricae, tricarum: trifles, nonsense; troubles (intricacy, extricate)

trudo, trudere, trusi, trusum: to push, press, urge on, force (extrusion, intrude, abstruse, protrude)

turbo, turbare: to disturb, unsettle (turbulence, turbinal, turbinate, turbine, turbojet, disturbing, perturb)

turpis: ugly (turpitude)

tussis: a cough (tussal, tussive)

ubi-: where (ubiquitous)

ulcus: sore, wound (ulcer, ulceration, ulcerous, ulcerative)

ulter: far, ulterior *ulterius* [comparative form]: farther, more advanced or remote (ulterior) *ultimus, ultima, ultimum* [superlative form]: most distant, farthest, extreme, original, last, final, greatest or meanest, lowest (ultimate)

ultra: beyond, on the far side of, farther than, more than (ultramarine, ultramicrometer, ultraconservative, ultramodern, ultrasonic, ultraviolet, ultramundane) *umbra*: shadow; protection; ghost (umber, penumbra, umbel, umbellate, umbelliferous, umbellule, umbra, umbrage, umbrella, adumbral, adumbrate, somber, sombrero)

umidus [humidus]: wet, damp (humidity, dehumidifier, humectant)

unda: wave (undulate, inundate, redundant, undine)

ungo [also *unguo*], *ungere, unxi, unctum*: to anoint, besmear (unguent, unctuous, anoint, ointment)

unus, una, unum: one, at the same time. Adverb is *una*: together. (united, union, unity, unification, universal, uniform, unicycle, unicorn, unilateral, unilocular)

urbs, urbis: city (urban, suburb, urbane)

urgeo, urgere, ursi: to push, press, drive; to beset, oppress, stress; to press on with, follow up (urge, urgent)

utor, uti, usus: to use, possess, enjoy, employ (useless, usualness, usury)

vaco, vacare: to be empty, free, at leisure (vacancy, vacation, evacuate, vacuum)

vado, vadere: to go, step (evade, invasion, evasive, pervasive)

valeo, valere: to be strong or well; to have force, be able or be worth. Participle is *valens, valentis*: strong, powerful, healthy (valence, prevalence, valerian, valiant, validity, invalid, valueless, convalescent, equivalent, prevailing)

vanus, vana, vanum: empty, vain, worthless; ostentatious, boastful, unreliable (vain, vanity, vanish)

vapor, vaporis: steam (evaporation, vapor)

varius: changeable, speckled (variant, variegated, variola, variety, invariable, variate)

vastus: empty (vast, devastation)

veho, vehere, vexi, vectum: to carry, convey; to ride, drive (convection, vector, vehicular, inveigh)

vello, vellere, velli [also *vulsi* or *volsi*], *vulsum* [*volsum*]: to pull, twitch, pluck out (convulsion, revulsion, divulsion, evulsion)

vena: a blood vessel, vein, artery; water course; vein of metal, vein of talent, disposition (vein, vena cava, veinlet, veinstone, venule, venosity)

vendo, vendere, vendidi, venditum: to sell (vendor, vending)

venio, venire, veni, ventum: to arrive, happen, grow, arise (convention, convenient, event, invention, adventure, advent, venue, avenue, convenient, eventual, intervention, misadventure, prevention, revenue, souvenir, supervene, circumvention, adventitious, covenant, provenance)

ventus, venti: wind, rumor, favor (ventilation, vent, ventage)

venus, veneris: charm, loveliness; love, a loved one (venerate, venerable)

verax, veracis: truthful (veracity)

verbum, verbi: word, expression (verb, verbal, verbatim, verbalize, verbiage, verbify, verbosely)

vergo, vergere, versi: to bend, verge, turn (verge, converge, divergence)

verto [also *vorto*], *vertere, verti, versum*: to turn, change (versatility, version, revert, subvert, subversive, vertigo, verse, vertebrate, vortices, adversity, conversely, adversary, anniversary, aversion, controversial, diversion, evert, extroverted, introverted, perverse, transverse, universal, vice versa, obvert)

vestis: clothing (vest, divest, travesty, revested, vesture)

veto [also *voto*], *vetare, vetui, vetitum*: to forbid (veto)

vexo, vexare: to shake, annoy (vexation)

via: way, road, means, method (viaduct, obviate, obvious, impervious, deviation, deviously, previously, viatic, viaticum, viator) *vibro, vibrare*: to shake or cause to shake (vibration, vibrant, vibraphone, vibratile, vibrato, vibrio, vibrissa)

vicinus, vicina, vicinum: near, neighboring (vicinity, vicinage, vicinal)

video, videre, vidi, visum: to see or seem (videotape, vision, visa, surveyor, videogenic, view, review, preview, visage, visibility, visit, visitation, vista, visualizer, evidence, voyeurism, clairvoyant, interview, provision, supervision)

vigil, vigilis: watchful (vigil, vigilance)

villa: house, estate, farm (village, villa, villain)

vinco, vincere, vici, victum: to conquer, master, surpass (invincible, victor, vincible, convincing, eviction, conviction, vanquish)

violo, violare: to violate, outrage, injure (inviolate, violation, violence)

vita: life (vital, vitality, vitamin, vitalism, vitamer, vitascope)

vivo, vivere, vixi, victum: to live, be alive, survive (survival, vivacious, revival, vividness, convivial)

voco, vocare: to call, name (invocation, vocal, vocation, revocation, vocabulary, vocalic, vocative, evocative, provocation, invocation, advocate, convocation)

volo, velle, volui: to wish, want, ordain. Participle is *volens, volentis*: willing, favorable (volition, voluntary, volunteer, benevolence, malevolence, volitive)

volo, volare: to fly, to move rapidly (volleyball, volitation, volitant, volplane, volant, volatility)

volvo, volvere, volvi, volutum: to turn, roll, twist; to turn over in the mind, consider; to experience (involvement, volution, devolvement, convolution, involution, revolution, evolution, revolve, volute, volvulus, volvox, voluble, circumvolve, obvolute)

voro, vorare: to eat greedily, consume, devour (voracious, devouring, carnivore, herbivore, omnivore) *voveo, vovere, vovi, votum*: to vow, pray for, wish (votive, vow, vote, votary, devotedness, devoutly)

vox, vocis: voice, cry, call; language; sound (vocal, vociferous, vociferate, voice)

vulgo, vulgare: to make common or accessible; publish, impart (vulgar, vulgate, vulgarian)

vulnus, vulneris: a wound, injury (vulnerable, invulnerability, vulnerary)

Finis-whose meaning you now know!

Evidence-Based Reading

People hate the Evidence-Based Reading, which is the new name for Critical Reading. Why? Well, for starters, it's boring. But this is one of those things you just have to get through, and you can do it! You just have to remember that you can't put your head down and take a nap, okay?

The most important tips to remember regarding the Evidence-Based Reading on the SAT are:

1. *Read the passages!* This sounds obvious, but I've heard too many people suggest skipping the reading and going straight to the questions. The questions are all about the passages, so if you don't read them, you're severely handicapping yourself.

2. All the answers are in the passage, either stated outright or implied.

3. Don't overanalyze, since often smart and creative people will talk themselves into picking the wrong answers because they can think of perfectly valid sounding reasons for doing so. Remember that you are to pick the *best* answer, not merely an acceptable one that you could defend if you were writing a terrific essay.

4. Read the answer choices without stopping to think about each one separately. Stopping to think over each one separately might cause you to make an emotional commitment to an answer; if you have done so, it is harder to ditch that answer even if a better one is revealed later.

5. If you are referred back to a specific line, read a little bit above that line and a little bit below it to get the context.

6. Keep working on vocabulary. If you don't know what *sardonic* means, how can you figure out if the passage's tone is sardonic?

7. Make yourself concentrate. The reading is boring, we know, but you *can* stay awake. Staying awake and alert is a prerequisite to getting into college! (The next bit will sound like stupid advice, but it works: practice catching yourself whenever your mind wanders, on any reading you're doing. If you keep practicing this skill, you will eventually catch yourself after a few words, rather than four paragraphs!)

8. Try to read quickly. Most people slow down when they're reading for comprehension, but usually people do better if they push themselves to read slightly faster; the sentences hang together better and people are less likely to lose their train of thought. Think of it as analogous to riding a bike: if you try to ride a bike really slowly, it's harder to balance than if you pick up the pace. Likewise, if you read a bit faster, you may find that you remember the beginning of the sentence when you get to the end of it! (If you have an opportunity to learn speed-reading, consider it; it can save you gobs of time for the rest of your life. There are books you can buy to teach yourself this skill. I took an Evelyn Wood course years ago, and you can google Evelyn Wood or go to Amazon and find books using that method.)

During your reading of the passages, focus on key ideas, style, tone, attitude and purpose of the passages. If a passage is very difficult for you, skip it and come back to it if you have time. Remember not to mess up your numbering on the answer sheet.

Avoid injecting your own knowledge into the answers. It is important to look at what the passage says or implies and not to choose answers based on other readings or ideas you have seen.

Select the best answer. There may be several choices that are partly correct, but only one answer will stand out. Therefore, it is important not to fill in the answer sheet until you have read all the answer choices and thought about which one is most appropriate.

If you become puzzled in answering a question, you may go back to look at the passage; you should also reread the question to make sure that you understand what is being asked. Sometimes people look at the answers and choose one that is certainly true according to the passage, but is not the answer to the particular question being asked. Another problem people have is losing track of the main idea of the passage; you may find secondary or tertiary ideas that are like side roads off a main highway. If you are asked about the main idea, try not to scoot off the subject.

Some questions might be of the following sort: "What idea would the author be least likely to have?" or "The author is mostly concerned with . . ." or "What can you infer from the passage?" It will be necessary for you to read the questions carefully, so that you don't, for instance, answer what idea the author would be *most* likely to have if the question wants the *least* likely idea.

Sometimes a question will say, "Which event, *if it happened,* . . . ?" or "Which fact, *if true* . . . ?" In such a case, don't look for the fact or event in the passage; they're trying to say, "If we added this new piece of information, how would it change everything?" They will not italicize it in the question, but you will probably see this sort of construction on the test.

There are sometimes dual passages on the SAT. The authors of the passages may be presenting conflicting ideas or at least showing different slants on the same subject. You will be asked some questions about the first passage, other questions about the second passage, and still further questions concerning both passages. Essentially, the methods for answering single-passage questions will still apply to the dual passages, except that you will need to be careful not to confuse which passage you are being referred to. The questions clearly denote whether the first and/ or second one is being addressed. We have found that most students do best if they read Passage One first and answer the questions about Passage One, then read Passage Two and answer those questions, and *then* do the compare-and-contrast questions.

You may have passages that are really only a couple of sentences long. Dealing with these is the same as dealing with the longer passages, except that you may be grateful for the brevity!

Vocabulary is often tested in context on the SAT reading selections, with an emphasis on how words are used in the passages. Sometimes all five choices are dictionary definitions of the word cited, so it is your job to figure out which definition works best in context.

Additional vocabulary testing occurs in the Sentence Completion questions, which are covered two chapters ahead.

Try to relax when reading the passages and to get a basic sense of content. Every reader has had the experience of getting all the way through a selection and not having the foggiest idea what he or she has read. It is also easy to focus on minutiae. Try to calm yourself down and focus your mind on the selection; remember that if you miss picking up something in the passage, you can always go back and get it later. But if you burn up lots of time trying to digest every word and nuance of the passage or taking notes, you may run out of time. In general, on the SAT (since all questions have an equal value), answer the easiest questions first and go back and pick up the harder ones later if you have time.

And one last little bit of advice about vocabulary: not only will it help you on all types of questions on these sections of the SAT, but you *will* use this vocabulary in college, graduate or professional school, in your career and in the rest of your life. In high school, I wondered why the heck they kept giving us more vocabulary words; didn't we have enough already to say everything we needed?

The short answer is a resounding "No!" If you ever hang out around a two-year-old, you know they are fascinating creatures, but their vocabulary consists of concrete nouns, maybe a few colors, *big* and *little* and so forth. They can't think in more complex terms at that phase of their development, but when they acquire a more complex vocabulary, their ability to express broader ideas also grows. Likewise, your thinking processes grow when you develop a more sophisticated vocabulary.

It isn't just showing off!

Writing and Language Sample

Sample passage for Writing and Language Test:

Directions: Some questions accompany the passage below; some questions ask you how you might improve the expression of key ideas and others deal with grammatical structure and syntax. You might need to focus on an underlined portion or have to consider the whole passage or a part of it. Your task is to pick the best answer in order to improve the writing or follow accepted standards in English. When "NO CHANGE" is an option, you should pick it if leaving things as is would be the best choice.

Questions 1-11 are based on the following passage:

Jeannie Rousseau was the beautiful young daughter of a high-ranking Parisian official when the Nazis [1] were marching into Paris. Recruited one night on a train by Georges Lamarque, she [2] was becoming a spy for the French Resistance as the code name AMNIARIX. Her father had "volunteered her" to work for the Nazis and she became privy to very classified German intelligence, information that she was able to absorb readily because of possessing a photographic memory.

[1]
A) NO CHANGE
B) had marched onto Paris.
C) marched into Paris.
D) walked into Paris.

[2]
A) NO CHANGE
B) became a spy for the French Resistance under the code name AMNIARIX. Her father
C) became AMNIARIX, a spy. For the French Resistance, her father
D) decided she liked the name "Amniarix" and subsequently worked for the French Revolution. Her father

Every night after work, she would travel to a [3] <u>safe house and essentially "upload" the information</u> to others in the Resistance movement, and the intelligence would find its way to [4] <u>Winston Churchill's desk within days. Probably the most important intelligence she gathered concerned the development of V1 and V2 rockets by Werner von Braun,</u> who after WWII came to the U.S. to work with the nascent space organization NASA to help develop America's space program. These V1 and V2 rockets would have been capable of traveling from the base at Peenemünde to stratospheric heights and then raining on London.

[3]

A) NO CHANGE
B) safe house and essentially "download" the information
C) safety house and essentially "upload" computer files
D) another city, where she would meet friends for dinner and conversation and then give notes of her findings

[4]

A) NO CHANGE
B) Winston Churchill's personal secretary within a few month's time. Probably the most important intelligence she gathered concerned the development of specialty laser rockets by W. von Braun,
C) Winston Churchill, who was the main leader in England. Probably the most important intelligence she gathered concerned Werner von Braun, a scientist
D) Werner von Braun, who was developing V1 and V2 rockets for Germany, and

[5] <u>Historians since WWII will someday almost have proven pretty decisively that</u> 50 of these rockets carrying bombs would have been capable of completely destroying London. Furthermore, Allied troops were massing on the southern shores of England in preparation for D-Day.

[6] <u>When Churchill received Jeannie Rousseau's report of stratospheric rockets that could travel such distances without a single German plane flying to deliver the bombs, he was able to act instantly; Jeannie Rousseau's intelligence contained relevant codes and enough detailed information that Churchill was able to set back the German rocket program months—long enough for D-Day to happen.</u>

[5]

A) NO CHANGE
B) Preposterously, Churchill himself speculated that
C) Truly, or not (Who really knows!)
D) Reportedly, Churchill himself estimated that

[6] The writer is considering eliminating this paragraph. Should it be kept or eliminated?

A) Kept, since it explains how valuable the intelligence Jeannie Rousseau provided was to the Allies.
B) Kept, since eliminating it would create an awkward gap between the 2nd and 4th paragraphs.
C) Eliminated, since it provides no new information to the rest of the passage.
D) Eliminated, since it's poorly written and contains a run-on sentence.

[7] <u>Ms.</u> Rousseau was captured as
Churchill attempted to bring her
to England for further debriefing.
She [8] <u>survived around three
concentration camps</u> including
the women's punishment camp,
Ravensbrück. She settled in
Paris, marrying and having
[9] <u>two kids, who lived into
their 90s in a flat overlooking
the Seine. Few knew that
the diminutive woman could
arguably have been considered
to have survived the war.</u>

[7]

A) NO CHANGE
B) Mademoiselle
C) Madame
D) Miss

[8]

A) NO CHANGE
B) lived in three concentration camps
C) survived three concentration camps
D) survived three high-density camps

[9]

A) NO CHANGE
B) two children.
A) (C) two children, living into her 90s on a level spot overlooking the Seine, a large mesh-like landmark in the French countryside. Few knew that the wee woman was more than the typical Frenchwoman.
C) two children, living into her 90s in a flat overlooking the Seine. Few knew that the diminutive woman could arguably have been considered one of the most consequential heroes of the war.

[10]<u>She occasionally was duly honored, once by the CIA for being the epitome of what a spy should be,</u> and once by then-President Sarkozy in a ceremony at the Élysée Palace.

[10]

A) NO CHANGE
B) She was doubly honored by the CIA for being the epitome of what a spy should be
C) She herself honored the CIA, praising the organization for epitomizing what spying should be
D) She occasionally was duly honored, once epitomizing spying for the CIA

[11]<u>I had the honor of meeting her on a number of occasions, and she bristled at taking any credit. Whether it was survivor guilt or something else, she was self-effacing to a fault; she refused to consider herself a hero.</u>

[11] The author of this passage includes this paragraph but is unsure of whether it should stay. What is the correct strategy to take?

A) Leave this paragraph where it is because it adds an interesting and personal anecdote.
B) Eliminate this paragraph completely because it is at odds with the informational tone of the rest of the passage.
C) Put this paragraph at the very beginning, because it provides a personal context and supports of main thesis of the passage.
D) Elaborate further on the fact that Jeannie Rousseau didn't consider herself a hero by including further sources.

Answer Key:

[1] C) is correct. D) is too casual-sounding, as though the Nazis were strolling through rather than taking over France. Tenses are incorrect as written in A) and in B).

[2] B) is correct. As written in A), it sounds as though Jeannie Rousseau was already becoming a spy, when she was actually recruited by Georges Lamarque. C) and D) change the information completely. She is not working for the French Revolution!

[3] A) is correct as written. B) is wrong because downloading means getting info, not giving it. C) The term for a place to go among one's own spies is "safe house," not "safety house," and computer files would not have existed during WWII the way they do today. D) makes all the spying sound more casual and fun than it was, by far; at every moment, spies risked death if they were caught and identified as spies. Georges Lamarque himself met such a death at the hands of the Nazis.

[4] A) is correct as written. Had intelligence taken months to get to Churchill, as in B), it would have been utterly useless. C) is wrong because the intelligence did not focus on Von Braun, but on the V1 and V2. D) is wrong because Rousseau was not providing info to a scientist working for the Nazis, but information *about* that scientist's work to Churchill.

[5] D) is correct. A) with its "will someday almost have proven pretty decisively" doesn't really make sense. B) makes the real possibility of 50 V-2 rockets with bombs destroying London sound like foolish guessing. C) makes the serious estimate sound silly and "(Who really knows!)" adds a light tone unbefitting the subject.

[6] A) is correct. It does substantiate how critical Jeannie Rousseau's intelligence was to the Allies. B) is beside the point. C) is wrong because there is new info added to the passage. D) is wrong because it's not poorly written nor is there a run-on sentence.

[7] B) is correct. "Ms." is a term developed after WWII to address women without referring to marital status the way "Miss" and "Mrs." do. C) is wrong, because it refers to a married woman in France and Mademoiselle Rousseau is the term for a single woman; Jeannie

did not marry until after WWII; her marriage is referred to in the fourth paragraph. D) is the term for a single woman in English, not in French.

[8] C) is correct. A) is wrong because the word "around" doesn't belong there. B) makes it sound as though these camps were merely three locations where she took up residence voluntarily. D) substitutes "high-density" for "concentration," but of course "concentration camps" refers to Nazi death camps during WWII, not to the concept of "concentration" relating to density.

[9] D) is correct. As written, A) makes no sense; she had her children after WWII, which ended in 1945, so they would not have lived till their 90s by the publication date of this passage in 2016. Also, Mademoiselle Rousseau did not merely survive the war but rather was a heroine due to her spying activities. B) leaves out key information. C) "Flat" refers to an apartment, not a level spot, and the Seine is the river running through Paris, not a "large mesh-like landmark."

[10] A is correct. B) is wrong because "duly" means "correctly" or "rightly" or "deservedly" and it makes more sense than "doubly," for she was honored only once by the CIA. C) is wrong because the CIA honored her and praised her, not vice versa. D) is wrong since she didn't spy for the CIA.

[11] B) is correct; it really doesn't fit with the tone of the rest of the passage. A) is wrong because it really is not all that interesting! C) is not right because the personal context is only interesting to the author, not critical to the main thesis. D) would take the passage in a different direction from the main thesis, which is a biographical summary of Jeannie Rousseau's spying activities during WWII, not her assessment of those activities.

Technical and Fictitious Reading

The Evidence-Based Reading passages of the SAT often seem tedious to students; they necessitate wasting precious moments wading through long passages before questions can be answered. Time is at a premium during the SAT and reading paragraph upon paragraph takes up far too much of it.

This impression is compounded when the material is not familiar. If you are lucky enough to be a biology whiz and the section concerns a biological issue, you will probably be able to grasp the material relatively quickly. But wait! The next passage is about the Spanish-American War, and the third passage concerns ethics in business.

Some of the passages will seem to be excerpted from the middle of a novel. In these cases, you will get brief glimpses of characters and/or action without necessarily knowing what exactly is happening. You may occasionally have a passage you recognize from a real book you've read.

In both the technical passages (whether scientific or political or historical) or the fictitious passages, you are asked to read only what is there and make no assumptions about what is not given. In both kinds of passages you are therefore presented with similar requirements: first, to read the passages; and second, to go back to answer the questions as best you can.

Since there really are not different requirements for different types of passages, this amounts really to a non-unit! The general methods covered under Evidence-Based Reading suffice for all types of passages.

Sentence Completion

(A Subset of the Evidence-Based Reading Sections)

Fill in the blanks . . .

The key to the Evidence-Based Reading sections of the SAT is "vocabulary, vocabulary, VOCABULARY." Now, I know that this test looks hard to most people, but please trust me that if you learn substantial amounts of the material herein, you will find the test getting easier and easier. Why? Because you'll know more and more of the answers. But you have to do your homework, in order to put all the material into your brain so that it's there when you take the darn test.

Sentence Completion requires that you look at a sentence with one or two blanks in it and determine which of five choices given will fill in the blank(s) best. The best choice will result in a sentence that, among other things, makes logical sense.

When you look at a question, you might try to figure out what word or words would make sense in the blank(s) before looking at the choices given. After you have figured out something that works, look at the selections; if your word is there, you are home free. If it's not there, but there's a synonym, you are still home free. Vocabu-toons™ is a good section for learning synonyms and antonyms, and those are useful in Sentence Completion. For example, let's say that you know you need a word meaning *afraid* and you know several synonyms. Won't that make it easier to come up with the right answer? Of course, if you draw a blank, it's time to move to the next question without any undue delay, and come back to this one later. Just remember not to mess up your numbering on the answer sheet!

You will often notice that there are word clues in the sentence. For instance, if you see the words *but, although,* or *however,* look for a word that when filled in creates a distinction or contrast with the rest of the sentence. Likewise, if you see the words *and, also,* or *in addition,* you must look for a word or words that reinforce the meaning in the rest of the sentence.

Note: sometimes there will be two or three possibilities that make sense, but only one will be the best. *The SAT is not a test on which you can settle for second-best!* Often, two or three or even four can be immediately eliminated because they form nonsensical sentences. Once you are down to two or three choices, your job is much easier.

Some Sentence Completion questions are nothing more than a request for the meaning of a word. For instance, you might get a sentence like the following:

The _____, a three-wheeler, is a viable means of transportation for the elderly as well as for preschoolers.

(A) bicycle (B) tricycle (C) scooter (D) car

(B) is obviously the correct choice, because it is the word defined in the phrase that follows the blank.

Sometimes a Sentence Completion fill-in will make sense of a number of examples or illustrations given elsewhere in the sentence. Here is an example:

Evan's _____ working knew seemingly no bounds; in addition to laboring many extra evening and weekend hours, Evan lugged home projects that he did in the wee hours of the morning.

(A) compulsive (B) greedy (C) excellent (D) senseless

(A) is the correct choice, since it presents the best generalization of the specific examples given. A case could be made for (D), since this sort of compulsive working seems senseless to more moderate souls, but (A) would be the best choice.

As in the other Evidence-Based Reading areas, vocabulary building is a critical part of your preparation for the Sentence Completion questions. Not comprehending the words given as choices makes it much more difficult to select the correct answer. When you know all the vocabulary words in a question, you will find that the correct answer almost leaps off the page in the time it takes you to read the question and the five answer choices.

Also, it can be important to practice drills of Sentence Completion problems, so that you become increasingly comfortable with them and so that you are able to look for appropriate word and punctuation clues in the sentences that will help you answer them correctly.

Strategy (A Game Plan)

At this juncture in the book, I want to talk about strategy, tips and such for a few chapters. Consider it a break from the heavy curricular material! But it is also really important material in its own way.

The Back Burner

If you've ever cooked rice, you understand the idea of the back burner. You put rice in a pot, add water, turn the heat on, and at some point, without actively doing anything more, *voila*! it has turned into rice.

The brain is a mysterious organ. While we don't know fully how it works or why, the brain definitely seems to have a "back burner." In creative thinking, if you put aside a tough or incomprehensible problem, move on to other things, and go back to the difficult problem later, you may discover that you now know how to solve it. You haven't been actively thinking about it, but the problem sat on the back burner and almost seemed to work itself out!

On the other hand, if you come back to it and you still don't have a flash of insight, that's okay too. Please remember that it is okay to guess on the test. Sometimes you just draw a blank every single time you look at the problem (until suddenly at 3PM, a few hours after the test, in the middle of nothing in particular, you have a brilliant flash of insight.... Oh well, can't win 'em all).

The important thing is that if you don't immediately know the answer or how to get it, you do not want to sit there staring at the question for five minutes. This is a timed test, so please move on and come back to the problem later. It will still be there. Honest!

When taking the SAT, do the easiest questions first and then go back and do the harder ones. Since time is of the essence during the test, you must maximize your use of it. Thus, you cannot afford to tarry on questions whose answers do not come swiftly to you.

Great thinkers and inventors throughout history have reported that solutions have come to them almost out of the blue, while they were in the middle of something completely different. The solutions that had eluded them as they struggled with the material suddenly presented themselves when their minds were away from the work.

Why does this happen? Nobody really knows for sure, but the phenomenon can work to your advantage during the SAT. Read a question, and if you know how to answer it, fine; do so and move on to the next question. After you have gone through the entire section and answered all easy questions, go back and look at questions that weren't easy. Some may now seem clearer. You may even do a third go-round.

Whenever you get really stuck, move on. It's not worth it to bang your head against a wall, getting nowhere. If the flash of insight hits you before your time is up, that's great, but if it doesn't, don't despair. Remember: you can still get a great score while guessing at some test questions, and you are better off making an educated guess (again, there's no penalty for guessing on the new test) than wasting absurd amounts of time on them.

Pacing Yourself

Take a watch into the test site. Make sure it works and doesn't have any bells or beepers that go off on an hourly or quarter-hourly basis.

When you are told to start on a section, check quickly to see how many questions you must answer. Then consider the available time for completing the section and figure out quickly how much time on average you may spend on each question. For instance, suppose there are thirty questions and you have thirty minutes; you therefore have one minute on average for each question. Now, once you've computed your time parameters, you need to recognize that you should spend significantly less time on easier questions; perhaps some of the simplest questions will take a mere ten seconds.

A word of caution: you should not get obsessed with the watch. It's there to help you, not take over your brain. Steal furtive glances at it, and use it to pace yourself. But don't adhere slavishly to the schedule suggested above or to any other. If you find it only takes you three minutes to run through the easy questions, by all means move on. The key thing about the watch is that it can help prevent you from figuring you have plenty of time left just as the proctor calls "Time's up!"

Waste Not, Want Not

Don't spend any time daydreaming, doodling, thinking about how neat college is going to be, etc., etc. Just focus your attention as thoroughly as you can on the task at hand: the test.

Pitfalls

I have learned a lot from my students. Sadly, a few of them have taught me some pitfalls:

Case #1: One student did her work in the test booklet, which is fine, but figured she'd transfer her answers to the answer sheet when she was done with the section. She was a real math whiz, always scoring 700+ on those sections in class by the end of the course. But before she could transfer one answer, the proctor called time. Not wanting to have her test confiscated by continuing to work on that section (a correct but sad call), she simply left that section blank. And she knew she had them all correct! Fortunately, it was only junior year, and she promised she wouldn't make this mistake again. Her next scores were great.

Case #2: Another student forgot his calculator. Again, it was only junior year, so he had the luxury of time.

Case #3: A third student (another math genius) skipped an early math problem in each of two 30-minute sections and forgot to skip that line on his answer sheet. He paid extra to get the Question and Answer service and all his answers were correct but in the wrong place: he put the answer to problem 6 where problem 5's answer was supposed to be, problem 7 where 6 was supposed to be, etc. Instead of the 700+ math score he would have had, he had a mid-400. The machine grading the test didn't understand that he really knew everything but messed up on the answer sheet, so it counted it all wrong.

Case #4: One student took another prep course prior to mine; the teacher had claimed that the last section never counted. So the student sat that section out! He was quite surprised to discover it most certainly *had* counted, and that he got zero for that whole section. He told this story in my class, and we all laughed. Sometimes these things make funny stories . . . later! As in the previous three cases, he was a junior and had another chance to raise his scores.

Case #5: Various students have cited irregular circumstances that compromised the test. If something goes wrong, you may have certain rights. You may ask politely for things to improve at the time. If they don't, you can complain; look at the College Board web site or call within a short period after the test (as of this writing, you have until the Wednesday after the test for them to receive your complaint by fax, overnight delivery or email). There actually must be something wrong; *e.g.*, you can't just *say* there was too little time given on a section.

Case #6 (a.k.a. The Reason for Checking Your Work): One student years ago got a defective test booklet. When she got to the first reading passage, it was mostly blank paper and not legible. She went to the proctor, who gave her a new test booklet. When she completed the reading, she checked earlier questions and discovered she had been given a whole different test. Afterwards, she told the proctor and he arranged for the test to be hand-scored, since she had taken parts of two different tests. She scored quite high, but if she hadn't checked her work, she'd have never noticed the different tests.

Case #7: Two students refused to work any problems out of order. If they were stumped on question two, they'd sit there for 10 minutes until they got it. I read them the riot act and told them half-facetiously that they could either (a) work in consecutive order; or (b) go to college. If a problem is confusing or frustrating, move on. That question should be toast! You can go back later if there's time, so please don't fret about it.

Guessing

Ideally, you will not need to guess on the SAT. If you know all the answers, guessing is not needed. But most people who take the SAT have moments when they are not sure of the correct answer.

On multiple choice questions, if you can eliminate two or three wrong answers out of five possibilities, your odds improve, and it generally makes sense to hazard a guess in such a case. One student crossed out in the test booklet any option that she knew was wrong, and would make little notations in the margins of the booklet like *A? or C? Maybe B*, or *B or D correct*. These notes saved valuable time when she went back over the test later and often then it was clearer to her which of two or three choices made the most sense. You can write *NO!* by answers you know are wrong, and circle the whole question in your booklet to save you time when you go back to it. And once again, please remember not to waste valuable time on any given question. This is-need we remind you?-a timed test.

In My Estimation . . .

On math problems, estimate the answer. If a question asks for 47% of a number like 1200, you should immediately note that 47% is a bit less than half, and consequently the correct answer will be slightly less than 600. So if the choices include

(A) 612; (B) 259;(C) 647; (D) 564; and (E) 470,

you can rule out the first three right away since they're way out of line. This eliminates a lot of time-consuming computation. Even E can be eliminated by estimation, since you know that 470 would be 47% of 1000, and you're starting with 1200. So (D) is it.

Drawn to Scale

Unless otherwise indicated, diagrams in the math section are drawn to scale. Thus, you can eyeball answers using diagrams just as you can estimate answers in the example above.

If you are looking at a rectangle that measures 10 by 4 inches, and it is cut in two by a line that creates what looks like a square on the left side and a rectangle on the right side, you can estimate the area of that square as being about 16 square inches. Then you can look at the answer choices and see if there is something close to that choice.

Failing to Panic

Please remember that the SAT is not the most important thing in the world. It is an important test for college entrance, but people work themselves into a froth over it. It's not worth it!

I cannot overstress the desirability of *failing* to panic. Panic involves runaway emotions, fear, dread, palpitations, cold sweats and such. Tell yourself to calm down; you'll be glad you did. FDR once said that we have nothing to fear but fear itself. He probably never took the SAT, and it does seem there are a few things worth fearing in today's world, but the advice nevertheless makes sense. It is very easy to waste an enormous amount of energy being afraid of, say, failing, looking foolish, etc. I believe it makes sense to prepare yourself to do well on the SAT by working hard ahead of time. Then when you take the actual test, you should be in great shape.

Nonetheless, even prepared students might run across a question that stumps them. Don't let this throw you. Even if you have to skip answering one or more questions, you can still have a great performance on the SAT.

Test Tips

Even it you loathe exams, wouldn't it make sense to learn to handle them better? You might surprise yourself by learning to cope so well that you almost look forward to them. Oh well,
let's not get carried away . . .

Before The Test

There are some helpful things you can do before you enter the test site:

1. Familiarize yourself with directions for each type of question since these directions are the same on each SAT. It is silly to spend test time reading directions and focusing on understanding instructions if you can do this work ahead of time. The book *The Official SAT Study Guide* (the current title; always make sure it's by the College Board) has real sample tests in it. Keep in mind that reference information is at the beginning of every math section, too. It would be a shame during the test to say, "Oh, I wish I could remember the formula for area of a triangle." It's right there at the top of the first page of every math section!

2. Study the material herein and learn it well. You may hate it while you're doing it but it *will* pay off.

3. Spend time doing drills. Practicing types of questions that arise on the SAT is invaluable.

4. If the location of your test site is unfamiliar to you, do a dry run before the test date so you know how to find it. Make sure you leave earlier than you think necessary to allow adequate time to get there the day of the test. You never know when you will hit traffic or bad weather, and it's better to arrive early than to

wonder whether you'll make it on time. Know where your ticket is and please remember to take it and picture ID.

5. Line up your clothes the night before, and make sure they're comfortable and loose-fitting. It's a good idea to wear or bring a removable sweater or sweatshirt, whatever the outdoor weather, since you may find the test site is on the warm or chilly side. Dressing in layers is the idea. A student once said he would wear shorts under long pants and take off the pants if he got warm during the test. I told him I wasn't sure the proctors would understand! He said, "Okay, but may I take off my shoes?" "Yes," I told him, "as long as you don't kick them off and they fly through the air and hit another student in the head." (You can't cause a ruckus since proctors *do* have the right to oust students they feel are disruptive.)

6. The night before the SAT is *not* a good time to stay out til 3AM. You'll need an adequate night's sleep before the test. You can plan something fun for *after* the SAT, but the night before should be pretty uneventful.

7. Speaking of the night before, I suggest you also round up sharp No. 2 pencils and take a few extra, with good erasers (none that have been ground down below the metal). Set them near your clothes along with a dependable watch and your trusty calculator (with fresh batteries or recharging).

8. Nutritionists generally recommend a good breakfast, including some complete protein and carbohydrates. Some students hate eating breakfast, but if you can do so, breakfast will raise and keep higher your blood sugar levels, which affect mental performance. Having a sinking spell halfway through the exam is not what you want. Do not drink 73 ounces of liquid just before the test! You get bathroom breaks, but they aren't long, and there are lines.

9. Take a snack. No, you can't eat or drink during the test and crinkle cellophane wrappers and smack your lips and slurp, but you'll be glad if you have a personal source of nourishment when you do have a break. Yes, there may be vending machines, but there are often long lines, and sometimes when you get to the front, they're out of everything except one package of stale

cinnamon gum and it's stuck and won't come out. Instead of taking your chances, take a snack. And make it something you like; since this is not a fun morning for most people, you might as well have something you enjoy! It may be the only thing you enjoy all morning! If you're taking the test at your home school, take extra snacks. Invariably, you'll run into a friend who says, "Oh, I'm so hungry. I didn't eat breakfast. May I please have some of your snack?" If you've only brought enough for yourself, you're giving away sustenance you need to keep up your energy during the test, or you're spurning your friend. And trust me, your friend will remember! You'll go back for your 25th high school reunion, and that person will say, "Hey, man, I remember you! You wouldn't give me part of your stinkin' snack and I never did get into college and I only got crummy jobs, and I'm on my third divorce, and I blame it all on you!" OR . . . "Hey! You're the person who shared your snack with me during the SAT! I got into Harvard, met the man of my dreams, got a great degree, and we have three wonderful children, and I'm President of the United States, but of course you know that because you read the papers!" Moral of the story: take extras, okay?

During The Test

Now that we've covered the stuff you should do before the test, there are things you should do during it. (This section should be used in conjunction with the modules entitled "Psyching Yourself . . ." and "Strategy").

1. One of the test sections may be used only for statistical data purposes and may not be scored, but you will not know which section it is and you cannot therefore afford to say that any of the sections don't matter.

2. Your question booklet is the place for working out answers. No stray marks or scratchwork should go on the answer sheet, since the mechanical scoring machines may register them as answers. But the question booklet can hold a great deal of work in the margins, and you can scribble notes to yourself in case you need to come back to a question of whose answer you are not sure. It is not necessary to show all your work and you don't want to waste time going through needless procedures if you already know the answer. Of course there is no credit given for getting a correct answer that's written in the question booklet; you have

to transfer that answer to the proper spot on the answer sheet in order to receive credit.

3. Feel free to cross out answers in the question booklet that you definitely know are wrong; this effort may save you the time of rereading pointless material.

4. All questions (except the grid-ins) have as their answers one of the multiple choices listed below it. While the SAT is a somewhat challenging test, it is not as tough as it would be if you had to generate all the answers and write them down. Sometimes you can eliminate clearly absurd answers right off the bat. Sometimes you can estimate the answer and then look for something similar in the choices. Sometimes you can plug in real numbers for variables. Sometimes, when you get stumped, you can merely plug in the answers one by one and see if any of them makes sense. *Use* the answer choices to help you take the test.

5. Don't waste too much time on any given question, because time is strictly limited. If you are stumped, skip it quickly. You can go back later.

6. Don't be too hasty either. There is no point to rushing through questions so quickly that you make silly mistakes. If a computation needs to be done, do it carefully, since the test makers often include as choices answers you would get if you made a careless mistake or omitted a step.

7. Be careful to keep questions aligned with answers and to double-check this alignment when you're done.

8. Look at all answer choices before you make your selection. You are looking for the best answer, and there may be a very close second choice which you would pick if you didn't read every choice.

9. It is important to look at how many minutes you are allowed per section, and how many questions you must answer during that time frame. Roughly, you need to answer about one question per minute, but some of these will go quickly, and some will take more time. For instance, you'll have to use up some of your available total test-taking time reading the Evidence-Based Reading selections.

Psyching Yourself for the SAT

Note: Some relaxation techniques are listed below. These are not usually considered physically dangerous, nor is there an attempt to practice any form of medicine by including them here. If you have concerns, it's a good idea to contact your family doctor to make sure they are safe for you to do.

The natural response of the typical student to standardized testing is something between *Yeccchhh!!!* and *Argghhhh!!* But you can reach a point at which you no longer register horror, fear, panic and all the other not-so-lovely emotions that arise when you confront a standardized test.

1. The first key is preparation. Since you are reading this material, you are already taking that step. When you have practiced sample problems, increased your vocabulary, learned the math rules, and done every conceivable thing you can do to get ready for the SAT, why should you feel pressured? After all, you're *ready*.

2. The next key is to learn a few relaxation techniques. A person who is able to relax during the SAT will be less likely to panic and clutch up when trying to find an answer. Some relaxation techniques are listed below:

    Deep breathing as long as you don't overdo it and hyperventilate. People who are nervous tend to hold their breath or take shallow breaths. A conscious effort against this tendency can help you relax.

    Imaging. Imaging involves putting a pleasant and relaxing picture in your mind. An example might be thinking of lying on a warm beach; another might be sitting by a quiet pool at sunset. You can find images that relax you and practice imaging in the weeks before you are ready to take the SAT.

    Conscious tensing and relaxing of muscles. We often don't notice we are tensing up until the process is so far along that we have a headache, stiff neck, or other bodily manifestation of tension. In this exercise, the student tenses, say, the shoulders, holds them tensed for several seconds and then relaxes them and notices the difference. Some typical places that people hold tension are the head, neck, shoulders, and stomach. Students who learn to notice and release muscle tension before it becomes an impediment to performance may have a better chance of doing well.

3. The third key is to remember to answer the easiest questions first. All questions on the SAT are scored equally; there are no bonuses for correctly answering the toughies, and the toughies do burn up a lot of time. Catch the tough ones only after you've done the easier ones.

4. Please remember that the SAT is not like the tests you take in school in that it is not designed so that people will get perfect scores, even though people occasionally do. In school, a test would be considered a poor measure of material if only a few people out of hundreds of thousands got a perfect score. But the SAT is designed to be a very hard test; most colleges will consider you to be doing very well if you get a 600–650 on Evidence-Based Reading and Writing and 600–650 on Math. But in school, that level of performance would often merit a low B or a C or below. Keep in mind also that many colleges accept lower scores and a few want to see higher ones.

   This is not-repeat, not-your normal test. You do not have to know how to do everything that shows up on the SAT, and you can still earn a very respectable score.

5. Try to take one thing at a time. If you focus during the test on how much you want to go to a certain college and how scared you are that you won't do well enough to get in there, you won't have time to figure out the circumference of that circle. Be where you are: you're taking the SAT and you're going to do as well on it as you can, give it the old college try, etc., and you're not going to bring in lots of extraneous concerns that interrupt your thought processes.

6. Try to develop an attitude of game-playing, of fun. Believe it or not, there are people who tackle a standardized test with the attitude that it's enjoyable, challenging and *not a big deal.* Now you should not be so cavalier that you make careless errors, but

do relax a bit and try to have a good time while you are working hard. We suspect the students who are having the best time are those who have the strongest grasp of the material. Those who have prepared to take the SAT can probably afford to have fun.

7. Cultivate in the weeks before the exam the mental image of yourself as doing well on the test, as being fully capable of mastering the material. Mental imagery is a powerful tool if it's used properly. Too many people have been given the message that they are "bad at math" or "not good with words," until they believe this label is written in stone. Many people, as children, just didn't *get* the material as quickly as others the first time it was presented and therefore decided they weren't as good at that subject as others were (who knows? Maybe some kids had older siblings or parents who taught them the material ahead of time). *Break those negative stereotypes and give yourself the positive messages that will precede future competence.* If you constantly say, "I can't" or "I'm no good at that," you excuse yourself from even having to try. Part of growing is breaking through old limitations. As you do so, you will find that some of your limitations were imaginary or self-inflicted.

8. It helps to allow yourself more than one chance to take the SAT. If you can, try to take the SAT at least once in your junior year; then if the scores are not what you wish, you still can try again. This approach allows you a reprieve if you are tired or ill, or if you just plain mess up. One friend of ours felt particularly lousy the first time she took the SAT and thought it was nerves until she got home and took her temperature: 103 degrees! Needless to say, her scores were less than optimal. Out of the thousands of students who take the SAT each time it's administered, many will be grateful that they have allowed themselves the luxury of trying again if necessary. While we hope your first try yields terrific results, try to leave yourself an opening in case your first try is a mess. Note: colleges tend to frown on people taking the SAT more than three times. They think it looks desperate, and, well, it *does*.

9. A few butterflies in the stomach are normal. For all our talk of relaxing, we also feel that a little stage fright or nervousness can create an edge and cause a student to try a little harder than he or she normally would. This is fine; it's when a tiny case of nerves

slides over into a monumental case of incapacitating tension that you need to worry (or, rather, to relax!). You be the judge of what is the right amount of tension to perform optimally.

The best of luck to you. You've worked hard. Break a leg.

Where We Go From Here

Now that you've arrived at this point, you are in one of several positions:

1. You are due to take the SAT tomorrow.

2. You take the SAT within days, weeks or months.

3. You have a year or more until you take the SAT.

If (1) is the case, we wish you the best of luck and suggest that you reread the section on test-taking tips called The Panic-Level Module and get reasonable amounts of sleep, especially the night before the SAT (but not during it!).

If (2) or (3) is your situation, you can prepare yourself further to do well on the SAT. If you devote a block of time once, twice or more per week, you will find that you can reinforce and even advance the learning herein. Here are our suggestions:

1. Try to sit down and do twenty or thirty Evidence-Based Reading questions and twenty or thirty Math problems in the book *The Official SAT Study Guide* (the current title; please look for the College Board name and acorn logo); if you can do that much at a sitting, several times a week, you should be able to cover at least one test per week.

2. Try to learn several new vocabulary words per day, and several Latin roots, prefixes or suffixes too.

3. Review a MathFacts™ module every day or two.

4. Occasionally reread sections herein on various kinds of questions on the SAT and on study skills and so forth.

5. Memorize directions for each test section so they are an automatic part of your repertoire and so you need not waste actual time during the SAT reading directions.

6. Practice Word Building and Discovery™ techniques. You will have opportunities to use these techniques in regular high school courses, as well as when you look over material we've covered in this program.

7. When taking foreign language courses: be alert, as you learn foreign vocab, to words that have English relatives. Doing so will help you cement your foreign vocabulary and English vocabulary.

8. As you learn new terminology in subjects like chemistry, biology, etc., try to analyze vocabulary using methods covered in this program and see how these technical words are constructed.

9. As you do math problems in school, analyze each problem to see what info you need to solve the problem. Try to work problems more quickly, and to avoid careless calculation errors. Circling relevant info like *positive, negative, sum, product, perimeter, area*, etc., can be a good idea.

10. When you take a test in school, practice psyching yourself up to do your best work. It's common for many otherwise bright students to slip up because they get careless during exams and thus fail to show the breadth of knowledge they truly have.

11. Try to find at least twenty minutes a day to study and review for the SAT. You should obviously not take time away from your regular studies, but most students find they have at least twenty or thirty spare minutes a day to review for the SAT and that this review pays off. You can give yourself a day off now and then; if you study five or six days a week, you'll thank yourself during the SAT.

12. Practice writing about some of the essay topics in this book or elsewhere. You can get much better at writing if you try!

The above suggestions can help you strengthen the progress you make. But it's your choice whether you put in the time or not. Most students find it helps enormously to review and solidify the knowledge they've gained, and feel they increase their skill levels by continued drill.

You can keep building up your vocabulary and exercising your math skills or you can put the material on a shelf and forget about it until the SAT looms over you. We hope you will do yourself the favor of continuing to make a little time each week. A few hours or so a week can do wonders.

Again, best of luck to each and every one of you.

Vocabu-Toons™

Yet Another Vocabulary Building Method

Another one? Well, yes. Sometimes it takes every bit of help you can grab to get where you want to go.

Some methods work better for one person, some for another, and some people benefit from combinations. This section is *not* a substitute for the Top 100 Words list or Words You Must Know! or Word Building and Discovery™ or the Latin dictionary. It's *extra*. It's a system that helps people group words effectively and associate them with silly cartoons. Sounds crazy, but it works. Personally, I've always believed that, if you could put all learning in cartoon form (*e.g.,* Theory of Relativity, organic chemistry, Russian, European history, and on and on), it would be much easier to absorb!

The key is to take the original cartoon, look at the key ideas below it, and then at the associated words. If you give this method a chance, I think you will discover that this is an effective way of getting vocabulary to travel into your brain, and that's the goal. No matter how much vocabulary you cover, it's the amount retained by your brain that will help you during the SAT and elsewhere. Of course, repetition is once again highly important, since going over something once does not usually commit the material to long-term memory; most people need to go over the material a bunch of times.

The cartoons are deliberately off-beat, since often memory is enhanced by making associations that are outlandish or weird. Because synonyms or closely associated words are grouped, you are giving yourself another solid aid to vocabulary development. There are also antonyms (opposites), since these help develop your vocabulary too.

Please suspend judgment for a bit, since oftentimes new techniques feel awkward, no matter how effective they will eventually prove to be. Students will tell me occasionally that they feel like they're not getting anywhere in their studying, but then I see the scores and they're *waaay* up. So don't get disheartened (definition below!) and *do* just keep plugging away.

Some students don't like Vocabu-toons™ and others love them and find them the best way to learn vocab they've ever seen. So try to use them, and you may be pleasantly surprised!

Wesley couldn't understand why his mother
(normally the soul of cheerfulness and enthusiasm)
was not pleased with his creative project.

KEY IDEAS: **understand, cheerfulness, enthusiasm, creative,** and **weary,** since that's what Wesley's mom is.

understand: grasp, comprehend, fathom, conceive.

cheerful: sunny, festive, joyful, lighthearted, riant.

enthusiasm: passion, fervor, zealousness, ardor.

creative: innovative, inventive, original, ingenious.

weary: bleary, exhausted, fatigued, drained, sapped, depleted, enervated.

"Oh, drat it all, this is just *not* my day!"
thought Agnes in disgust. "First I drop my new
pocketbook and then I turn into an elm tree!"

KEY IDEAS: Agnes has (quite improbably) changed into a tree, so **change** is a key idea. She's having a bad day and is **discouraged**. And she is **annoyed** or **crabby** about it all. The opposite of **change** is **sameness** or **staying the same**.

> **change**: metamorphosis, transfiguration, transmutation, mutation, modification, transmogrification.
>
> **discouraged**: disheartened, dispirited, dejected, depressed.
>
> **annoyed**: petulant, snappy, irascible, peevish, testy.
>
> **crabby**: cantankerous, carping, surly, cross, fussy.
>
> **sameness**: tedium, monotony, boredom, uniformity.
>
> **staying the same**: constancy, consistency, uniformity, invariability, evenness.

Alien Poker

KEY IDEAS: What we have here is a lively poker game among an a bunch of aliens, a game of **chance** or **risk** or **randomness** combined with **skill**. Being **unskilled** is the opposite of having **skill**.

chance or **risk** or **randomness**: hazard, gamble, fortuity.

skill: proficiency, artfulness, dexterity, expertness, aptitude.

unskilled: incompetent, inexpert, inept, incapable, amateurish, dilettantish.

Angels sneaking off to eat junk food.

KEY IDEAS: The angels are **eat**ing junk **food**, which is presumably **harmful**. Since angels are presumably kind, we'll do the concept of **kind** too. The opposite of kind is **nasty**.

eat: consume, digest, devour, ingest.

food: fare, comestible; also edible, which means *eatable*.

harmful: detrimental, injurious, deleterious, noxious.

kind: benevolent, humane, humanitarian, benign, kindly.

nasty: evil, villainous, malicious, malevolent, spiteful, venomous, poisonous, malignant.

Anthony knew he had to pass the test
to graduate, but how? He though of studying,
but quickly ruled that out.

KEY IDEAS: Anthony is being **lazy**. If he decided to **work** hard and be **diligent** (applying steady effort), he might succeed. He's **think**ing about it, but has decided to avoid studying.

lazy: idle, slothful, indolent, shiftless, otiose.

work: strain, endeavor, exertion, effort.

diligent: industrious, assiduous, studious, painstaking, sedulous.

think: consider, cogitate, deliberate (as a verb), conceive, ideate, ponder, intellectualize.

Billy was cornered. His mother read him his rights, among which was the right to remain silent, which, all things considered, seemed like a pretty good idea.

KEY IDEAS: Billy was cornered, so we have the concept of **trapped**. He's remaining **silent**, and his **idea** is a good one. The opposite of silent can be **talkative**. The opposite of trapped could be **free** (in the sense of having liberty).

trapped: snared, webbed, enmeshed.

silent: reticent, tacit, taciturn, tight-lipped, mum.

idea (in this context): strategy, scheme, design.

talkative: loquacious, garrulous, chatty, conversational, voluble.

free (in the sense of having liberty): emancipated, loose, unconstrained, liberated, manumitted, unconfined, unrestrained, unfettered.

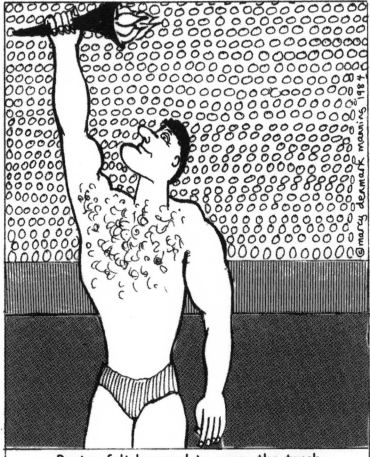

Brutus felt honored to carry the torch
in the opening ceremony but couldn't remember
to hold it upright.

KEY IDEAS: This depicts a person who's rather clueless. Key concepts are **honored**, **ceremony**, **remember** and **upright**.

> **honored**: distinguished, elevated, ennobled, graced.

> **ceremony**: rite, ritual, observance.

> **remember**: recollect, recall.

> **upright** (in physical terms): perpendicular, plumb, vertical; (in moral terms): honest, honorable, true, incorruptible, moral, forthright.

"Keep your lip buttoned, Rodney," they said, but did they realize what a big damper this put on his social life?

KEY IDEAS: Rodney is **quiet** or **using few words** (we've done this concept before, but remember, repetition is good for you!). He's concerned about his **social** life. The opposite of being social is being **unsociable**.

> **quiet** or **using few words**: terse, laconic, tacit, taciturn, uncommunicative, close-mouthed, wordless, mute, speechless, mum.

> **social** (as an adjective modifying a person): convivial, companionable, gregarious, outgoing, extroverted.

> **unsociable**: insular, reticent, reserved, secluded, unaccompanied, aloof, standoffish, remote, isolated.

Charlie was in dire need of a charisma transplant.

KEY IDEAS: Poor Charlie. He has a **dire** need for **charisma**. And behind him is a **building**.

dire: dreadful, terrible, appalling, alarming, grave, awful.

charisma: magnetism, glamour, charm, appeal, attractiveness.

building: edifice, structure.

KEY IDEAS: Sylvester is **dense**, asking **questions** that make no sense to Marjorie. She is therefore **wonder**ing about him. The opposite of wondering about something is being **sure**; if you're sure, you have **certitude**.

dense: doltish, half-witted, dimwitted, obtuse.

question: inquiry, query, interrogation.

wonder and **doubt** (as nouns): skepticism, dubiousness, mistrustfulness, incertitude.

certitude: confidence, sureness, conviction, certainty, assurance.

Lucy appeared at the interview wearing
her "Dress for Failure" clothes.

KEY IDEAS: Lucy's outfit is not the typical "Dress for **Success**" look, but the "Dress for **Failure**" mode. Her outfit is definitely **eclectic**-looking.

success: achievement, triumph, accomplishment, victory, eclat.

failure: fiasco, washout, deficit, insufficiency, disaster, debacle.

eclectic (a Top 100 Word), which means *coming from a variety of sources*: motley, diverse, variegated, multifarious.

Harry was a trifle dismayed that the ship's mice
had decided to bunk with him, but then Harry
thought, "Well, heck, they're so small,
I probably won't even notice them!"

KEY IDEAS: Harry is **dismayed**, but then he **reconsider**s and thinks he won't even be **aware** of the mice. The opposite of aware is **unaware**.

dismayed: horrified, aghast, thunderstruck, shocked, appalled, consternated.

reconsider: reexamine, rethink, reevaluate.

aware: cognizant, sentient, mindful, awake, perceptive.

unaware: oblivious, unwitting, uninformed, innocent, unconscious, unacquainted, unfamiliar, ignorant, unperceptive.

"Yeah! It's really wild! I've got the snowball right in my hand, I'm wearing long johns and boots, and, well, the old joint finally seems to have frozen over!"

KEY IDEAS: Since this is a devil, **evil** is a key idea. Since the netherworld is supposed to be consumed by flames, **hot** is a key idea.

> **evil**: wicked, nasty, malevolent, venomous, loathsome, revolting, immoral, nefarious, iniquitous, diabolical, depraved, pernicious.

> **hot**: fiery, sultry, scalding, scorching, torrid, sweltering, sizzling, broiling.

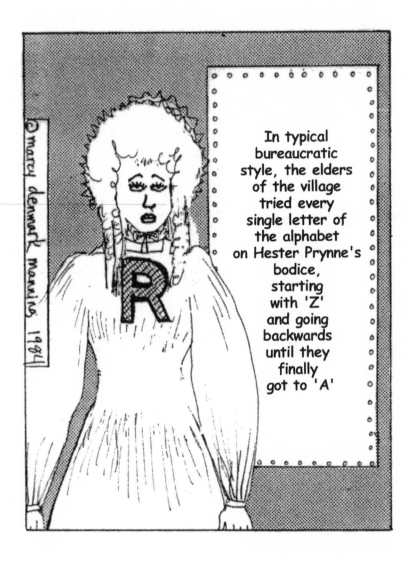

KEY IDEAS: Of course this is a riff on the idea of *The Scarlet Letter*, which was an *A* that Hester Prynne was made to wear. Since bureaucrats sometimes adhere rigidly to rules, **rigid** is a concept. **Backward** is too. The opposite of rigid is **flexible**. The opposite of backward is **forward**.

rigid: adamant, inflexible, unyielding, brassbound, obdurate, inalterable, ironclad.

backward: retrograde, retrogressive, reactionary.

flexible: supple, pliant, plastic, malleable, workable, moldable, ductile, resilient, elastic, pliable.

forward: precocious, progressive, advanced.

Try though she did, Hilda could not shake off
the feeling of impending doom.

KEY IDEAS: Hilda is having **feelings** of **doom impending (about to happen)**. The opposite of doom can be **salvation**.

feeling: emotion, sentiment, intuition, impression, hunch, perception.

doom: fate, destiny, destruction, ruination.

impending or **about to happen**: imminent, looming, proximate, menacing.

salvation: deliverance, rescue, salvage.

Jessica was disturbed by the repeated attempts
of her shadow to bolt in the opposite direction
as she jogged.

KEY IDEAS: Jessica is **disturbed** by the **repeated** or **persistent attempt**s of her shadow to bolt in the **opposite** direction.

disturbed: uneasy, disquieted, troubled, nervous, agitated, unsettled.

repeated or **persistent**: stubborn, unremitting, persevering, protracted, prolonged.

attempt: endeavor, undertaking, trial.

opposite: reverse, polar, diametric, converse, contrary, antithetical, contradictory, opposing.

What owls in their wisdom are really pondering.

KEY IDEAS: We think of owls as proverbially **wise**, but this one is **ponder**ing his own **tired**ness. On top of the insomnia type of tiredness, there's a kind of tiredness meaning *overused or stale*, so let's do that too. Since owls are night animals, let's focus on assorted words having to do with **animal habits**.

wise: scholarly, erudite, shrewd, astute, perspicacious, discerning, sagacious, sapient.

ponder: cogitate, cerebrate (think of *cerebrum*, part of the *brain*), mull, ruminate, contemplate.

tired: somnolent, slumberous, soporific, drowsy. The second kind of *tired* meaning *overused* gives us stale, hackneyed, cliche, platitudinous, trite, musty, banal.

animal habits: *nocturnal* animals stay up at night, *diurnal* animals stay awake during the day, and *circadian* rhythms are the 24-hour cycles on which organisms operate, whether they're nocturnal or diurnal.

Lewis found flight to be oddly exhilarating
but very hard on the eyeglasses.

KEY IDEAS: **exhilarating** and **hard** or **difficult**. The opposite of hard is **easy**.

exhilarating: inspiring, intoxicating, buoying, cheering, elating.

hard or **difficult**: arduous, burdensome, taxing, laborious, demanding, backbreaking, onerous.

easy: gentle, fluid, effortless, cursive, moderate, simple, smooth, facile.

A Monster Family Portrait

KEY IDEAS: Here's an unusual family portrait. Key concepts are **familial** or **related,** and **portrait**.

> **familial** or **related**: domestic, homely, related, akin, kindred, allied, consanguineous, household.

> **portrait**: image, depiction, delineation.

How William Shakespeare's neighbor let out her dog on bad mornings.

KEY IDEAS: Lady Macbeth? No, this is the playwright's next-door neighbor saying the immortal lines from *Macbeth*. She **neighbor**s or **border**s Shakespeare and she's **eject**ing her dog, named **Spot**, which could be a stain as well as a dog's name. And even though she isn't acting like it, she does have a **welcome** mat.

neighbor or **border** (as a verb): abut, juxtapose, verge.

eject: oust, evict, expel, bump, banish, discharge, dislodge.

spot: blemish, stigma, taint, tarnish, stain.

welcome: congenial, pleasant, greeting, embracing.

One of the questions on the philosphy midterm had Margaret completely stumped: "If the eyes are the windows of the soul, what is the nose?"

KEY IDEAS: Margaret is stumped or **baffled** or **confused** by a **question** on a **test**.

baffled or **confused**: addled, befuddled, confounded, fazed, bewildered, perplexed, disconcerted.

question: problem, issue, query.

test: trial, quiz, catechism, examination.

Long ago, if a pizza dropped on the floor, the party was ruined. Now pizza restoration and repair can save the day!

KEY WORDS: Pizza restoration? What will they think of next? Key concepts are **ruin**, **restoration** or **making like new** and **repair**.

ruin: destruction, deterioration, devastation, degeneration, downfall, ruination, demolition, wreckage, havoc.

restoration or **making like new**: renewal, refurbishing, renovation, rejuvenation, reinstatement, revival, reparation, restitution.

repair (as a verb): patch, mend, fix, revamp, overhaul.

Seymour the writer wasn't altogether certain,
but all in all he did seem to be getting
a better class of rejection letters.

KEY IDEAS: This writer is well acquainted with rejection. Key concepts are **certain, class** and **rejection**. The opposite of rejection is **acceptance**.

certain: positive, undoubting, definite.

class: caliber, rank, tier, classification, quality, grade.

rejection: refusal, disallowance, negation, disaffirmation.

acceptance: approval, favor, acquiescence, approbation.

While waiting at the starting line, Sydney suddenly got a bad feeling about the race.

KEY IDEAS: Sydney is dismayed to discover that he is racing against Aesop's tortoise. Key words are **starting** and **sudden**ly. The opposite of start is **stop**. The opposite of sudden is **gradual**.

> **starting**: originating, incipient, undertaking, beginning, commencing, embarking, initiating, triggering.

> **sudden**: precipitate, hasty, abrupt, rash, unexpected.

> **stop** (as a noun): conclusion, completion, termination, closure, cessation, termination, halt, standstill.

> **gradual**: moderate, piecemeal, step-by-step.

It says, "This monolith stands in honor of all those slain on the Dread Day of the Exploding Watermelon."

KEY WORDS: **honor, dread,** and the concept of **disaster,** since that's what the Dread Day of the Exploding Watermelon was. The opposite of honor (as a noun) is **dishonor.**

> **honor**: regard, consideration, esteem, admiration, appreciation, homage, deference, obeisance, kudos, accolade.

> **dread** (as a noun, instead of the adjective in the cartoon): panic, alarm, fearfulness, trepidation.

> **disaster**: tragedy, cataclysm, calamity, catastrophe.

> **dishonor**: shame, ignominy, disgrace, disrepute, disesteem, opprobrium.

Weight loss camp for birds.

KEY IDEAS: Since these birds are **overweight**, let's do that concept, as well as **thin** and **fly** (since most birds can fly).

overweight: fleshy, corpulent, obese, porcine (think of Porky Pig, since *porcine* means *relating to pigs*), stout, portly, chunky.

thin: angular, gaunt, bony, meager, rawboned, scrawny.

fly: flit, flutter, wing, aviate, skim, dart.

"Do you know, Ralph, sometimes I think you're a little flaky."

KEY IDEAS: Snowflakes don't last long, so **temporary** is a key idea. *Flaky* is a pun on *snowflake* but it also means **odd** or **crazy**. Snowflakes occur in winter, so **cold** is a concept. The opposite of crazy is **sane**. The opposite of temporary is **permanent** or **unending**.

temporary: ephemeral, temporal, fleeting, evanescent, transitory.

odd: eccentric, bizarre, idiosyncratic, quirky, outlandish, outre, uncommon.

crazy: insane, lunatic, maniacal, demented, preposterous, nonsensical, harebrained, raving.

cold: gelid, polar, frosty, glacial.

sane: prudent, judicious, level-headed, commonsensical, sagacious, wise, balanced.

permanent or **unending**: eternal, perpetual, immortal, everlasting, ceaseless, interminable, illimitable, uninterrupted, changeless, infinite.

Words You Must Know

Words You Must Know is a must for studying for standardized tests like the SAT. Here you will find words, many of which have found their way onto these tests, and simplified definitions that cut to the chase.

Learning this vocabulary may not be the most exciting thing you do this year (or even today!). But it *will* help you grasp and hold onto a collegiate-level vocabulary, something which not only should help you on entrance exams, but which will be very important for you when you head for college. These words should assist you in reading more difficult texts and treatises, and should help you write better (the goal is not to write ostentatiously, but to express yourself more lucidly).

How to use this list: You should look at the words on this list daily, if possible. Test yourself on whether you've learned the meaning of a word by covering up the definition. If you are typical, it will take you many repetitions over days or weeks before you really have made each definition part of your permanent repertoire.

Most students have vocabulary quizzes in school and study for such quizzes by cramming wildly up until a few seconds before the test. This process puts the definitions into short-term memory (if you're lucky), so that you can get a decent grade on the quiz.

But how many people even look at those words and definitions after the quiz is past? The answer: close to zero. So a week or two after the quiz, almost nobody can define the words correctly.

But the SAT and other standardized tests depend on what you've put into long-term memory. Long-term memory can perhaps best be understood if you consider a friend's phone number. The first few times you dialed the number, before you were good friends, maybe, you needed to look up the number. But after you were friends for a while, you didn't have to look up the number. If, in fact, you were to go away for a few weeks, you'd still remember the number when you returned. (This example doesn't work if the number is stored in speed-dial!)

Long-term memory, then, works by repeating things over a long enough time that they become part of our permanent repertoire, and we know the answer not merely five minutes before the quiz, but two days later and two weeks later and even two or twenty years later.

So, your task with this list is as follows: Go over and over and over and over (repeat as necessary) these words, testing yourself by covering up the definitions, and then looking to see if you got them right. If you did, great. If you didn't, don't despair. After enough repetition, you might be able to learn all these words. But you must keep on coming back to this list day after day, week after week, and be faithful about continuing to do it even after you think you know something. Something that you have barely learned today will be reinforced by coming back tomorrow. If you skip a week after starting to learn something, you'll merely have put the information into short-term memory, and you'll find yourself rusty a week later. But if you do skip a week or more, please don't give up; go back to the lists and keep trying!

And if you learn only a tenth or fifth of these words, you'll still be better off. Start with the Top 100 Words list and get those under your belt. Then, because those are part of the Words You Must Know! list, you'll have 100 fewer words to learn when you come back to the bigger list. But please read the directions below to help you before you head for the Top 100 Words.

How should you study the words? Different students of mine have used different methods, all with great results. Some suggestions:

1. Make flashcards. What else are index cards good for?!

2. With parental permission, tape word lists on walls or mirrors so you pass and look at them many times a day.

3. Put words in audio format if this is your best learning style. One student listened to vocabulary in his car. He insisted he could concentrate on driving, and he made all his friends listen to vocab rather than music (I bet their scores went up too!).

4. One student color-coded the words. This wouldn't work for me at all, but to her, different colors expressed certain emotions, and by grouping the words according to hue she was able to memorize them more easily.

5. Another creative student found cartoons helped her to memorize this material.

6. Use foreign language ability, assuming you have studied a Romance language (French, Latin, Spanish, Italian, Portuguese, Romanian or English). Yes, English is a Romance language, derived from Latin. So if you look at a word like *indefatigable*, associate it with the root *fatig-* and *fatigue*, which you already know. This will make it easier. One time a student was baffled by the word *facile* in English. Asked if it reminded him of any word he knew in Spanish, he said yes and cited the Spanish word for *easy*. I said, "Guess what! The English word means about the same thing!"

7. Use words in sentences, poems, short stories, jokes, etc.

8. Anytime you are able to create a mnemonic (a memory-enhancing trick or technique), you're ahead of the game. If you make up a really silly sentence and memorize it, it sticks in your head, and the sillier the better. One of my students had everyone laughing uproariously with a description of her very effective mnemonics. But the word *effective* is key, since she did know the material. If it can help you learn the material, it's valid.

9. Calling all parents, friends, grandparents, *et al.*! If you practice with someone else and let the other person test you, this is highly effective. Make sure you show your appreciation and best manners, though, since nobody *has* to do this for you!

10. Latch vocabulary onto *anything* you already know. If you know from your Chemistry I class that infrared is *below* the red in the spectrum, then use that information to remember that *infra* means *below*, and to help you define words that have *infra* in them. Whatever the association in your brain, if you hook new info up to info already sitting there, you will learn faster and better and you'll more easily retrieve the information at a later date (perhaps even during the SAT!).

11. But the biggest piece of advice is just to do it *somehow*. If you put in the time and energy, you *will* see results.

Don't get discouraged. Sometimes when people are trying to learn tedious things (you may substitute *vocabulary* for *tedious things*!), they get bored (which is understandable) and crabby (which is also understandable). And they want to quit (yes, yes, we do understand!). But anytime you quit, you're accepting defeat. It's okay to put the words away today and feel discouraged, disgusted, and say, "I'm *never* looking at these darn words again." And then tomorrow, pick them up anyhow and try again. If you stick with it, it *will* pay off.

Don't hesitate to add words of your own as you read and to look up dictionary definitions so that you can expand upon what's here. But you will find that this list is an excellent start.

Some people find it helps to highlight 5-10 words starting with each letter of the alphabet and focus on those, since it can be discouraging to work and work, and still be only up to C or D. After those words are mastered, add some more from each letter. Obviously, some letters have almost no words, so you'll pick more words from the letters that are represented more often.

I realize it may not be possible to study material every day. Do the best you can, and you'll see results if you put in time.

I do not promise you great fun. I do not promise you excitement. But I do promise that, if you put in the time, you will develop a much better vocabulary than you already have. In the unlikely event that you already know all the words herein, you don't need this material. But if you do need it and you do study it, you will improve your vocabulary greatly.

Remember that the trick is just to plug away at material over and over and just put in the time. Don't spend energy worrying about whether you feel like you're making progress. If you keep putting in the time, you *will* make progress as the days go by.

abatement
1. reduction
2. lessening

abbreviate
1. to shorten
2. to reduce

abet
1. to help a criminal
2. toassist in wrongdoing

abhor
1. to loathe or to regard with horror
2. to reject

abolition
1. an act of doing away with something; elimination
2. slavery's end in the U.S.

abstemious
1. moderate
2. tending to abstain from excessiveness in food and drink

abstract
1. theoretical
2. not concrete

acclaim
1. to clap or applaud
2. to praise, recognize

acclimated
1. adapted
2. accustomed to one's surroundings

accolade
1. praise
2. approval

accumulate
1. to pile up
2. to amass

acerbic
1. biting
2. bitter

acoustical
1. pertaining to sound
2. having to do with music

acrid
1. bitter
2. harsh or caustic

adaptable
1. flexible
2. tending to adjust

addendum
1. something added
2. a book supplement

adequate
1. sufficient or satisfactory
2. often having the sense of barely acceptable

adherence
1. devotion
2. faithful following of rules

adherent
1. believer (as a noun)
2. sticking to something, e.g., to an idea or a belief (as an adjective)

adhesion
1. attachment, devotion, loyalty
2. scar tissue adhering to itself or organs

adjunct
1. auxiliary or subordinate
2. attached

admonition
1. warning or caution
2. reproof

adorn
1. to decorate
2. to enhance or to make more beautiful

adversary
1. a foe
2. an enemy

advocate
1. to endorse
2. to recommend

aerial
1. pertaining to flight
2. pertaining to air

aesthetic
1. artistic or pertaining to beauty
2. having a faculty for discerning beauty

affinity
1. attraction
2. inborn similarity between people or things

affirm
1. to declareas true
2. to confirm

aggregate
1. collection
2. total

aggression
1. hostility
2. assault

agile
1. coordinated
2. mentally adept

agrarian
1. agricultural
2. pertaining to farming

alacrity
1. eagerness
2. speed

alienate
1. to dissociate oneself or to estrange
2. to turn away

allay
1. to ease
2. to mitigate

alleged
1. supposed
2. unproved

allegory
1. a symbol-filled literary genre

allot
1. to allocate
2. to apportion or mete out

alloy
1. mixture of metals
2. combination that implies less than total purity

allude
1. to refer
2. to mention obliquely

allusion
1. a reference
2. an indirect mention

ally
1. a friend or supporter (as a noun)
2. to join with (as a verb)

aloof
1. standoffish
2. distant

altruistic
1. thinking of others
2. unselfish

amateurish
1. unprofessional
2. unskilled

ambiguous
1. unclear
2. uncertain

ambivalent
1. feeling at least two different ways about something
2. experiencing contradictory emotions

ambush
1. a surprise attack (as a noun)
2. to make a surprise attack (as a verb)

ameliorate
1. to make better
2. to improve

amenities
1. pleasant behavior
2. courtesies

amorphous
1. shapeless
2. formless

amplification
1. the act of increasing, or the act of making sound louder
2. sometimes, clarification

amulet
1. talisman
2. charm

anachronism
1. something happening out of its proper time frame

anarchy
1. lack of political leadership, political disarray and confusion
2. utter disorganization

anchorage
1. stabilization
2. act of securing

anecdote
1. a short tale, usually amusing

anemia
1. a lack or insufficiency of oxygen in the blood

anguished
1. in torment
2. in agony physically or mentally

angular
1. having sharp edges
2. lean, in referring to a person's body build

animate
1. to enliven or to fill with life
2. to encourage

annex
1. to add (as a verb)
2. something added, e.g., a room to a house (as a noun)

annul
1. to void or cancel as though something never happened
2. to nullify

anomaly
1. abnormality
2. irregularity

antagonism
1. hostility
2. resistance

antagonist
1. foe
2. adversary

anticipate
1. to expect, await or look forward to
2. to foresee

anticipation
1. expectation
2. sense of awaiting

antidote
1. an agent that works against a poison
2. something that combats or remedies a harmful situation

antigen
1. a substance that makes the body produce antibodies
2. irritant to the system

antiquated
1. aged
2. obsolete

antiseptic
1. sterile
2. lacking in germs

antithesis
1. opposite
2. the co-existence of very contrasting words, thoughts, actions, etc.

antithetical
1. opposite
2. contrasting

apathetic
1. emotionless
2. uncaring

appalled
1. dismayed or outraged

apparel
1. clothes or attire
2. adornment

appeal
1. a plea
2. a request

append
1. to add
2. to attach

appraise
1. to rate
2. to evaluate

appreciable
1. large or considerable
2. noticeable

apprehend
1. to catch orarrest
2. to understand

apprehension
1. fear or dread
2. understanding or grasp of a subject

apprehensive
1. uneasy
2. anxious

approbation
1. approval
2. praise

arable
1. farmable, plowable
2. fit for growing things

arbiter
1. judge
2. arbitrator

arbitrary
1. by whim or discretion
2. not dictated by law

arboretum
1. a place where many kinds of trees and bushesare exhibited and studied

archaic
1. ancient or antiquated
2. characteristic of an earlier period

archive
1. an collection of records
2. an amassing of historical material

aristocrat
1. a noble
2. blue blood

arouse
1. to wake up
2. to excite or stimulate

arrogant
1. overly proud or egotistical
2. haughty

articulate
1. to pronounce or to enunciate
2. to say

artisan
1. skilled person
2. craftsman

ascendancy
1. dominating or lording it over someone (note: when oneascends, one rises above other things)

ascertain
1. to prove
2. to discover via experiment

aspire
1. to hope for
2. to aim for

assent
1. agreement or consent (as a noun)
2. to agree to (as a verb)

assertion
1. affirmation, claim
2. positive statement

assess
1. to evaluate or rate
2. to charge a tax

asset
1. a plus; a valuable thing, or a positive trait
2. something owned by a person

assiduous
1. diligent or sedulous
2. persistent

assign
1. to dole out
2. to giveas homework

assimilate
1. to absorb
2. to become like one's surroundings

assuage
1. to ease
2. to calm
3. to satisfy

astrological
1. concerning the zodiacal signs
2. pertaining to the belief that stars ordain our personalities and destinies

asylum
1. safe haven
2. refuge

atrocity
1. something horrible
2. act of evil

atrophy
1. wasting away
2. diminution

attribute
1. toascribe or assign (as a verb)
2. to consider someone theartist or author of a work (as a verb)
3. a characteristic (as a noun)

audacious
1. bold or daring
2. fearless

audacity
1. brashness
2. boldness or daring

augment
1. to increase
2. to add to

austere
1. stern, strict, orascetic
2. bare

authenticate
1. to prove
2. to show something is real

authenticity
1. genuineness
2. the quality of being real

authoritarian
1. expecting absolute obedience
2. minimizing personal freedom

autoimmune
1. pertaining to diseases in which the immune system attacks and often destroys parts of the body.

automation
1. operation by machinery
2. robotics

automaton
1. robot
2. person functioning mechanically

avarice
1. greed
2. cupidity

averse
1. reluctant
2. loath

aversion
1. dislike
2. repugnance

aviary
1. a zoo cage for birds
2. a huge birdhouse

awe
1. respect or reverence
2. sense of wonder

babble
1. chatter or meaningless talk (as a noun)
2. to talk nonsense (as a verb)

balm
1. an ointment
2. something soothing

banter
1. playful talk
2. light conversation

barbarity
1. cruelty
2. coarseness

barren
1. dull or sterile or fruitless
2. incapable of producing children

bastion
1. fort
2. stronghold

becloud
1. to obscure
2. to darken

beguile
1. to amuse or delight
2. to pass time enjoyably

belittle
1. to put down
2. to disparage

belligerent
1. aggressive or warlike
2. hostile or tending to pick fights

beneficial
1. helpful
2. advantageous

benevolent
1. kindly
2. charitable, full of good will

benign
1. kindly or mild
2. non-malignant

bicker
1. to quarrel
2. to have a pettyargument

bizarre
1. odd or outlandish
2. far-fetched or unusual

blasphemous
1. hugely disrespectful
2. often, disrespectful of a religious idea

bleak
1. barren
2. dreary or gloomy

bleat
1. the cry of a sheep (as a noun)
2. to make such a cry (as a verb)

blueprint
1. plan
2. architectural drawing

bluff
1. to deceive
2. to pretend to have a stronger position than one does

blunder
1. to err or bungle
2. to say or do something stupid

blunt
1. insensitive or brusque
2. dull

boggle
1. to be overcome
2. to mess up

bolster
1. to support
2. to prop up

bolt
1. cloth measure in bulk in fabric stores, or metal fastener (as a noun)
2. to flee or abandon, or to lock, or to eat hastily (as a verb)

bombardment
1. a seemingly unending attack of events, questions, orarms
2. a barrage

bombastic
1. pompous, overbearing (usually referring to speaking or writing)

boom
1. a prosperous time economically
2. a deep sound

braggart
1. a boaster
2. a person who is prone to brag or crow

breach
1. break or rift or estrangement
2. breaking of a law

brevity
1. briefness or shortness
2. terseness

bristle
1. to be agitated
2. to react negatively to a threat or a slight

broad-minded
1. tolerant
2. liberal

brutal
1. harsh or cruel
2. disagreeable

bucolic
1. rural
2. pastoral

buffoon
1. jokester or clown
2. unserious person

bulky
1. clumsy or unwieldy
2. large or heavy

buoyant
1. lively
2. capable of floating

bureaucracy
1. red tape
2. layers of organization in business and government

burgeon
1. to thrive or grow
2. to flourish

burnish
1. to polish
2. to rub

bustle
1. activity
2. noise

busybody
1. meddler
2. nosy person

bystander
1. onlooker
2. non-participant

callous
1. unfeeling or hardened emotionally
2. toughened

camaraderie
1. friendship
2. comradeship (*camaraderie* and *comrade* are etymologically related)

camouflaged
1. hidden or concealed
2. having a pattern similar to one's surroundings, so as to disguise oneself

candid
1. open, honest, straightforward
2. unrehearsed
3. unbiased

candor
1. openness or honesty
2. lack of prejudice or bias

cantankerous
1. crabby or quarrelsome
2. disagreeable or unpleasant

capitalism
1. a free-market economic system, encouraging competition, private and corporate ownership and investment

capitulation
1. surrendering
2. giving in

captive
1. held prisoner or restrained (as an adjective)
2. a prisoner (as a noun)

caricature
1. a cartoon or exaggeration
2. a poor imitation

carnal
1. pertaining to the body
2. worldly

carp
1. to complain
2. to find fault

cataclysm
1. a disaster
2. a violent upheaval

catchword
1. a handy phrase

causal
1. pertaining to cause and effect
2. making something happen

cavernous
1. huge or vast
2. deep, like a cave

celerity
1. speed
2. swiftness

censor
1. a person deleting subjectively objectionable material (as a noun)
2. to eliminate material deemed objectionable (as a verb)

censorious
1. criticizing harshly
2. blaming

censure
1. blame
2. rebuke or disapproval

ceremonious
1. formal
2. extremely polite

champion
1. supporter
2. winner

chant
1. a rhythmic monotone
2. a song done mostly in one note

chaos
1. absolute disorganization
2. disarray

charade
1. a mockery
2. exaggerated imitation

charismatic
1. having great magnetism
2. attracting loyalty from huge numbers of people

charlatan
1. a fake or fraud
2. a quack

chary
1. wary, cautious
2. shy

chaste
1. pure or virginal
2. moral

chasten
1. to restrain or punish
2. to purify

check
1. to stop or restrain
2. to control or rein in

cherish
1. to adore
2. to hold dear

chimerical
1. fanciful, fantastic
2. imaginary

chisel
1. to cheat or deceive
2. to carve

choked
1. clogged or slowed down
2. failed to perform under pressure

chronic
1. lingering
2. prolonged or lasting a long time

chronological
1. in order in terms of time
2. in consecutive order, historically

circumspect
1. careful or cautious
2. paying attention to circumstances

circumstance
1. condition
2. environment

civil
1. polite or civilized
2. non-military

civilian
1. a non-military person

clamorous
1. noisy
2. loud

clarity
1. clearness
2. lucidity

classical
1. having stood the test of time; of standard form
2. relating to Greek or Roman literature, architecture, or life

cleave
1. to cling to
2. to be true to

clemency
1. leniency, mercy or merciful act
2. mildness of personality or weather

cliché
1. a stale idea or usage (as a noun)
2. overused (as an adjective). Synonyms (for noun use): banality; triteness; (for adjective use): banal; trite; hackneyed; overused

client
1. a customer
2. a patron

clique
1. exclusive set of friends
2. aloof bunch of people

closefisted
1. miserly
2. stingy, tight with money

cloudburst
1. downpour
2. sudden rainstorm

coarseness
1. rudeness or roughness
2. a lack of manners

cocksure
1. overconfident
2. egotistical

coddle
1. to baby
2. to spoil or indulge

coercion
1. force
2. duress

cohere
1. to stick together
2. logically, to make senseas part of a whole

coiffure
1. hair style
2. arrangement of hair by a beautician

coincide
1. to agree, correspond precisely or be the same
2. to happen at the same time

collaborate
1. to cooperate
2. to work with others

collage
1. anartistic compilation of different pasted pieces

collective
1. actingas a group
2. massed into a whole

combustible
1. easily ignited
2. excitable

commence
1. to start
2. to set out or begin

commentator
1. a newsperson who analyzes what happens
2. one who remarks on or analyzes events

commercialism
1. emphasis on profit
2. focus on business and commerce

commitment
1. pledge
2. deep involvement

compassionate
1. caring deeply
2. sympathetic

compatriot
1. person from the same country
2. colleague

compel
1. to force
2. to pressure

compensate
1. to pay
2. to make up for

compile
1. to put together
2. to compose or combine

complacency
1. smugness
2. satisfaction or self-satisfaction

complement
1. something that completes or makes perfect
2. a component that makes up a whole

compliance
1. acquiescence or a tendency to give in to others
2. flexibility

complimentary
1. favorable
2. free of cost

component
1. a part
2. a section of a system

composure
1. calmness
2. control of oneself; poise

comprehend
1. to understand
2. to make sense of

comprehensible
1. understandable
2. intelligible

comprehensive
1. extensive
2. complete or full

compressed
1. compacted
2. pressed together into a smaller space

comprise
1. to consist of or constitute
2. to contain or to be composed of

compromise
1. the making of concessions or the settlement of differences
2. agreement with all sides giving in on some issues

compulsion
1. irresistible need to behave a certain way

concave
1. curved inward
2. opposite of convex

concede
1. to admit
2. to yield

conceive
1. to develop, form, or make
2. to understand or ideate

concerted
1. involving a combined effort
2. accomplished together

concession
1. point of giving in during negotiations
2. compromise

conciliate
1. to placate
2. to make up after a fight

concise
1. terse
2. succinct or to the point

concomitant
1. concurrently happening (as an adjective)
2. simultaneous event (as a noun)

concur
1. agree or coincide
2. cooperate

condensation
1. compression of a piece of writing or other thing
2. having water molecules form on the surface of an object from the air

condense
1. to abridge
2. to compress

condolence
1. sympathy expressed to a grieving person

condone
1. to ignore, forgive, or overlook an offense

configuration
1. arrangement of parts into a whole

conflagration
1. a huge, destructive fire

conformist
1. someone who goes along with customary behavior
2. one who follows tradition

conformity
1. similarity or agreement
2. adherence to certain forms of behavior

confound
1. to confused or bewilder
2. to mix things up

congeal
1. to clot or coagulate
2. to gel

congruent
1. corresponding

conjecture
1. a guess
2. an inference

conjunction
1. joining
2. agreement or concurrence

connotation
1. implication
2. suggested, secondary meaning

conquest
1. conquering
2. taking over something

consecrate
1. to bless or make sacred
2. to dedicate

conservationist
1. one who believes in preserving natural resources
2. ecologist

conservative
1. traditional
2. cautious or moderate; not showy

consign
1. to entrust
2. to commit or deliver

consistent
1. uniform
2. in agreement, compatible, or fitting together

consolidation
1. coherence
2. combination of elements, or merger

consonance
1. peace or harmony
2. agreement

conspiracy
1. a pact to perform something illegal
2. people banding together to perform such an act

constellation
1. group of stars
2. assemblage

constituent
1. component
2. voter

constrict
1. to narrow, shrink or contract
2. to squeeze

constructive
1. useful
2. purposeful

construe
1. to interpret
2. to translate

consultation
1. exchange of views
2. conference

consumption
1. the act or process of using up
2. a diseased condition of the body in which it wastes away

contamination
1. impurity or taintedness
2. corruption

contemporary
1. modern (as an adjective)
2. a person born about the same timeas another (as a noun)

contemptuous
1. disdainful
2. scornful

contend
1. to compete or fight
2. to claim

contention
1. assertion or claim
2. act ofcompeting

contiguity
1. the state of being next to something else, of touching it

continuity
1. lack of interruption
2. the state of having an unbroken series

contraction
1. shortening of words
2. any process of shortening or abbreviating

contradiction
1. denial
2. discrepancy or inconsistency

contrary
1. opposite, opposed or contrary
2. adverse

controversial
1. subject toargument
2. subject to dispute

convene
1. to meet
2. toassemble formally

conventional
1. ordinary
2. customary, common

convergent
1. coming together
2. intersecting

convey
1. to communicate
2. to transport, carry or deliver

conviction
1. belief
2. process of finding someone guilty

convincing
1. believable

convivial
1. lively
2. sociable, friendly

convoke
1. to meet
2. to call together, to convene

cordial
1. sincere
2. warm, friendly

cordiality
1. friendliness
2. warmth

corporeal
1. pertaining to the body
2. material or real

corroborate
1. to confirm, to supply evidence or proof for
2. to support

corrugated
1. arranged in rows of folds (as in corrugated cardboard, for instance)

corrupt
1. depraved
2. immoral

coterie
1. a small tightly-knit group of people
2. collection of closeassociates

countenance
1. face
2. appearance or bearing

counterbalance
1. counteraction
2. a weight that equals another load opposite it

counterfeiter
1. faker, imitator, maker of false copies
2. producer of phony money

counterpart
1. complement
2. match

courier
1. a messenger

coven
1. anassembly
2. usually, a group of witches

covenant
1. pact

covert
1. secret
2. hidden or covered

cower
1. to cringe
2. to avoid because of fear

crafty
1. sly
2. shrewd

crass
1. coarse
2. lacking in sensibility

credence
1. believability
2. trust
3. credential

credible
1. believable or reliable
2. trustworthy

credulity
1. gullibility
2. the quality of being overly trusting

critique
1. criticism or review
2. comments made about, e.g., a work of art

crucial
1. critically important

culpable
1. guilty
2. deserving of blame
3. responsible

cupidity
1. greed, avarice
2. excessive desire

curmudgeon
1. a grouchy person
2. a crab

curt
1. abrupt
2. terse

curtail
1. to shorten
2. to abbreviate

dainty
1. delicate
2. refined

dampen
1. to deaden a sound
2. to depress or sadden
3. to moisten

damper
1. restraint (as a noun)
2. to restrain or depress (as a verb)

daredevil
1. foolishly bold person
2. risk-taker

daunt
1. discourage

dawdle
1. to move slowly or take too long in accomplishing something
2. to be lackadaisical

deadpan
1. blank face
2. lack of emotion

dearth
1. lack
2. shortage

debase
1. to put down
2. to lower

debatable
1. questionable
2. disputable

debilitate
1. to make feeble
2. to weaken

debit
1. a negative quality
2. something subtracted on a balance sheet

debunk
1. to disprove
2. to exposeas false

decadent
1. decaying
2. morally declining or abased

decant
1. to pour

decapitate
1. to remove the head from

deceit
1. deception
2. trickery

deceive
1. to trick or entrap
2. to mislead

deception
1. deceit or trickery
2. ruse

decipher
1. to decode
2. to make sense of

declivity
1. a decline
2. a slope

decorative
1. ornamental
2. serving no important purpose

decorum
1. polite behavior
2. propriety; good manners

decoy
1. a lure
2. an enticement into danger

deface
1. to disfigure or spoil
2. to mar or damage

defect
1. imperfection
2. flaw

defiant
1. oppositional
2. going against authority

deflect
1. to turnaside

deforestation
1. ridding a location of trees
2. cutting down trees

delectable
1. delicious
2. delightful or pleasing

delegate
1. to use an agent to carry out one's wishes
2. to pass along duties that others will handle for oneself

delete
1. to erase
2. to wipe out or cancel

deleterious
1. harmful
2. injurious

deliberation
1. thought, discussion
2. careful consideration of an idea or option

delineate
1. to depict
2. to draw

delude
1. to deceive
2. to trick

demagogue
1. a false leader
2. a leader who appeals to the emotions of followers

demolition
1. destruction
2. wrecking

denote
1. signify
2. stand for or mean

denounce
1. to put down or condemn
2. to accuse

dense
1. crowded
2. compact
3. thick
4. hard to understand

depiction
1. picture
2. representation

deplete
1. to use up
2. to empty or exhaust

deplore
1. to regret or disapprove
2. to feel sorrow

depopulation
1. sharp drop in residents due to catastrophe

depraved
1. corrupt
2. immoral

depravity
1. wickedness
2. evil, corruption

deranged
1. unbalanced, disturbed
2. insane

derivative
1. originating from something else
2. not original

derogatory
1. negative or pejorative
2. putting someone or something down

desolate
1. dreary or forlorn
2. friendless, lonely

despondent
1. depressed
2. sad or dejected

despot
1. tyrant, czar
2. absolute ruler

desultory
1. random
2. haphazard

detonation
1. explosion
2. blowing something up

detour
1. an indirect route
2. a wayaround a problem

detract
1. to diminish
2. to lessen

detriment
1. harm
2. loss

detritus
1. junk or garbage
2. ruins

devastate
1. to destroy
2. to overwhelm

deviation
1. divergence
2. variation from the norm

devise
1. to form
2. to make

devout
1. very religious
2. pious

dexterous
1. coordinated
2. adroit

dialect
1. a branch of a language
2. a particular or idiomatic way of speaking

dictator
1. absolute ruler
2. czar

didactic
1. meant to instruct
2. having a moral message; being preachy

differentiate
1. to distinguish between things
2. to discriminate

diffuse
1. scattered or spread out (as an adjective)
2. to scatter or spread out (as a verb)

digression
1. steppingaside from the main topic

dilatory
1. late or slow
2. procrastinating (think of *dilating* the time in which one does something, which would make the action slower.)

dilute
1. to thin or weaken
2. to lower the concentration of a solution

diminution
1. the act of making smaller
2. a decrease

diminutive
1. wee
2. tiny

disability
1. handicap

disaffected
1. discontented or resentful
2. disillusioned

disarray
1. mess
2. disorder

disburse
1. to pay out
2. to distribute money from a fund

discerning
1. perceptive
2. having good taste, good judgment

disciple
1. a student
2. a believer in a philosophy or religion

disclaimer
1. denial of responsibility

disclosure
1. revelation

discord
1. disharmony or disagreement
2. confusion

discordant
1. characterized by disharmony
2. tense or full of strife

discourse
1. discussion
2. conversation

discredit
1. to disgrace
2. to damage the reputation of

discrimination
1. discernment; the making of fine distinctions
2. prejudice, bias

disenchanted
1. rid of false belief
2. not fooled by illusions

disillusion
1. disenchantment (as a noun)
2. to disprove or ruin the beliefs of someone (as a verb)

disinclination
1. unwillingness
2. reluctance

disintegration
1. fragmentation or separation
2. falling apart

dismantle
1. to take apart
2. to disassemble

dismemberment
1. complete dissection
2. total destruction by tearing or cutting apart

dismissal
1. discharge
2. firing

disown
1. to repudiate
2. to deny responsibility for

disparage
1. to belittle
2. to put down

disparity
1. inequality
2. difference

dispel
1. to scatter
2. to clear up a doubt

dispense
1. to give or deliver
2. to administer

disperse
1. to dispel
2. to scatter

disposition
1. inclination
2. mood or temperament

disproportionate
1. having the wrong relative size or importance

dispute
1. toargue
2. to question or doubt

dissemble
1. to lie
2. to pretend

disseminate
1. to spread
2. to promulgate

dissent
1. disagreement
2. lack of assent or approval

dissertation
1. formal treatise
2. thesis

dissipate
1. to scatter or dispel
2. to waste

dissociation
1. separation
2. removal

dissolution
1. disintegration
2. too much liberty and not enough restraint
3. death

dissuade
1. to urge a person not to do something
2. to deter

distend
1. to stretch out
2. to dilate

distill
1. to purify
2. to extract unimportant material

distinct
1. clear
2. separate

distinctive
1. characteristic
2. distinguishing

distortion
1. misrepresentation
2. warped image

distraction
1. diversion or amusement
2. obsession

divergence
1. deviation from a norm
2. difference

diverse
1. varied, various
2. unlike

diversification
1.   a branching out into differentareas
2.   in business, the development of different kinds of business focus

divest
1.   to get rid of
2.   to dump

divine
1.   godlike
2.   magnificent

divulge
1.   to reveal or tell
2.   to announce publicly

docile
1.   tame
2.   gentle

doctrine
1.   belief
2.   principle

documentation
1.   provision of records, evidence
2.   the collection and storing of reference material

dogmatic
1.   authoritative
2.   rigid, unyielding

dominance
1.   having a superior position

doodle
1.   to scribble
2.   to write aimlessly

dour
1.   gloomy or glum
2.   ill-humored or forbidding

drab
1. dull
2. dreary

draft
1. mandatory selection into the military or other organization
2. selection process

dreary
1. bleak
2. dull or dismal

dross
1. worthless stuff
2. trivia or garbage

dubious
1. doubtful or questionable
2. skeptical

dupe
1. someone easily deceived, a goat (as a noun)
2. to deceive, fool or mislead (as a verb)

duplicitous
1. two-faced
2. double-dealing or deceptive

durability
1. long-lastingness
2. sturdiness

dynamics
1. the study of motion
2. the forces at play in a situation

earnest
1. sincere
2. serious

eccentric
1. odd

2. erratic or deviant

eclectic
1. from many different sources
2. having diverse parts or styles used together

ecstatic
1. extremely happy
2. blissful

edifice
1. a building
2. often, a huge and impressive building

efface
1. to wipe out
2. to be inconspicuous

effervescent
1. bubbly (pertaining to soft drinks and to personalities)

egalitarian
1. someone who believes in parity for all people
2. human rights champion

elaborate
1. detailed or intricate (as an adjective)
2. to explain or give details (as a verb)

elaboration
1. detail
2. filling a description with details

electorate
1. voters

elegy
1. a lament
2. a melancholy poem or song

elementary
1. basic
2. easy

ellipse
1. an oval

ellipsis
1. omission of a word or phrase

eloquent
1. graceful in conversation
2. expressing things beautifully

elucidate
1. to clarify
2. to make clear

elusive
1. hard to understand
2. difficult to describe or pin down

embed
1. to set firmly

embellishment
1. beautification
2. adornment

embezzler
1. someone who gets another's money through dishonest means

embitter
1. toarouse animosity
2. to make very unhappy

embody
1. to represent
2. to make concrete

embolden
1. to encourage
2. to enhearten

embroider
1. to embellish or adorn
2. to do needlework

embroil
1. to entangle
2. to involve, often in something unpleasant

emigration
1. an exit from a country

eminent
1. outstanding
2. noteworthy or prominent

empathy
1. deep feeling in common with someone else
2. identification with another person's feelings and thoughts

empirical
1. relying on evidence, not relying on theory
2. practical, provable, verifiable

employ
1. to use
2. to hire

enactment
1. the act of making into law

encode
1. to put into a secret language

endorse
1. to sign or approve

enervate
1. to weaken
2. to sap energy from

enhance
1. to improve
2. to augment

enigma
1. a puzzle
2. something confusing

enlightenment
1. being informed
2. being in the know

enmity
1. hatred
2. mutual dislike or animosity

ennoble
1. to lift up
2. to raise

enterprise
1. business
2. undertaking

entice
1. to lure
2. to attract

entity
1. existence
2. being

entrap
1. to snare or catch
2. to tempt or lure into a bad situation

entreat
1. to petition
2. to request

entreaty
1. plea
2. request

envenom
1. to embitter
2. to make toxic

ephemeral
1. short-lived
2. transitory

epic
1. a long narrative poem, like *The Iliad* (as a noun)
2. having the character of such a long poem (as an adjective)

epiphany
1. a key event or watershed
2. eye-opening time that changes one's life

epitome
1. an ideal or example
2. a representative

equanimity
1. calmness
2. poise or composure

equilibrium
1. balance or stability
2. coordination, poise

equivalent
1. alike
2. identical or equal

equivocal
1. doubtful
2. uncertain

eradicate
1. to erase
2. to get rid of entirely

erosion
1. weathering
2. corrosion or wearing away

erratic
1. irregular or eccentric
2. inconsistent or undependable

erroneous
1. wrong
2. mistaken

erudition
1. learnedness
2. high level of education

escalation
1. increase or rise
2. enlargement

escapade
1. adventure
2. lark

escapism
1. a focus on fantasy instead of reality
2. seeking out entertainment to get away from day-to-day concerns

esoteric
1. difficult to understand
2. understood by few people

espouse
1. to support
2. to be a proponent

esteemed
1. regarded with respect
2. prized

estrangement
1. alienation

ethereal
1. light, heavenly
2. unearthly, spiritual

ethical
1. moral
2. professionally, having to do with principles of right and wrong

eulogy
1. a favorable speech or tribute, often given at a funeral
2. large amount of praise

euphemism
1. the substitution of a harmless word for an unpleasant one
2. sugar-coated terminology

evacuate
1. to empty
2. to vacate or withdraw

evoke
1. to call forth or summon
2. to jog the memory or imagination

evolution
1. gradual change, usually toward increasing complexity

exacerbate
1. to worsen
2. to irritate or aggravate a situation

exalted
1. lofty
2. noble or high

exasperation
1. irritation or annoyance
2. anger; being fed up

excess
1. too much of something or overindulgence
2. remainder or residue

excise
1. removal by cutting out
2. type of tax

exclusion
1. rejection
2. keeping someone or something out

exclusive
1. keeping others out
2. not sharing

excommunication
1. censure
2. formal ousting from a church

excretion
1. elimination of waste
2. the waste matter itself

exemplary
1. servingas a good example
2. excellent, worthy of emulating

exemplify
1. to actas an example
2. to set an example

exhaustive
1. comprehensive
2. covering everything

exhilarating
1. stimulating
2. exciting

exhortation
1. incitement
2. urging

exonerate
1. to absolve or pardon
2. to relieve of a responsibility

exorbitant
1. expensive or extravagant
2. improper or immoderate

exotic
1. not locally bred
2. unusual, alien or foreign

expansive
1. outgoing or extroverted
2. broad

expatriate
1. someone living in exile (as a noun)
2. to leave one's native country (as a verb)

expedient
1. appropriate
2. promoting one's interest.
3. having a concern for policy instead of principle

expedite
1. to handle efficiently or speed up a process

explication
1. explanation
2. clearing up

explicit
1. clear
2. defined, definite

exploit
1. to use to greatest advantage
2. to take advantage of someone unfairly

expulsion
1. the state of being thrown or driven out

expunge
1. to erase
2. to wipe out or obliterate

expurgate
1. to censor
2. to take out subjectively offensive parts of a piece of work

extant
1. not extinct
2. still in existence

extemporaneous
1. impromptu
2. unpracticed

extensive
1. wide
2. broad

extinction
1. the process of becoming non-existent
2. non-existence

extol
1. to praise

extortion
1. the illegal use of power to obtain money
2. coercion

extraction
1. taking something out
2. pulling something out with force

extradite
1. to surrender to another country

extraneous
1. not essential
2. irrelevant or not pertinent

extrapolate
1. to project from known information
2. to extend orexpand from a position

extravagant
1. unrestrained
2. imprudent or spending too much money

extricate
1. to get out of
2. to disentangle or disengage

exuberance
1. joy
2. enthusiasm

fable
1. legend
2. story

fabricate
1. to make up
2. to make or create

facilitate
1. to ease
2. to help

faction
1. a collection of people with particular beliefs
2. a section of minority views within an organization or nation

fallacious
1. false
2. deceptive or misleading

fallow
1. inactive, idle
2. uncultivated (referring to land left idle for a growing season)

fanaticism
1. irrational zeal
2. excessiveness

fatalism
1. the belief that eventsare predetermined
2. passivity

fathom
1. to understand
2. to grasp

fecund
1. fertile
2. productive

federalist
1. believer in the system of national government (as a noun)
2. pertaining to belief in the national government (as an adjective)

feisty
1. spirited
2. somewhat nervy and brazen

felicitous
1. delightful or happy
2. apt, appropriate

fellowship
1. friendship or companionship
2. union

fertile
1. rich for growing things
2. productive or prolific

fervid
1. impassioned, full of zeal
2. burning

fervor
1. intense feelings
2. passion or heat

fiasco
1. disaster
2. failure

figurehead
1. person with no real power, only a title
2. authority in name only

finesse
1. tact
2. refinement

fiscal
1. financial
2. pertaining to government finances or the treasury

flaccid
1. not firm, loose
2. unenergetic

flaunt
1. to show off

flawless
1. perfect
2. having no faults

fleet
1. rapid (as an adjective)
2. anassemblage of ships or other vehicles (as a noun)

fleeting
1. transitory, passing quickly
2. evanescent

flourish
1. prosper
2. thrive

fluctuate
1. to waver
2. to vary or to go back and forth

fluid
1. smooth, flowing, pliable
2. uninterrupted

flushed
1. reddened
2. blushing

focused
1. concentrated
2. centered

foil
1. to thwart or frustrate
2. to confuse

foliated
1. leafy
2. covered with foil

foolhardy
1. rash
2. foolish or unwise

foolproof
1. infallible
2. error-proof

foreboding
1. a premonition
2. an omen or portent

forestall
1. to prevent
2. to delay

forethought
1. the act of planning ahead
2. the act of thinking of the future

forgery
1. fake copy
2. counterfeit

forlorn
1. sad
2. pitiful, hopeless or wretched

formulaic
1. following ordinary or mundane ideas
2. characterized by a set, expected pattern

forswear
1. to disavow
2. to renounce

founder
1. to sink (as a verb)

fracture
1. breakage
2. rupture

fragmented
1. in pieces
2. incomplete

framework
1. structure
2. support

frankness
1. openness
2. candor, directness or honesty

fraudulent
1. deceitful
2. phony, engaging in misleading or illegal activities

frivolity
1. fun
2. lightness or triviality

frugal
1. thrifty
2. inexpensive

full-fledged
1. mature
2. having complete status

fundamental
1. basic
2. central

furrow
1. trench
2. rut

furtive
1. stealthy
2. surreptitious or sneaky

fuse
1. to blend or mix
2. to weld

futility
1. uselessness or pointlessness
2. desperation

gag
1. to restrict speech
2. to censor

gallant
1. courageous
2. polite

garble
1. to render unintelligible
2. to deliver a confused message

garish
1. loud and flashy
2. gaudy
3. dazzling

garrulous
1. talkative

generalize
1. to draw inferences
2. to universalize

generate
1. to beget
2. to produce, create or make

genre
1. category or class
2. literary form

gesture
1. expression or motion
2. sign

ghastly
1. unpleasant
2. frightening or repellent

giddy
1. light-headed or dizzy
2. frivolous

gimmick
1. scheme
2. ruse

girth
1. circumference
2. waistline

glum
1. gloomy
2. sad

gluttony
1. excessive food consumption
2. being piggy in thearea of eating

gnarl
1. to knot
2. to tangle

gourmet
1. someone who loves fine food

grandiloquence
1. pompous speech

grandiose
1. grand
2. pompous and affected

gratification
1. pleasure
2. feeling of satisfaction

gratuitous
1. unnecessary
2. extra or free

gravitation
1. attraction
2. magnetic movement toward a source of attraction

graze
1. to brush lightly against something
2. to abrade

gregarious
1. friendly
2. sociable

grievance
1. complaint
2. protest

grotesque
1. bizarre
2. odd
3. ludicrous and unseemly

groundless
1. unfounded
2. unsubstantiated

gullible
1. easily fooled
2. readily duped

gust
1. a sudden wind
2. an outburst

hamper
1. to get in the way of
2. to restrict progress

haphazard
1. by chance
2. not organized

hardiness
1. sturdiness or ruggedness
2. courage

hardship
1. suffering
2. great difficulty

harmonic
1. pleasant to the ear
2. concordant

haste
1. rashness or overeagerness
2. speed

haughty
1. overly proud and egotistical
2. arrogant

hazy
1. unclear
2. foggy

headlong
1. rash
2. impetuous

hearten
1. encourage

heckle
1. to badger or annoy
2. to boo

hedonistic
1. pleasure-seeking
2. concerned with physical gratification

hefty
1. heavy or weighty
2. rugged

hence
1. therefore
2. from this time forward

heresy
1. unorthodox event or behavior
2. controversial opinion or theory

hereupon
1. immediately
2. now

heritage
1. tradition
2. inheritance

hiatus
1. a gap
2. a pause, break or space

hideous
1. horrible or ugly
2. disgusting or despicable in a moral sense

high-handed
1. snooty, overbearing orarrogant
2. egotistical in manner

histrionic
1. overly dramatic
2. theatrical, like a ham

hoard
1. a hidden supply (as a noun)
2. to save, often with a compulsive sense to it (as a verb)

hoax
1. deception or trickery
2. fraudulent behavior

homage
1. honor or respect displayed in public

homely
1. plain, simple, unrefined, unsophisticated
2. not attractive

hotheaded
1. excitable
2. easily angered

humane
1. merciful
2. compassionate

humdrum
1. boring
2. monotonous

humility
1. lack of pride, having a small level of ego
2. simplicity

hunch
1. an intuition
2. a guess

hyperbole
1. exaggeration
2. extravagant statement, suchas "I could eat a horse."

hypnosis
1. sleep-like state
2. suggestible condition during a trance

hypocritical
1. insincere
2. pretending to be someone other than who one is

hypothesis
1. assumption
2. theory or unproven concept

idealist
1. not a realist or a pragmatist
2. one who operates on ideas of how things should be

identity
1. personality
2. individuality

idiom
1. a particularized or peculiar form of speech
2. expressions and characteristics of a particular language

idiosyncrasy
1. particularized behavior
2. peculiar habit

idolatry
1. blind worship
2. excessive adoration

illumination
1. lighting
2. spiritual knowledge

illusion
1. wrong belief
2. wrong concept of reality

illusory
1. unreal
2. deceptive

illustrious
1. famous
2. noted

immaculate
1. pure or clean
2. spotless or perfect

imminent
1. impending
2. ready to happen

immunity
1. the state of being unaffected by something
2. resistance to illness

immutable
1. unchanging
2. not alterable

impartial
1. fair
2. unbiased

impassable
1. impossible to get through or past

impasse
1. deadlock or stalemate
2. roadblock

impeccable
1. perfect
2. flawless

impediment
1. something that gets in the way
2. hindrance or obstruction

imperative
1. mandatory
2. obligatory

imperceptible
1. not visible
2. too subtle or small to be seen

imperious
1. haughty
2. overbearing

impermeable
1. impassable

impertinence
1. sassiness
2. lack of respectfulness

impervious
1. impenetrable
2. unable to be affected by an external source

impetuous
1. rash
2. impulsive

implant
1. to set firmly or embed
2. to instill

implausible
1. unbelievable
2. impossible

implicate
1. to incriminate
2. to imply

implicit
1. understood or implied
2. unquestioning

impoverished
1. needy
2. poor

impregnation
1. fertilization
2. act of filling or permeating

impromptu
1. unrehearsed
2. spontaneous

impropriety
1. poor manners
2. improper behavior

improvidence
1. lack of caution
2. not planning for the future

improvisation
1. invention
2. creating something on the spot, without a rehearsal

imprudence
1. lack of wisdom
2. rashness

impudence
1. impertinence
2. disrespect

impugn
1. to attackas false
2. to disprove byarguing

impulsive
1. without thinking
2. sudden

inane
1. empty, stupid, pointless
2. nonsensical

inarticulate
1. speechless
2. not eloquent; clumsy with words

incentive
1. reward
2. a spur to accomplish something

inception
1. beginning
2. start or commencement

incessant
1. constant
2. unending, uninterrupted

incidental
1. by chance
2. unpredictable

incisive
1. sharp or perceptive
2. direct

incite
1. to urge on
2. to instigate

inclement
1. stormy
2. not calm

inclusive
1. comprehensive
2. containing everything

incoherent
1. inexpressive
2. unclear or lacking organization

incongruous
1. discordant
2. inconsistent

inconsequential
1. unimportant
2. petty

incontrovertible
1. indisputable
2. impossible to question

incorporate
1. to merge with something already in existence
2. to combine with something else into a whole

incorrigible
1. not controllable
2. not correctable

increment
1. gain
2. increase

incur
1. to bring upon oneself

indecipherable
1. unreadable
2. impossible to decode

indefatigable
1. unable to be tired
2. full of endless energy

indictment
1. accusation
2. formal charge against a person for a crime

indigenous
1. native
2. innate or intrinsic

indignation
1. anger spurred by injustice or other negative condition

indignity
1. affront to one's pride
2. abusive treatment

indiscernible
1. not able to be perceived
2. unseeable

indispensable
1. necessary
2. essential

indistinguishable
1. imperceptible
2. bland or having no detectable difference between things

induce
1. influence
2. lead or cause

indulgence
1. privilege
2. lenient treatment or the allowance of liberal behavior

industrialism
1. a system in which business and factoriesare prominent

inebriated
1. drunk
2. intoxicated

ineffectual
1. ineffective
2. vain, not producing a result

inept
1. incompetent or clumsy
2. unsuitable

ineradicable
1. impossible to get rid of
2. not erasable

inertia
1. resistance to motion or tendency not to move
2. inaction, unchangingness

inexorable
1. unyielding
2. not able to be persuaded

infallible
1. perfect
2. unable to fail

infer
1. to deduce logically
2. to conclude based on evidence

infraction
1. violation
2. law-breaking episode

ingenious
1. brilliant or original
2. magnificent

ingrate
1. an ungrateful person

inherent
1. essential
2. inborn

inhibit
1. to hold back
2. to restrain

initiative
1. opening move
2. enterprisingness

innate
1. inherent
2. inborn

innovation
1. something new, an invention
2. the act of introducing something new

innovative
1. creative
2. new

inopportune
1. inconvenient
2. poorly timed

inordinate
1. immoderate
2. excessive

inquisitive
1. curious or nosy
2. wanting to learn or know things

insensitivity
1. unfeelingness towards others
2. inability to react caringly toward suffering

insidious
1. treacherous
2. sneakily spreading harm; harmful

insightful
1. perceptive

insinuation
1. hint
2. subtlety

insipid
1. dull
2. flavorless

insolent
1. impudent, sassy
2. impertinent

insolvent
1. having no funds
2. bankrupt

instantaneous
1. immediate
2. happening with no delay

instigate
1. to stir up or to start
2. to urge on

instinctive
1. impulsive
2. spontaneous, done without thinking about it

insular
1. isolated
2. like an island (*insula* means *island*)

insurgent
1. rebel
2. revolter (usually politically speaking)

intact
1. whole
2. undamaged

integration
1. the act of making whole
2. organization of disparate parts into one thing

intemperate
1. immoderate
2. excessive

interconnect
1. to relate to other things
2. to interact

interminable
1. endless
2. drawn out to the point of boredom

intervene
1. to come between or interfere
2. to enter a situation and try to modify it

intimate
1. close acquaintance, trusted friend (as a noun)
2. innermost, private (as an adjective)

intractable
1. stubborn
2. hard to control

intransigent
1. uncompromising
2. unyielding, unbending

intricacy
1. detailedness
2. elaborate organization

intrigue
1. a secret plot or scheme (as a noun)
2. to stimulate curiosity or spark interest (as a verb)

intrinsic
1. inherent
2. inborn

invalidate
1. to make void
2. to nullify

inventiveness
1. creativity
2. resourcefulness or skill in making things

inverted
1. having a reversed order
2. upside down or inside out

inveterate
1. ingrained
2. persistent

invidious
1. offensive

invigorate
1. to give energy to
2. to animate

iridescent
1. brilliant
2. shining

irk
1. to annoy
2. to irritate

ironbound
1. rigid
2. unbending

ironhanded
1. strict
2. firm

ironic
1. containing a deliberate gap between real and apparent meanings

irrelevant
1. not pertinent
2. having no relationship to a subject at hand

irrepressible
1. uncontrollable
2. unrestrained

irresolute
1. indecisive
2. unresolved

irrevocable
1. irreversible
2. not retractable

isolationism
1. a national policy of avoiding involvements in other countries' affairs

jaunty
1. perky
2. buoyant

jester
1. fool
2. joker

jettison
1. to throw overboard
2. to get rid of

jubilee
1. big celebration or a special anniversary
2. a state of rejoicing

junta
1. military leaders after a coup or takeover

jurisprudence
1. the study of law

juvenile
1. childish
2. immature

juxtaposition
1. the act of placing things next to each other
2. side-by-side relationship or comparison

kaleidoscope
1. a toy with continually changing shapes and colors
2. a set of endlessly changing events

kindhearted
1. gentle
2. generous

kinsfolk
1. relatives
2. family

kudos
1. praise, acclaim
2. honor or prestige

laborious
1. difficult
2. hard-working

laceration
1. a tear
2. a jagged or rough wound

lackadaisical
1. lacking energy
2. spiritless

laconic
1. using few words
2. terse or to the point, concise

lament
1. to bemoan
2. to regret or to deplore

lavish
1. extravagant
2. spending wildly

lax
1. loose, lenient, slack
2. not strict

legible
1. readable
2. capable of being understood or interpreted

lenience
1. mercy, lightening of a penalty
2. generosity, tolerance

lethargic
1. sluggish or lazy
2. indifferent

levity
1. lightness
2. frivolity or humor

liability
1. debt
2. responsibility

liberal
1. free, tolerant or broad-minded
2. believing government can change people's lives for the better

linguistic
1. pertaining to language

lionize
1. to treatas a celebrity
2. to praise

lipid
1. fat
2. fatty cell

listless
1. lacking energy
2. lethargic

litany
1. a responsive prayer
2. an endless list

literate
1. educated or knowledgeable
2. able to read and write

loath
1. reluctant
2. disinclined or unwilling

locomotion
1. movement
2. travel or motion

loquacious
1. talkative, chatty
2. garrulous

lull
1. to soothe or relax
2. to calm down with intent to deceive

lurid
1. shocking or gruesome
2. sensationalized

lustrous
1. shiny
2. radiant

luxuriant
1. rich or abundant
2. elaborate

lyrical
1. expressing deep emotion (often in music, poetry, dance)

lyricism
1. intense emotion, usually expressed in thearts

magnanimous
1. literally, large-spirited
2. generous

magnate
1. a powerful person
2. an important person in business

magnetism
1. attraction or power
2. allure

maladjustment
1. inability to adapt or imbalance
2. poor adaption to one's environment

malapropism
1. funny misuse of a term or word
2. wrong word

malcontent
1. a rebel (as a noun)
2. dissatisfied with the status quo (as an adjective)

malevolence
1. spite
2. ill will

malignant
1. evil
2. deadly, very harmful

mandate
1. a clear message from the electorate about what it wants

mandatory
1. required
2. obligatory

manifestation
1. reality or evidence of existence
2. embodiment

manipulation
1. shrewd management
2. devious control of a situation for one's own purposes

mar
1. to spoil
2. to damage

marvel
1. astonishment or wonder
2. amazing person

masonry
1. stonework
2. brickwork

masquerade
1. disguise (as a noun)
2. to put on a disguise or mask (as a verb)

mass
1. a large amount or an aggregation
2. majority (of something)

matchless
1. having no equal
2. peerless, unmatched, without a rival

materialism
1. a focus on acquisition of things
2. worldly concerns

maxim
1. a pithy saying
2. a short statement of a rule or idea

meager
1. lean
2. scanty or deficient

meddlesome
1. interfering
2. nosy

mediator
1. an intermediary
2. someone who seeks to reconcile opposing parties

medieval
1. concerning the Middle Ages

medley
1. mixture or hodgepodge
2. musical piece patched together from many sources

melancholy
1. depressed or gloomy
2. deep in thought

mellow
1. gentle
2. relaxed

melodramatic
1. histrionic or overly emotional
2. showing fake emotion

menacing
1. threatening or causing trouble
2. annoying

mercenary
1. a person who works only for monetary reasons (as noun)
2. money-hungry (as adjective)

meritorious
1. praiseworthy
2. excellent

metamorphosis
1. marked change
2. dramatic transformation

metaphor
1. a figure of speech where one thing is said to be equivalent to something one normally wouldn't associate with it: *e.g.,* saying someone is a monolith

methodical
1. organized
2. systematic

meticulous
1. careful or precise
2. overscrupulous

migratory
1. nomadic or wandering
2. seasonally moving

milestone
1. turning point
2. important or crucial event

minimal
1. least
2. smallest

minuscule
1. very small
2. tiny

mirth
1. glee
2. gaiety, joy

misanthrope
1. someone who hates mankind

miscalculation
1. a wrong move
2. error

miscarry
1. to go wrong
2. to abort

misconceive
1. to understand incorrectly

misconstrue
1. to misinterpret
2. to misunderstand

miscreant
1. wrongdoer
2. scoundrel

misdemeanor
1. a wrong deed
2. a petty crime (less serious than a felony)

miser
1. a stingy or greedy person

misfire
1. to err
2. to commit a mistake

misnomer
1. wrong name

mitigate
1. to lessen or ease
2. to moderate

mnemonic
1. an aid to memory (as a noun)
2. pertaining to memory (as an adjective)

mobile
1. movable
2. not fixed in one place

mobilize
1. to organize and put into operation
2. to start a motion

modest
1. moderate or reserved
2. humble

modification
1. change
2. adjustment

molt
1. to shed feathers
2. to shed skin

monarch
1. sovereign or king
2. absolute ruler

monotony
1. sameness
2. boringness

monumental
1. huge
2. outstanding and enduring

moralize
1. to sermonize or to preach
2. to reform

morbid
1. unhealthy, diseased or gruesome
2. unhealthy, psychologically speaking

mosaic
1. a design patched together from small pieces (often of tile)

muffle
1. to deaden a noise
2. to make unclear or vague

mundane
1. ordinary
2. everyday

munificent
1. generous
2. having a giving nature

munitions
1. weapons
2. ammunition

musty
1. moldy
2. trite, hackneyed

mutability
1. changeability
2. inconsistency or inconstancy

mystical
1. spiritual in a manner not apparent to the mind or senses
2. having communion with a reality beyond the senses

naive
1. innocent
2. lacking worldliness

narrative
1. story (as a noun)
2. descriptive (as an adjective)

nebulous
1. cloudy, unclear
2. vague (a *nebula* is a cloud)

necromancy
1. black magic
2. sorcery

negation
1. invalidation
2. denial or erasure

negotiate
1. to settle something by discussing and working out terms

neophyte
1. a newcomer
2. a beginner [synonyms: tyro, novice, greenhorn]

nobility
1. aristocracy
2. blue bloods

nocturnal
1. pertaining to night
2. active at night

noisome
1. foul, disgusting
2. harmful

nomadic
1. roving
2. wandering

nonchalance
1. carefreeness
2. coolness

noncombatant
1. non-fighter
2. civilian

nondescript
1. bland or blah
2. not distinctive

nontraditional
1. unusual
2. not relying on what's been done in the past

nostalgic
1. homesickness
2. longing for the past in a bittersweet way

novel
1. new
2. original

novice
1. newcomer or beginner
2. tyro or neophyte

nuance
1. subtlety
2. slight difference

nullify
1. to make void
2. to render ineffective

numb
1. unfeeling
2. paralyzed

nurtured
1. fed or nourished
2. helped to develop

oath
1. promise
2. pledge

obdurate
1. hard-hearted
2. intractable, stubborn

objective
1. verifiable or real, as distinguished from *subjective*, which relates to how one feels about something (used as an adjective)
2. an aim or goal (used as a noun)

obliterate
1. to erase
2. to wipe out

oblivion
1. forgetfulness
2. obscurity

oblivious
1. unaware
2. forgetful

obscure
1. dark or inconspicuous
2. far away, hard to find

obsequious
1. fawning
2. servile

obsolescence
1. outdatedness
2. the state of fading from active use

obsolete
1. no longer used
2. outmoded or outdated

obstinate
1. stubborn or hard to control
2. persistent

obtrusive
1. pushy
2. protruding or noticeable

odious
1. hateful
2. causing repugnance or disgust

offspring
1. child or children
2. product

ominous
1. menacing or threatening
2. pertaining to an omen

onus
1. burden
2. blame or responsibility

opalescent
1. iridescent
2. resembling an opal

opaque
1. not letting light through

opportune
1. advantageous
2. convenient, suited

opportunist
1. someone who takes advantage of circumstances
2. often, someone with no principles

oppress
1. to persecute
2. to subjugate or to press down on or depress

opulence
1. affluence
2. richness or state of plenty

orientation
1. inclination
2. adaptation to environment

ornamentation
1. embellishment
2. making something fancier

ornate
1. fancy
2. showy or highly decorated

ostentatious
1. showy
2. pretentious

ostracize
1. to shun
2. to avoid or to exclude

otherworldly
1. eerie
2. transcendent

outdated
1. obsolete or passé
2. old-fashioned

outlandish
1. bizarre
2. alien
3. weird

outwit
1. to be cleverer
2. to outsmart

ovation
1. applause
2. public appreciation

overindulgence
1. doting treatment of another
2. excessive consumption (usually of food or drink)

overt
1. open or unconcealed
2. direct, unhidden

overwhelming
1. overpowering
2. awesome

oxidation
1. the process of rusting
2. rust

pacifism
1. belief in peace
2. opposition to war

paltry
1. scant; insignificant
2. worthless; poor

panorama
1. wide view
2. vista

paradigm
1. a model
2. an example

paradox
1. something that is self-contradictory

paragon
1. a model or an ideal
2. something perfect or excellent

parallelism
1. correspondence or similarity
2. analogy

paramount
1. supreme
2. of highest importance

paraphrase
1. to restate or clarify (as a verb)
2. a restatement or clarification (as a noun)

parch
1. to make thirsty
2. to dry

parity
1. equality (*par* is the same root found in *peer,* meaning *an equal*)
2. fairness

parochial
1. provincial
2. narrow

parody
1. a comic work ofart that imitates an author's style
2. an awful performance

parry
1. to ward off or to block
2. to evade

partisan
1. devoted to a cause(as an adjective)
2. one who is dedicated to a particular ideology (as a noun)

passionate
1. intensely emotional
2. having strong feelings of love

pastoral
1. bucolic or rural
2. countrified

patronage
1. support
2. a business's client base

patronize
1. to support or to be a customer
2. to condescend or talk down to

paucity
1. scarcity
2. dearth, lack

pedantic
1. narrow
2. formalistic or intellectually ostentatious

pedestrian
1. ordinary, common or everyday (as an adjective)
2. walker (as a noun)

peer
1. an equal
2. a compatriot

pejorative
1. negative (the Latin word *peior* means *worse*)
2. derogatory

penchant
1. liking
2. inclination

penury
1. neediness
2. poverty or lack

perfunctory
1. routine
2. just going through the motions, without caring

periphery
1. edges
2. outside boundaries

pernicious
1. very harmful
2. evil

perpetuate
1. to lengthen the existence of
2. to cause to be remembered

persevering
1. persisting
2. keeping going

persistence
1. perseverance or tenacity
2. sticking with something

perspective
1. point of view
2. realistic appraisal of a situation

perturbation
1. agitation
2. disturbance

pervasive
1. widespread
2. present throughout or permeating

perverse
1. stubborn
2. oppositional

petty
1. small-minded
2. narrow in views

phalanx
1. a compact line of people
2. in ancient Rome, an organization of soldiers

phenomenon
1. a marvel or unusual event
2. an outstanding person

philistine
1. ignorant person
2. uncivilized person

philosophy
1. belief system

physiology
1. study of life functions
2. a physical being's vital functions

pithy
1. short and to the point
2. compelling and terse

pivotal
1. essential in determining direction or outcome
2. of critical importance

placate
1. to appease
2. to allay the anger of someone

placid
1. peaceful, calm
2. composed or unruffled

pneumatic
1. pertaining to air

podium
1. platform
2. dais

poignant
1. intense or painful
2. incisive or piercing
3. stimulating

poise
1. composure or social grace
2. coordination, balance

polarized
1. characterized by two opposite positions (e.g., like north and south poles being on opposite ends)

policymaking
1. high-level governmental planning

pompous
1. self-important
2. bombastic

ponderous
1. massive or heavy
2. unwieldy or not graceful

pore
1. to ponder
2. to study

porous
1. having holes

portly
1. hefty
2. stout, obese

positivism
1. a belief that sense perception is the sole basis of knowledge
2. the quality of being sure of something

pout
1. to sulk
2. to push the lips out and make a sad, moping face

prattle
1. to babble
2. to speak meaninglessly

precarious
1. unstable
2. dangerous or uncertain

precede
1. to be in front of
2. to come before

precedent
1. example
2. template

precept
1. a rule concerning a standard of behavior
2. a writ

precipitate
1. to throw down, to cause to occur unexpectedly or to rain (as a verb)
2. rash or overly hasty (as an adjective)

precise
1. exact, correct or definite
2. detailed

precocious
1. showing early development

precocity
1. early development

preconceived
1. formed ahead of time
2. having notions shaped prior to seeing something

precondition
1. prerequisite

precursor
1. predecessor
2. forerunner

predator
1. one that feeds off others
2. looter

predecessor
1. forerunner
2. ancestor

prejudice
1. bias
2. preconception

preliminary
1. in rudimentary form
2. preparatory or first

premature
1. early
2. existing prior to the expected time frame

preposterous
1. ridiculous
2. absurd

prescient
1. knowing something ahead of time
2. capable of foresight

prescription
1. a formulaic method
2. medicine dosages dispensed by a doctor

preside
1. to actas chairperson
2. to be in control or charge

presume
1. to take for granted
2. to behave in a brazen manner

presumptuous
1. overly bold
2. arrogant

prevalent
1. common
2. widely practiced and accepted

primeval
1. ancient
2. original

primitive
1. simple, crude or unsophisticated
2. representative of ancient societies

pristine
1. pure
2. uncorrupted

proclaim
1. to declare
2. to make clear

procrastination
1. the act of putting off until later
2. the act of delaying the completion of a task

prodigal
1. wasteful
2. lavish, extravagant

profane
1. blasphemous
2. vulgar or unholy

professionalism
1. having standards befitting one's career choice

proficiency
1. ability
2. competence

profound
1. deep
2. far-reaching
3. wise

profuse
1. abundant or plentiful
2. extravagant

progenitor
1. the ancestor at the start of a lineage
2. the first person in a family tree (the one at the top)

progressive
1. proceeding or moving forward
2. liberal

prohibition
1. banning something
2. forbidding something

proliferate
1. to spread rapidly
2. to grow

prolonged
1. lasting a long time (as an adjective)
2. lengthened (as a verb or adjective)

prominence
1. conspicuousness
2. fame

prone
1. lying face down
2. tending in a certain direction

propel
1. to move forward
2. to push

propensity
1. tendency or inclination

prophetic
1. telling the future

proposition
1. a plan or idea offered for acceptance, or subject needing analysis
2. an immoral offer

propound
1. to put forth for consideration

prosaic
1. ordinary, everyday or straightforward
2. unimaginative

proscribe
1. to forbid or to prohibit
2. to outlaw

prospect
1. possibility, expectation or chance of success
2. potential client

prospective
1. expected
2. likely to happen

protagonist
1. lead character or hero
2. performer of the action in a play

prototype
1. a model for later inventive developments

protract
1. to lengthen
2. to stretch out

provincial
1. unsophisticated or unfashionable
2. narrow or limited in views; self-centered

prowess
1. strength
2. superior skill

prudent
1. wise
2. careful, circumspect

prudish
1. priggish
2. morally judgmental in a very picky way

puerile
1. childish
2. immature

pugnacious
1. tending to pick fights
2. quarrelsome

pungent
1. acrid or biting
2. sharp

purport
1. to profess
2. to intend

quack
1. a fake
2. a charlatan

quagmire
1. marsh, bog
2. predicament or difficulty

quaint
1. old-fashioned
2. charming, sometimes in an odd way

qualify
1. to give an exception to a general rule or to moderate
2. to have the skills and experience necessary to gain admission or acceptance

quandary
1. dilemma
2. confusion or uncertainty

querulous
1. complaining

quibble
1. to object
2. toargue in a trivial way

quiescent
1. quiet, still or inactive
2. dormant

raconteur
1. storyteller

radical
1. extreme
2. revolutionary

ratify
1. to approve or to validate
2. to make into law

rationalism
1. belief in the power of reason

rationalization
1. the act of justifying something
2. thought process

raucous
1. loud
2. disorderly

ravage
1. to destroy
2. to ruin or pillage

ravishment
1. enchantment
2. forceful seizure

reactionary
1. opposing liberal thought
2. often ultraconservative

ream
1. a measure of paper in quantity

reapportion
1. to allot anew
2. to redistribute

rebuff
1. to snub
2. to repel

rebuke
1. to criticize harshly (as a verb)
2. a reprimand or criticism (as a noun)

rebuttal
1. opposingargument
2. legal response (also anargument against a particular view)

receptive
1. ready to react favorably
2. willing to listen

reciprocal
1. involving give and take
2. interchangeable

recluse
1. a solitary person
2. a hermit

reconcile
1. to make up after a fight or to resolve a dispute
2. to accept or come to terms with a situation

recuperate
1. to recover health or strength
2. to recover financially

recurrent
1. occurring again
2. reappearing

reform
1. to change
2. to improve

refute
1. to disprove
2. to deny

regimen
1. highly organized system or governmental rule
2. dietary or exercise system

regimented
1. organized or ordered
2. pertaining to the organization of troops in the military

regress
1. to return to a previous phase, e.g., a four-year-old reverting to babyish behavior
2. literally, *re* (meaning *back* or *again*) and *gress* (meaning *step* or *walk*), thus stepping backwards

regulate
1. to control
2. to adjust

rejuvenate
1. to make younger
2. to restore youthfulness

relativity
1. the lack of absolutes
2. the theory that existence is dependent on the mind

relevant
1. pertinent
2. relating to the subject at hand

relic
1. vestige
2. keepsake or remnant from the past

relinquish
1. to leave or abandon
2. to surrender or give up

reluctance
1. disinclination
2. unwillingness

reminiscence
1. memory
2. recall or the act of remembering

remission
1. abatement or lessening
2. situation in which a disease temporarily goes away

remnant
1. remainder
2. leftover

remonstrate
1. to protest
2. to object

remorse
1. regret
2. repentance from prior sins

render
1. to give
2. to make something a certain way (e.g., to render unintelligible)

renounce
1. to give up
2. to reject

repellent
1. pushing something away
2. making impervious to

repertoire
1. a collection of artistic material that a group can perform
2. a set of talents or abilities

repertory
1. a collection of skills
2. a set of achievements

replete
1. complete with everything one needs
2. amply supplied

replicate
1. to copy
2. to duplicate

reprehensible
1. guilty
2. worthy of blame

repression
1. restraint
2. the psychological tendency to push ideas into the subconscious

reprisal
1. retaliation

reprobate
1. a sinful person
2. an incorrigibly immoral person

reprove
1. to find fault
2. to scold

repudiate
1. to reject or disown
2. to refuse

repugnance
1. dislike
2. aversion

rescind
1. to void, annul
2. to repeal

residual
1. remaining
2. leftover

resignation
1. submission, passivity, or giving in
2. formally leaving a position

resiliency
1. elasticity
2. bounce; the ability to return to a previous form

resolute
1. firm and unbending
2. determined

resonance
1. richness of sound
2. acoustics

responsive
1. reacting
2. involved

restorative
1. rejuvenating
2. having the ability to revive or repair

restraint
1. limitation
2. loss of freedom; restriction

retaliate
1. to get back at
2. to repay

reticent
1. restrained or reserved
2. quiet

retraction
1. drawing back
2. recanting a story

retrograde
1. going backward
2. changing back to an prior state, or reversed

retrospection
1. looking back
2. thinking about the past

revelation
1. manifestation
2. disclosure

revere
1. to respect greatly
2. to worship or to be in awe

reverential
1. feeling awe
2. deeply respectful

revolting
1. disgusting
2. abhorrent

revulsion
1. disgust or loathing
2. turning away from something

rhetorical
1. said for effect
2. not meant literally

ripple
1. to make tiny waves on the surface
2. to oscillate
3. to rise and fall gently

robust
1. sturdy
2. healthy or strong

romantic
1. impractical or imaginative
2. having to do with love

rostrum
1. a speaker's platform
2. a dais

rotund
1. round
2. overweight

rouse
1. to awaken
2. to incite

rubble
1. ruins of a building
2. wreckage

rudder
1. a steering mechanism
2. guide or director

ruddiness
1. redness
2. rosy color

rueful
1. regretful or sorry
2. inspiring pity

ruffle
1. to fluster
2. to fold or to disturb the smoothness of

rustic
1. countrified
2. unsophisticated

ruthlessness
1. the quality of showing no compassion or pity

sallow
1. pale
2. yellowish in complexion, sickly

salubrious
1. healthful
2. good for one

salutary
1. favorable
2. healthy or wholesome

salutation
1. a greeting

sanctify
1. to bless
2. to make holy

sanction
1. approval, validation or encouragement
2. punishment or penalty (an oddly opposite meaning from 1.)

sardonic
1. mocking
2. scornful or derisive

satiated
1. filled
2. satisfied or sated

satirist
1. one who writes using irony, humor and derision

satrap
1. a petty ruler

saturation
1. filling to capacity
2. soaking

savor
1. taste, distinctive quality (as a noun)
2. to enjoy, taste or relish (as a verb)

scant
1. meager or inadequate
2. deficient

scapegoat
1. person blamed for something
2. symbolic receptacle for guilt or blame

schematic
1. a diagram showing structure

schizophrenia
1. a particular diagnosis of psychosis
2. inability to distinguish reality from fantasy

scintillate
1. to sparkle
2. to be lively

scorn
1. to reject
2. to look down upon or to treat with contempt

scrupulous
1. conscientious or principled
2. exacting

scurrilous
1. coarse
2. foul-mouthed

seamless
1. fitting together perfectly
2. flawless

sect
1. persons forming a distinct unit with different beliefs within a larger group
2. a religious group that separated from a larger denomination

sectarian
1. narrow-minded
2. parochial

sedative
1. soothing, calming (as an adjective)
2. a tranquilizing drug (as a noun)

seductive
1. drawing someone into improper conduct
2. leading someoneastray

seethe
1. to boil
2. to ferment or to agitate

segment
1. part
2. portion

seismic
1. relating to earthquakes

sentimentalism
1. expression based on feeling
2. emotionalism or tendency not to employ reason and thought

sentry
1. a guard

serene
1. peaceful
2. tranquil

serf
1. a slave
2. an indentured servant

serpentine
1. sly
2. sinuous, snaky

servile
1. submissive
2. acting like a slave

shackle
1. a handcuff or ankle restraint to curb a prisoner's movement (as a noun)
2. to restrict or restrain movement of (as a verb)

shear
1. to cut
2. to strip or to remove hair or fur

shoddy
1. of poor quality or cheap
2. dishonest

shorthand
1. rapid system of writing with shortened words and symbols
2. abbreviation
3. stenography

sieve
1. a sifter
2. a kitchen utensil used for ricing, etc.

simpleton
1. a fool
2. a stupid person

simultaneous
1. happening at the same time
2. coexisting

sinuous
1. winding
2. having many curves

skepticism
1. doubt
2. an attitude of questioning everything

skinflint
1. stingy person
2. miser

skulk
1. to lurk or to sneak about
2. to avoid work

slag
1. residue from smelting

sliver
1. a splinter
2. a thin piece of something

smirk
1. to smile in a simpering way

sneer
1. to look down upon or scorn
2. to make a mocking expression while curling the lip

snub
1. to scorn
2. to ignore

sober
1. serious
2. abstaining from alcohol

solemn
1. grave
2. serious or somber

somber
1. melancholy
2. dark, gloomy, sad

sonority
1. resonance
2. sound

soothsayer
1. a seer
2. someone claiming to predict the future

sophisticate
1. a worldly person
2. someone who's not naive or green

sophomoric
1. immature
2. stupid

sorcerer
1. a wizard
2. a magician

sordid
1. base
2. lowly, debased, dirty

sovereign
1. ruler (as a noun)
2. having the highest rank or self-governing (as an adjective)

spare
1. to save
2. to be lenient

sparse
1. scantly occurring
2. widely spread out,as in a sparse population density

specific
1. particular
2. definite or distinctive

spectrum
1. range

spiteful
1. mean-spirited
2. malicious

spitfire
1. hothead
2. highly excitable person

splendor
1. glory
2. grandeur

spontaneity
1. impulsiveness
2. freshness

sporadic
1. not widespread
2. irregular or occasional

spur
1. incentive
2. goad

spurious
1. false
2. inauthentic

spurn
1. to reject
2. to be disdainful

squander
1. to waste
2. to scatter

stagnation
1. staying in the same place, usually a rut
2. failure to move or develop

stalemate
1. deadlock
2. situation in which no one can move

stalwart
1. strong, hale
2. uncompromising, sturdy

standardize
1. to regularize

statistical
1. using special numerical systems to organize data

stature
1. status
2. height

status quo
1. as thingsare today
2. the existing state of things

steadfast
1. loyal, constant
2. unchanging, steady

stealthy
1. sneaky
2. characterized by secretive action

stereoscope
1. an instrument that creates two-dimensional effects

stereotype
1. an oversimplification
2. a view of a group without regard to any individual characteristics
3. often a prejudicial, biased, negative characterization of a group

stratagem
1. military maneuver
2. deception

stratified
1. layered
2. often pertaining to class levels in a society

stupefaction
1. astonishment
2. amazement; the state of being stunned

stylized
1. conventionally portrayed

stymie
1. to get in the way of; to block (as a verb)
2. an obstacle (as a noun)

subjective
1. not objective; personal
2. illusory

subjugation
1. enslaving or subduing others
2. literally, *sub* (meaning *under*) and *juga* (meaning *yoke*), referring to oxen which were under the yoke to perform work

submission
1. compliance
2. meekness

subordinate
1. underling (as a noun)
2. secondary or lesser (as an adjective)

subscribe
1. to pledge or to agree
2. to sign up

subservient
1. subordinate
2. servile

subside
1. to settle down
2. to abate

subsidiary
1. secondary
2. auxiliary

subterranean
1. underground
2. hidden

subtle
1. not obvious
2. elusive

sufficient
1. enough
2. adequate

suffrage
1. the right to vote
2. franchise

summon
1. to call or to send for
2. to command the appearance of in court

sumptuous
1. lavish
2. expensive or posh

superficial
1. shallow, on the surface
2. insubstantial; trivial; unimportant

superfluous
1. more than necessary
2. extra

supersonic
1. above the speed of sound

supplement
1. something that is added (as a noun)
2. to add (as a verb)

supplication
1. prayer
2. the act ofasking for something

surfeit
1. excess (as a noun)
2. to fill to excess (as a verb)

surmise
1. to guess

surplus
1. something extra or an excess (as a noun)
2. extra (as an adjective)

surreptitious
1. secret
2. stealthy

sustain
1. to support, encourage
2. to nourish

suture
1. a seam created during surgery (as a noun)
2. to sew up after surgery (as a verb)

swagger
1. to behave in anarrogant way
2. to boast

sweltering
1. very hot and humid
2. tropical

swindler
1. a cheat or fraud
2. someone who obtains money dishonorably

sybarite
1. a person who loves luxury
2. a hedonist or pleasure lover

symmetry
1. balance or harmony
2. having anarrangement that is identical on both sides

symptomatic
1. having to do with manifestations of a condition
2. displaying signs of an illness

synthesize
1. to combine parts into a more unified or complex whole
2. to make

synthetic
1. fake
2. artificial

taboo
1. prohibition
2. something disallowed, a "no-no"

tabulation
1. organization into a table
2. computation

tacit
1. implicit or understood without being stated
2. silent or not talking

taciturn
1. quiet
2. not at all talkative

tact
1. diplomacy
2. ability to express oneself without offending

talon
1. claw

tangential
1. beside the point
2. divergent

tantamount
1. equivalent to

tatters
1. rags
2. ruined, torn clothing

taunt
1. to mock
2. to jeer

technocracy
1. government by technical advisors

tedious
1. wearisome
2. uninteresting or proceeding slowly

tempestuous
1. stormy
2. tumultuous

temporal
1. pertaining to time; short-lived, temporary
2. worldly

tentative
1. uncertain
2. provisional

tepid
1. lukewarm
2. neither hot nor cold

terse
1. concise or employing few words
2. to the point

testify
1. to declare under oath
2. to witness

theocracy
1. government by religion or a god
2. a state governed in such a fashion

thickset
1. overweight
2. stout

thrifty
1. frugal, careful with money
2. economical

thunderous
1. loud

thwart
1. to frustrate
2. to challenge

tinge
1. to color slightly

tirade
1. angry speech
2. abusive critique

top-heavy
1. unsteady
2. inclined to fall over

torrid
1. burning
2. passionate

tourniquet
1. a band tightened to halt blood flow

tranquility
1. peace
2. serenity

transcribe
1. to write out from notes
2. to transfer from one medium to another

transform
1. to convert dramatically
2. to change thoroughly

transfusion
1. injection of fresh blood to a patient during surgery

transgression
1. sin
2. act of wrongdoing

transient
1. passing
2. transitory, temporary

transitional
1. changing
2. going from one place (or conversation or condition) to another

transitory
1. passing, temporary
2. short-lived

translucence
1. the quality of letting light through

transmit
1. to send
2. to impart or to hand down

transmutation
1. transformation
2. change

transplantation
1. replanting
2. transfer or relocation

trauma
1. sudden injury (usually serious)
2. shock

trigger
1. to start
2. to initiate

trite
1. overused or banal
2. hackneyed or cliché

trivial
1. unimportant
2. insignificant

troupe
1. group of actors

tumult
1. to-do; ruckus
2. stormy revolt or emotional upheaval

turbulence
1. agitation
2. disturbance

turmoil
1. chaos
2. great confusion in a situation; commotion

tyrannize
1. to employ absolute power
2. to use such power witharbitrariness and often cruelty

tyrant
1. absolute ruler
2. oppressor or cruel leader

ultimate
1. last, farthest or maximum

unanimous
1. in full agreement
2. without dissent

unconditional
1. absolute
2. with no exceptions or limitations

undermine
1. to weaken
2. to wear away or sap

uniform
1. consistent
2. same or identical

unintelligible
1. not understandable
2. garbled

unionization
1. the act of organizing labor into a cohesive bargaining power

unkempt
1. messy
2. disorganized

unleash
1. to loose
2. to release

unproductive
1. not useful
2. not effective

unresponsive
1. not answering
2. not reacting

unruly
1. misbehaving
2. difficult to control

unsung
1. unpraised
2. unhonored

untenable
1. indefensible
2. not maintainable

unwarranted
1. groundless
2. baseless

unwieldy
1. bulky
2. clumsy

uproarious
1. hilarious
2. raucously funny or boisterous

upsurge
1. a quick rise or increase

usurp
1. to seize power
2. to take authority illegally

utility
1. usefulness
2. a public service, e.g., electric company

vacillation
1. wavering or indecision
2. swinging back and forth between options

vacuity
1. emptiness or idleness; vacuum
2. unoriginality of ideas

vacuous
1. empty
2. stupid or unserious, silly (a *vacuum* is *empty*)

vague
1. unclear
2. indefinite

validity
1. soundness
2. effectiveness

valve
1. regulator of flow and pressure
2. mechanical device that shuts off the flow

vanquish
1. conquer
2. defeat

vaporize
1. to change into gaseous form

variant
1. differing
2. variable or deviating

vehement
1. forceful or strong
2. insistent

vengeful
1. wanting to get back at someone
2. desirous of revenge

vent
1. to express
2. to release pressure, let off steam

verbose
1. wordy

verdict
1. conclusion
2. judgment; jury's decision

verification
1. proof
2. the process ofascertaining the truth of a theory

vexation
1. irritation
2. annoyance

viable
1. able to survive outside the womb
2. capable of being alive

vibrant
1. lively
2. full of energy

vigilance
1. alertness
2. watchfulness

vigor
1. energy or enthusiasm
2. health

vim
1. energy
2. liveliness or vitality

vindicate
1. to justify
2. to clear from blame

vindictive
1. vengeful
2. spiteful

virtuoso
1. master, skilled expert, often in music
2. brilliant person with a finely honed skill

virtuous
1. pure
2. righteous

viscosity
1. thickness (pertaining to liquid)
2. the makeup of oil or any dense liquid that pours slowly

vitality
1. energy or pep
2. ability to thrive

vociferous
1. loud
2. making an outcry

vogue
1. fashion
2. style

volatile
1. capable of being vaporized easily
2. unsteady, changeable

voluble
1. talkative
2. fluent in language

voluminous
1. huge
2. great in size or number

voracious
1. insatiable
2. ravenous or greedy

vulnerable
1. woundable
2. susceptible to injury or attack

waiver
1. relinquishment of a claim

wan
1. pale
2. weary or weak

wanderlust
1. a strong desire to travel

wane
1. to ebb
2. to decrease

wariness
1. caution
2. carefulness

warranted
1. justified
2. guaranteed

waterlog
1. to soak
2. to overfill with liquid

watery
1. thin
2. diluted

wayward
1. unpredictable
2. unruly; stubborn, intractable

whim
1. a fancy
2. an idea that's not serious, a caprice

wince
1. to flinch
2. to start involuntarily

wisp
1. a thin piece
2. a hint

wither
1. to fade away
2. to shrivel, to droop, to dry out

withhold
1. to refrain from giving
2. to hold back

writhe
1. to squirm, contort, to twist
2. to be in pain

yearn
1. to long for
2. to desire or pine

zeal
1. enthusiasm
2. fervor

zealot
1.   a fanatic

zenith
1.   uppermost point
2.   peak

Top 100 Words

Really important. Even if you can't stand learning the words in the previous section, you should master these 100, which have shown up so often on SATs that you will severely handicap yourself if you don't know them.

aesthetic
1. artistic, or pertaining to beauty
2. having a faculty for discerning beauty

altruistic
1. thinking of other
2. unselfish

ambivalent
1. feeling at least two different ways about something
2. experiencing contradictory emotions

amorphous
1. shapeless
2. formless

anachronism
1. something happening out of its proper time frame

annul
1. to void or cancel as though something never happened
2. to nullify

anomaly
1. abnormality
2. irregularity

antiquated
1. aged
2. obsolete

antithesis
1. opposite
2. the co-existence of very contrasting words, thoughts, actions, etc.

arable
1. farmable
2. plowable or fit for growing things

assiduous
1. diligent
2. persistent

asylum
1. safe haven
2. refuge

atrophy
1. wasting away
2. diminution

audacious
1. bold
2. fearless or daring

austere
1. stern, strict or ascetic
2. bare

authoritarian
1. expecting absolute obedience
2. minimizing personal freedom

belligerent
1. aggressive or warlike
2. hostile or tending to pick fights

benevolent
1. kindly
2. charitable, full of good will

camaraderie
1. friendship
2. comradeship (*Camaraderie* and *comrade* are etymologically related.)

candid
1. open, honest
2. straightforward

cantankerous
1. crabby or disagreeable
2. unpleasant or quarrelsome

carp
1. to complain
2. to find fault

censure
1. blame
2. rebuke or disapproval

charlatan
1. a fake or fraud
2. a quack

chimerical
1. fanciful, fantastic
2. imaginary

cliché
1. a stale idea or usage (as a noun)
2. overused (as an adjective). Synonyms (for noun use): banality; triteness (for adjective use): banal; trite; hackneyed; overused

compatriot
1. person from the same country
2. colleague

comprehensive
1. extensive or complete
2. full

concise
1. terse
2. succinct or to the point

curmudgeon
1. a grouchy person
2. a crab

dearth
1. lack
2. shortage

deleterious
1. harmful
2. injurious

demagogue
1. a false leader
2. a leader who appeals to the emotions of followers

depraved
1. corrupt
2. immoral

despot
1. tyrant, czar
2. absolute ruler

detriment
1. harm
2. loss

dilatory
1. late or slow
2. procrastinating (think of *dilating* the time in which one does something, which would make the action slower.)

disparity
1. inequality
2. difference

dogmatic
1. authoritative
2. rigid, unyielding

dubious
1. doubtful or questionable
2. skeptical

eclectic
1. from many different sources
2. having diverse parts or styles used together

edifice
1. a building
2. often, a huge and impressive building

elucidate
1. to clarify
2. to make clear

enigma
1. a puzzle
2. something confusing

ephemeral
1. short-lived
2. transitory

epitome
1. an ideal or example
2. a representative

esoteric
1. difficult to understand
2. understood by few people

frugal
1. thrifty
2. careful with money

garrulous
1. talkative

gregarious
1. friendly
2. sociable

haughty
1. overly proud and egotistical
2. arrogant

hedonistic
1. pleasure-seeking
2. concerned with physical gratification

heresy (also heretic, heretical)
1. unorthodox event or behavior
2. controversial opinion or theory

hyperbole
1. exaggeration
2. extravagant statement, such as "I could eat a horse."

illusory
1. unreal
2. deceptive

imperious (i.e., like an emperor)
1. haughty
2. overbearing

impromptu
1. unrehearsed
2. spontaneous

indigenous
1. native
2. innate or intrinsic

infer
1. to deduce logically
2. to conclude based on evidence

ingrate
1. an ungrateful person

innate
1. inherent
2. inborn

jettison
1. to throw overboard
2. to get rid of

laconic
1. using few words
2. terse or to the point, concise

magnanimous
1. literally, large-spirited
2. generous

malevolence
1. spite
2. ill will

mercenary
1. a person who works only for monetary reasons (as noun)
2. money-hungry (as adjective)

misanthrope
1. someone who hates mankind

monumental
1. huge
2. outstanding and enduring

munificent
1. generous
2. having a giving nature

neophyte (synonyms: tyro, novice)
1. a newcomer
2. a beginner

opulence
1. affluence
2. richness or a state of plenty

ostentatious
1. showy
2. pretentious

paradox
1. something that is self-contradictory

paragon
1. a model
2. an ideal; something perfect or excellent

paucity
1. scarcity
2. dearth, lack

pedestrian
1. ordinary, common or everyday (as an adjective)
2. walker (as a noun)

pejorative
1. negative (the Latin word *peior* means *worse*)
2. derogatory

penury
1. neediness
2. poverty or lack

primeval
1. ancient
2. original

pristine
1. pure
2. uncorrupted

prosaic
1. ordinary or everyday
2. straightforward or unimaginative

puerile
1. childish
2. immature

quack
1. a fake
2. a charlatan

quagmire
1. marsh, bog
2. predicament or difficulty

querulous
1. complaining

recluse
1. a solitary person
2. a hermit

salutary
1. favorable
2. healthy or wholesome

sanctify
1. to bless
2. to make holy

spurious
1. false
2. inauthentic

stymie
1. to get in the way of; to block (as a verb)
2. an obstacle (as a noun)

superfluous
1. more than necessary
2. extra

surfeit
1. excess (as a noun)
2. to fill to excess (as a verb)

tacit
1. implicit or understood without being stated
2. silent or not talking

taciturn
1. quiet
2. not at all talkative

tempestuous
1. stormy
2. tumultuous

tepid
1. lukewarm
2. neither hot nor cold

terse
1. concise or employing few words
2. to the point

tirade
1. angry speech
2. abusive critique

voluminous
1. huge
2. great in size or number

zealot
1. a fanatic

Mnemonics

Mnemonics are tricks to help you memorize. Once you get the hang of it, you can make up your own mnemonics for other words! Here are some to get you started.

Penitent means *sorry, apologetic*. This is where they get the word *penitentiary*. It's a place where people are supposed to go to feel sorry for what they did wrong. I don't know if it works, but that's where they get the name.

Arid means *dry*. Think of the deodorant, named similarly so you will think it can keep you dry and therefore buy it.

Glacial means *icy, cold* (in terms of temperature or personality). Think of a glacier, made of ice, and thus cold. It can also mean *slow*, since glaciers move very slowly.

Haughty means *overly proud, snooty, full of oneself*. Think of the word *high*, with the same consonants and different vowels. Thinking that someone is haughty means the same as thinking that someone is on a high horse: "She thinks she's so high and mighty!"

Jollity is *the quality of being jolly, happy or merry*. It has the word *jolly* with *it* in the middle, so think of *it* being a pro*noun*, and *jollity* being the *noun* form of the word *jolly*.

Compliant means *going along with things, obeying, being cooperative*. *Complaint* has the letters *a* and *i* reversed, so it means the opposite of *compliant*.

Debasement means *lowering*. Say to yourself, "De basement is de lowest room in de house." That will tip you off to the fact that *debasement* means *a lowering of one's standards or morals*.

Opulent means *richly appointed or looking as if it costs much money*. Think of an opal (jewel); if something had many jewels, it would be richly appointed and cost big money.

Wily means *sneaky, tricky*. So think of Wile E. Coyote, the cartoon character that was always being tricky.

Incantation means *magic words,* like *Shazam!* or *Abracadabra!* Think of someone *chanting* those words, since *chant* is only one letter different from the *cant* in *incantation.*

Complemented means *completed* or *went with* or *filled a deficiency.* It even has the word *completed* in it, with *ment* in the middle, which is similar to *meant.* So think that they *meant* to say *completed* when they said *complemented.*

Extant means *still in existence.* Something extant IS. So put the word *is* after the *ex,* and you (almost) have *existent* (slightly different spelling, but you get the idea!).

Extinct means *not still in existence;* think of the word *extinguish,* which one does to a flame to get rid of it.

Eclectic means *from a variety of sources.* One might eat an eclectic meal of Chinese egg rolls, French crepes and English toffee. One might decorate in an eclectic manner, choosing modern furniture, colonial-style quilts, and hand-hewn, craft-like items. To remember *eclectic,* notice it almost has *collect* in it: *clect.* If you were collecting things from all different places, they could have an eclectic style.

Adorn means *to decorate.* Think of *add*ing *orn*aments to make things decorated.

Ornate means *adorned, decorated;* it has the *orn* of *ornament* in it.

Facade means *a building face or front* or *a show meant to deceive someone.* Think of the word *face* which has an *ad* in it; the person is advertising what he wants people to see. *Face* is close to *fake,* so this is a fake front too.

Potable means *drinkable, suitable or safe for drinking.* As a noun it means a *beverage.* Think of being able to put liquid into a *pot* of vegetables to make soup. You wouldn't add water to soup if it weren't drinkable (*pot* is the same root in *hippopotamus,* which is *a river horse; pot* means *river* as well as *water.* Think of Mesopotamia, the land in the middle or *meso* of two rivers, the Tigris and Euphrates).

A **raconteur** is French for a *recounter* (teller) or a *story-teller.*

A **protege** is *one supported and protected by another.* From French, this word and *protect* have almost the same letters.

Camaraderie is French for *comradeship, friendship.* Consonants of *camarad*—and *comrade* are identical; when this happens, vowels can be different, but the meaning is often the same.

Efficacious means *effective or getting results.* The consonants of both *effective* and *efficacious* are f-f-c, so they mean the same thing.

Hoi polloi is Greek for *the common people.* It is possibly etymologically related to the word *polis,* meaning *state or city;* a *polis* was the kind of place where *people* would live.

Remuneration means *reward, payment or compensation.* You could pronounce *mun-e* and *money* the same.

Munitions and **ammunition** mean *weaponry.*

Laud means *to praise;* think of it as being part of the word *applaud.* If you app*laud* a performance, you are praising it.

To **amplify** is *to increase.* Think of amps a band uses to increase sound level.

Enervated means *exhausted.* E-, like *ex-*, is a prefix meaning *out of* or *from.* Think of the word *nerve.* If you imagine someone who is *out of nerves, i.e.,* whose nerves are shot, that person would be exhausted.

Bilk means *to cheat someone out of money.* Think of it as being one letter away from the word *bill,* which is a legitimate way of getting money.

Cerebral means *mental, intellectual or rational;* it comes from the fact that the cerebrum is part of the brain.

Deleterious means *harmful.* Think of writing a term paper and accidentally deleting it from your computer. That would be harmful to you, since you'd have to do it over!

Repel means *to push away.* Think of insect repellent, meant to push bugs away.

Florid means *flowery or fancy.* Think of a florist's shop, which sells flowers.

Circumlocution means *talking in circles or never getting to the point.* Think of *circum*—being like a *circle. Locu*—and *loqu*—mean *to talk or to speak. Loquacious* means *talkative.*

Novelty means *newness or something new. Nov*—means *new.* Ditto for *neo. Neo* is just one letter different from *new.* And *nov*—is similar to *new* because *v* and *w* are often interchanged, and vowels can change from word to word.

Longevity means *long life.* It has *long* in it. Think of someone having good vital signs (pulse, blood pressure, etc.); one gets vital signs from a person who's alive. *Vitality* is another word with this root; it means *liveliness.*

Mundane means *ordinary or everyday.* It's related to the French word *monde,* meaning *world.* So think of things that are ordinary or everyday being part of the world. By contrast, words that mean not ordinary are: *otherworldly, bizarre, outlandish.* These all indicate things you don't see in your everyday world.

Alleviate means *to ease or lighten.* That's why they named a pain medicine to sound like the first two syllables.

Remedial should evoke *remedy,* meaning *cure.* **Therapeutic** should evoke *therapy,* meaning *cure.* Both adjectives mean *curative or healing.*

Derisive means *sneering or making fun of something*; it's related to the French word *rire, to laugh.*

Taint means *to sully or make impure*. Think of some hillbilly saying, "This water? ÔTain't good enough to drink!" *Tainted* means *impure.*

To **bridge** is to *connect*. Think of the fact that that's exactly what a bridge does; it connects two points of land.

Vociferous means *loud and noisy, usually protesting*. Think of the fact that *voci* is almost *voice* or *vocal. Fer* means *to carry*; think of the fact that a ferry carries passengers. So if your voice is really carrying, that's the sense of the word!

Evanescent means *temporary, fleeting, passing away quickly*. Think of *vane* being almost like *wane*, and of course v and w are often substituted for one another.

Bereft is related to the word *bereave*. A bereft person is sad; so is a bereaved person.

Punitive means *harsh or tending to punish*. The first four letters of *punish* and *punitive* are the same.

Olfactory means *pertaining to the sense of smell*. Think of the fact that *odor* also starts with an o, and your nose is a factory that processes odors.

Carp means *to complain or criticize*. All three words start with c. *Carp* is also a fish. Think of complaining about the fish dinner you've just been served in a restaurant.

A **gap** is *a hole*. Think also of *gaping*, meaning *wide open.*

Wretched means *deplorably bad, miserable, suffering greatly, afflicted*. Think of *retch*, which means *to make an attempt to vomit*. If you were retching, you would feel wretched.

Affront means *insult*; think of someone getting in your face (in front of you) and insulting you.

A **charlatan** is a *fake*. Think of the sentence *Charles is faking getting a tan.*

Dupe means to *fool. Dupe* looks like *dope*. So you might think that only a dope would be fooled by something.

Totalitarian*:* think of someone being *totally* in control of your thoughts, of the information you receive, and that's what often happens in a totalitarian government.

Waver means *to move back and forth or vacillate*. Think of wave; when you wave, your hand goes back and forth.

Phlegmatic means *sluggish* (or *slow*; think of a slug moving slowly) *or dull or unenergetic*. Think of having a lot of phlegm when you're sick, a time you don't have energy.

Grammar, Usage, Punctuation, Etc.

Writing: A Learnable Skill

Many students find writing a chore, to be avoided unless needed to pass a course. But you may find that, as with so many things in life, writing gets easier with practice. As you read and write more, you naturally develop your own style, your own voice.

I know it's tedious to learn rules of grammar, spelling, and punctuation. But the reality is that, when you learn the rules, you become a better writer. Having rules in your brain rather than having to look them up as you go, allows for a more natural style to develop. I know this sounds counterintuitive, but it's true. If you look at people who are excellent at a sport, they practice a lot of skills that, in and of themselves, are fairly dry and boring. But having this mastery of components allows the players to perform at peak level.

Ditto for writers.

Arguably the best book on grammar and usage is *The Elements of Style*, by William Strunk and E.B. White. The current edition is a succinct and flawless book, saying what many authors of grammar books take hundreds of pages to say. Therefore I recommend that you pick up that little book if you don't already have it, read it through and memorize the rules. It will improve your writing greatly if you take it to heart.

For the purposes of this book, I will include some of the format of the Writing Section of the SAT and a few of the more common rules of grammar. But do pick up *The Elements of Style* and study it and your writing will improve enormously. It is a good book to take to college and graduate or professional school and even past school. By the time you get done with it, it will be suitably dog-eared, showing the mark of years of grateful usage.

And if you ever have an opportunity to learn how to diagram sentences, you'll find that that skill is useful in helping you figure out just what modifies what, and how to figure out agreement between subject and verb, and so forth.

Some Important Rules

Make sure you don't take one sentence and break it into two or more parts:

> Jason was a straight-A student. Doing all his studying on time. Working into the night.

Instead, it should be:

> Jason was a straight-A student, doing all his studying on time and working into the night.

If you have two independent clauses, they are really like two separate sentences; thus, it's inappropriate to put a comma between them. Either they are two sentences or you may use a semicolon between them. For example:

> Rafael enjoyed Thai food most; he also was somewhat fond of Mexican, Chinese and French cuisine.

An exception to the semicolon rule comes when you have short phrases. Then commas are ok:

> It bends, it breaks, it snaps.

That tends to have a power lacking with the semicolon.

Colons can be effective punctuation in a sentence. A colon may be used if the second clause amplifies, restates or illuminates the first clause or gives a list of examples:

> Sanders filled the flower pots with various plants: coleus, lavender, mums, gardenias, and lilies.

> The meal was eclectic: Thai spring rolls to start, French crepes for the entree, and English toffees for dessert.

The team was irretrievably lost: it had fallen so far behind that all hope of catching up in the remaining 5 minutes was unrealistic.

I'd like the following items at the store: eggs, cheese, bread, and doughnuts.

You must have subject-verb agreement. A singular subject requires a singular verb and a plural subject requires a plural verb. Thus:

Melanie and John pick flowers in the field.

(You have a plural subject and verb; please note that the plural word *flowers* is an object, not a subject, so it's irrelevant whether they pick one or more flowers.)

John picks wildflowers for his project.

(You have a singular subject and verb.)

Singular verbs get used after *either, everyone, everybody, nobody, neither, either, someone, somebody*:

Nobody was late.

Everybody in the school, whether he or she is a good student or not, is eligible to apply for these scholarships.

It's best to learn all the rules, but if you forget something, sometimes you can rephrase something to avoid an error!

When you link two subjects with *and*, you need a plural verb:

Marie and Frank were close friends.

But when you use phrases like *together with, as well as, in addition to, and with*, you must keep a singular verb:

Her clothing as well as her hair was unkempt.

A lot of people have trouble with personal pronouns, especially in figuring out whether to use the subjective or objective form of a pronoun:

Will Harry or she be recruited by the company?

(Leave out *Harry or* and see if the sentence sounds right. It does, because it is!)

"Who's there?"
"It is I!" (not *me*)

We tall people find that furniture is often not made for us.

(Leave out *tall people* and it's easier to figure out that *We* is correct. The words *for us* are right, because you need the objective form after the word *for*.)

Whom are you mocking?

(Substitute the word *him* or *her* for *whom* and twist the sentence order around: "Are you mocking her?" You would not say "Are you mocking she?" so you need the objective form *whom* in the original sentence.)

Nancy Parkinson is the person who we suspect will do the job.

(If you try, "We suspect she will do the job," you'll see that the subjective form *who* is needed.)

It's better to use *I* as the subject instead of *myself*, and likewise *you* instead of *yourself*:

Bob, Caitlyn and I are going to the football playoffs. If Mandy and you would like to go, please let us know!

If you have a phrase at the beginning of the sentence, you have to be careful that it modifies the subject:

Strolling by the store, he saw four children.

It's the *he* that's strolling. If you want to say that the four children are strolling, you have to say: "He saw four children strolling by the store."

> WRONG: A student of extraordinary talent, Beth's teachers declared her valedictorian

> RIGHT: A student of extraordinary talent, Beth was declared valedictorian by her teachers.

Despite the example given immediately above, active voice usually works better than passive; *e.g.,* instead of

> A good time was had by all.

it's better to say

> Everyone had a good time.

Specifics are good:

> It snowed or sleeted 4 out of every 5 days all winter long.

gives more detail and information than:

> We'd had unpleasant weather for months.

because it tells what kind of unpleasant weather and to what extent.

One of the best student essays I ever saw was one sparked by a tiny event: the discovery of a box of letters written by a relative during World War II. The essay contained a wealth of detail from the letters; the student was fascinated with history, and her ability to bring alive this small piece of it was striking.

Thus, it's important to use colors, specific card games being played, the type of clothing worn, etc. If you are writing an essay on an abstract topic like freedom or responsibility, it will still be important to come up with concrete examples that enliven your writing. Details are important. Examples are important. Too many students say vapid things like "I learned teamwork from being on my soccer team," or "I learned responsibility from my summer job." A better example might be:

Last summer, I had to master skills ranging from setting a table to slicing a baked potato, from polishing silverware to placating a tired businessman with a fresh cup of coffee. I learned to make small talk with the best of them, to make myself invisible when a couple wanted privacy, to amuse a 2-year-old on the verge of a tantrum and to keep orders for six tables straight while balancing a tray and smiling broadly at everyone.

Instead of

The trip to Africa taught me about getting along with people despite cultural diversity.

you might say:

When we stopped at the Masai village, the children clustered around with great grins on their faces. I could not speak their language, and they knew only the word *Hi!* but there was a palpable warmth in our meeting.

Many students use excessive verbiage and repeat things unnecessarily without adding any new thought:

Many people before myself have considered the matter of whether freedom is a subject that has any meaning at all in the modern-day world. Philosophers and statesmen have looked at this subject. Good men and bad men have pondered it. I suspect that the reason is that it's a compelling subject. Certainly there is no doubt that throughout the ages it's been a topic of conversation, from thousands of years ago til the present.

Well, this is clearly a lot of verbiage! We can shorten it significantly and move on to the point at which something new is actually said!

Throughout history, people have pondered and debated the concept of freedom. It is reasonable, then, to consider what relevance freedom has in the modern world.

(and then go on to give examples).

A lot of high schoolers and other less experienced writers tend to write only in simple declarative sentences. Varying sentence length and structure makes for more interesting writing.

Please pay attention to the following. You should say

by air, by sea or by land
OR
by air, sea or land

NOT: by air, by sea or land.

You put *by* in front of each, or only in front of the first word. *Both . . . and, Not only . . . but also, Either . . . or, Neither . . . nor,* all have to exist using the same rule. Thus:

> Both by birth and by education, she had a very high status in the society.

OR

> By both birth and education, she had a very high status in the society.

rather than:

> WRONG: Both by birth and education, she had a very high status in the society.

Also:

> Ellie must either make her bed or lose her allowance for the week.

The idea is that you have equivalent structures: *make her bed* fits the same form as *lose her allowance*. So the *either . . . or* part must fit before those equivalent structures.

Make sure that words modify what you mean them to. Often this means putting words closer to what they modify. An example of unclear modification:

> The scientist noticed that there was a hole in the ozone layer that was right in the middle.

Better:

> The scientist noticed a hole right in the middle of the ozone layer.

Why? You want the hole in the middle of the ozone layer, not something that implies that the ozone layer is in the middle of something else.

Subjects and main verbs shouldn't be separated by other words or phrases. Thus:

> Shakespeare, in *A Midsummer Night's Dream*, weaves a comical story combining elements of magic and farce.

can be improved:

> In *A Midsummer Night's Dream*, Shakespeare weaves a comical story combining elements of magic and farce.

Switching tenses is taboo, unless you are doing it accurately:

> Mr. Mountebanks rushed to the front. He raises his binoculars and then shouts to the others.

We've started out with past tense and switched to present tense. You can do either of the following:

> Mr. Mountebanks rushed to the front. He raised his binoculars and then shouted to the others.

OR:

> Mr. Mountebanks rushes to the front. He raises his binoculars and then shouts to the others.

Important words of a sentence should often go at the end or beginning:

> Since the dawn of time, nothing has been more critical than survival.

OR

> Disorganization and laziness Mary could not abide.

OR

> Gone are the roses.
> Untamed are the seas.

Varying the order of important words can give emphasis to them. "The roses are gone" has less power as a sentence.

Parentheses can be used to set off part of a sentence:

> Rolf revisited Antarctica (his fourth visit) during the short summer season when planes could actually land.

> After, his disastrous scores in May, Manny took the SAT again (his third try) after learning the entire contents of *Boot Camp For Your Brain*™.

Quotations are usually introduced by a comma (or more formally, a colon) before the first set of quotation marks and a comma or period before the last set of quotation marks:

> The first line of the *Aeneid*, translated, reads: "I sing of arms and the man."

> "Watch what you say," she warned. "Even the walls have ears."

> "I don't know why I'm still here," said Pop. "I just keep waking up every day."

The commas go inside the quotes. Ditto for the periods.

If you include a quotation that's in common usage, you don't necessarily need quotes:

> A rose by any other name would smell as sweet.
> I think, therefore I am.

Titles of books appear in italics. Author's names do not:

> Garcia Marquez's *One Hundred Years of Solitude.*

There are many common mistakes people make: misspelling words, using the wrong word, etc. You'll commonly see people use *their* (the possessive) instead of *there* or vice versa. Try to be careful and check your writing for mistakes. Spell-checkers on computers will not catch sound-alike word substitutions! The following are some common mistakes:

To *imply* is to suggest or hint. To *infer* is to draw a conclusion from some facts given. For example:

> Harold implied that Beth was his date Friday night.

> Dennis inferred from the passage that the author was an ultraconservative.

Between is used when speaking of two things. *Among* is used when speaking of more than two things:

> She divided her prized possessions between her two teenaged children.

> The lottery winnings were divided among seven people who'd picked the winning number.

Can connotes ability. *May* is used when asking permission.

> Can I juggle four bowling pins? You betcha!

> May I please have a drink of water?

(If you say, "Can I have a drink of water?" you're saying, "Am I physically able to have a drink of water?").

Comprise means *to consist of.* Thus,

> A university comprises students and faculty.

All ways and *always* are different. *All ways* means *all methods* and *always* means *forever.*

> Ms. Perkins always maintained her innocence in the insider-trading scandal.

BUT:

> All ways of studying for the SAT can be effective for various students.

There are numerous plurals derived straight from Latin (or Greek in the case of *phenomena* and *phenomenon*). Some examples are *data, media, phenomena,* and *dicta.* These take plural verbs. The singular (*datum, medium, phenomenon, dictum*) take singular verbs:

> When the data were analyzed, it became clear that the hypothesis was untenable.

(*i.e.,* it was unkeepable, or it needed to be thrown out).

> The phenomenon of an eclipse caused enormous fear before people understood what was happening.

By the way, the plural of *hypothesis* is *hypotheses.* The plural of *thesis* is *theses.*

> *Uninterested* means *not having an interest in (something),* but *disinterested* means *impartial or fair.*

> The election is monitored by disinterested parties.

> Meredith was uninterested in the science fiction series about mutated koala bears taking over Parliament.

Less pertains to quantity, and *fewer* to number. Thus,

> I had fewer pupils in 10th grade this year than last.

> Our team has less talent than theirs.

Etc. (literally, the Latin *et cetera*) means *and other things. Et al.* (literally, the Latin *et alia*) means *and other people.*

> Nan and Bud packed up the china, silverware, kitchen tools, etc.

> Frank, Pete, Joe, John, et al., were planning on going to the big game.

Enormity does not refer to great size; it refers to great evil. It is often misused.

> RIGHT: The enormity of the crime hit them on a visceral level.

> WRONG: The enormity of his bonus elated Chris.

All right means *okay.* It is two words.

> "Mom, is it all right if I borrow $20.00?"
> "Yes, dear, but are you going to get a job and pay me back?"

Illusion is something that's not real. *Allusion* is a reference.

> The mirage of an oasis was an illusion that teased the weary caravan travelers into believing they would soon find water and food.

> Our teacher made an allusion to the *Iliad.*

Farther and *further* are often used as synonyms, but *farther* refers to distance in space, and *further* refers to extra amounts of something, *e.g.,*

> I hit the ball farther than anyone else on my team.

> I'd like to do further research on the Pleistocene.

When you are creating a comparison using the word *than*, you have to make sure you're being clear. If you say

> I'm friendlier with Bob than Theresa.

the sentence can be interpreted two different ways. You must clarify what you mean:

EITHER: I'm friendlier with Bob than Theresa is.

OR: I'm friendlier with Bob than with Theresa.

Very, so, etc. as modifiers are tiresome and one should avoid them or at least limit their usage.

OVERDOING IT: I'm so very pleased and so very happy you attended this very momentous occasion.

BETTER: I'm grateful for your attendance after all the practice we've done for this concert.

However, there are times when gushing can be appropriate, as in expressing great gratitude.

Regardless is a word. *Irregardless* is not.

Regardless of the strenuous practice sessions, Joann loved being on the hockey team.

Lots of students confuse *than* and *then*. *Than* is used for comparisons; *then* is used to denote a time or consequence:

Marlene got better grades than her friends.

If you study hard, then you will get better grades.

Sort of, kind of, and *like* make for mushy English if used indiscriminately. Exceptions are when one is creating colloquial speech quotes. It is all right to use *sort of* in the following sense:

Pat hated the sort of task where one just did the same thing hour after hour.

Many people confuse *lay* and *lie*. To lie is to recline. To lay is to put down. It's important to note the present, past and past participle:

lay, laid, laid
lie, lay, lain

Note that the past tense of *lie* is the same as the present tense of *lay*. Yes, we know English is confusing! But you can memorize these facts and sound intelligent for the rest of your life.

He had lain down on the cot for 15 minutes to rest before his presentation.

She had laid her car keys on the piano on her way into the den.

Effect means to cause. *Affect* means to move or influence.

The senators effected a change in the appropriations bill.

Bill was deeply affected by the new novel written by his favorite author.

Free gift is redundant. A gift is something given to one, and thus by definition is free.

Use *first, second* and *third* when enumerating a list, not *firstly, secondly, thirdly*.

First, you fasten your seat belt. Second, you adjust your mirror. Third, you check behind you.

Split infinitives are allowable, but they should be avoided unless one is trying to stress the adverb inserted into the infinitive, *e.g.,*

to hold
to tightly hold

But normally, one might say:

to work assiduously
rather than
to assiduously work.

Unique means *one of a kind.* Thus, you don't use modifiers like *most* or *very* to amplify that uniqueness.

RIGHT: Her prom dress was unique.

WRONG: Her prom dress was the most unique we'd ever seen.

It's important to use the proper construction for forms of the verb *to be*

I was, you were, he (she, it) was, we were, they were.
I am, you are, he (she, it) is, we are, they are.

There are some irregular verbs in English that give a lot of people fits. The following three columns show present, past and past participle:

| Present | Past | Past Participle |
		(used with have, had)
eat	ate	eaten
leave	left	left
drive	drove	driven
become	became	become
know	knew	known
fall	fell	fallen
make	made	made
fly	flew	flown
am	was	been
go	went	gone
do	did	done

The subjunctive is something that many people misuse. Normally the past tense operates as follows:

I was the captain of my ship.

If you are using the subjunctive, you are indicating a possibility or contingency, and the verb *was* is not used:

If I were the captain of my ship, I'd sail around the world for years and stop at every port of call.

Please note the use of *were.* You would never correctly say "I were the captain of the ship," but it belongs in the subjunctive. Some words that introduce a subjunctive are: *if, lest, unless.*

Commas are a commonly misused type of punctuation.

WRONG: "Those, who live by violence, often die by it."

RIGHT: *The Pirates of Penzance,* written by Gilbert and Sullivan, is one of their best-known works.

The first example needs no commas, but the second example does require you to set off the clause in the middle of the sentence.

When you have separate clauses, you generally put a comma between them. Also, if you have a dependent phrase, you usually must do the same thing; *e.g.,*

The shop, which had been at that site for fifty years, had repaired bicycles for several generations of riders.

Schools are excellent at lots of tasks, but one thing that I think they do less well is teaching the difference between short-term and long-term memorization.

In general, to make the possessive, you add an apostrophe, then an *s:*

Brandy's doll
Da Vinci's drawings
Weiss's book
Bob's bicycle the movie's theme my life's joy

but there are no apostrophes in these possessives: *its, hers, his, yours, ours, theirs.* You say "It was her book," but you can also say "It was hers." Other examples:

It was his.
It was ours.

It was theirs.
It was yours.

A common error is putting an apostrophe in the word *its*, as a possessive. An apostrophe indicates that a letter has been left out: *it's* means *it is*. Thus, you might say,

It's astonishing that a cat always lands on its feet.

You see above two different uses with the same pronunciation.

Double negatives are not allowed, in general. Two negatives make a positive.

We weren't doing no harm to the dogs. (This literally means, "We were doing harm to the dogs.")

Exceptions: if you're writing dialogue and trying to capture the tone of a character, you are allowed to say things like:

Jed spat, shuffled, and finally said, "Aw, we wasn't doing nobody no harm."

Run-on sentences are bad, and they sound rather manic, as though someone isn't calm enough to catch a breath:

First you said you would do this and that then you broke your promise I don't know why I trusted you you weren't fair with me I am so angry I could pop a vein why didn't you tell me the truth?

When someone writes this way, we have a tendency to duck.

Sentences begin with a capital letter (unless you're e.e. cummings, the poet known for using lower-case when capitals would normally prevail).

Whenever he spied himself in a mirror, he flinched.

Proper names start with a capital, unless you're writing about, say, e.e. cummings. Thus, The United States, the University of Virginia, Hawaii,

Italy, Albert Schweitzer, Sonny and Cher, Bill Clinton, Senator Warner. If you are referring to a senator, you can say

> The senator said, off the record, that he supported the arms reduction bill.

But when the title is accompanied by the name, you capitalize:

> Senator Rodomontade opposed the Arms Reduction Act (ARA).

Sometimes (not often), there may be cause to end a sentence with four dots, perhaps when someone is being wistful, or something is unresolved or left hanging.

> Sharon sighed. She was exhausted this evening. Maybe tomorrow, there'd be another opportunity . . . .

Italics or underlining can be overused. But each has a place: when using foreign words, when listing titles, when referring to a word, or when stressing something.

> She had a certain *je ne sais quoi.* (French for *I don't know what.*)

> Marlon watched the final episode of *Friends* with his friends.

> The word *banshee* is of Irish and Gaelic origin.

> His heart went *ba-dum, ba-dum, BA-DUM.*

As you practice, you'll get better at all of this. The grammar worksheet that follows can help enormously.

Grammar Worksheet

Part 1

The sentences below test correctness of expression. You must change (or keep the same) the underlined part of the sentence.

1. Despite living next door to each other, Wendy and <u>Bill, who can be argumentative, apparently have no use</u> for one another, and they take every opportunity to avoid socializing.

    A. Bill, who could be argumentative, apparently has no use
    B. Bill, argumentative, apparently has no use
    C. Bill apparently have no use, on account of his argumentativeness,
    D. No change

2. Correct usage of grammar, spelling and punctuation <u>rules are something</u> that every student should have.

    A. rules is something
    B. rules are anything
    C. rules are nothing
    D. No change

3. "Please tell me; I wish <u>to have known</u> your problems," said the counselor.

    A. I will know
    B. you-all could tell me
    C. to know
    D. No change

4. Nancy went to the store to buy the ingredients <u>for enchiladas, knowing we were all</u> hungrily awaiting her return.

   A. that we all craved,
   B. since she knew that we were all
   C. that were all
   D. No change

5. Alice Johnson is <u>the one person who we suspect will receive</u> a full scholarship.

   A. the one person whom we suspect will receive
   B. the one person who will receive
   C. the only person who can receive
   D. No change

6. <u>Bob and myself are going</u> to catch a bus to the concert.

   A. Bob and myself went
   B. Bob and myself would go
   C. Bob and I are going
   D. No change

7. <u>A person wise beyond her years, Amy's</u> teachers gave her the philosophy award.

   A. Since Amy was a person wise beyond her years, her
   B. Being wise beyond her years, Amy's
   C. Wise beyond her years, Amy was thrilled when her
   D. No change

8. By regular mail, <u>by parcel mail or telegraph,</u> the message was delivered.

   A. by telegraph or parcel mail
   B. by parcel mail or by telegraph
   C. parcel mail and telegraph
   D. No change

9. First, Mr. Calabasas railed against the establishment, <u>and then he gnashes his teeth.</u>

A. and his teeth he gnashes.
B. before he gets into teeth-gnashing.
C. and then he gnashed his teeth.
D. No change

10. Alice divided the piece of chocolate cake <u>between the three girls who she was babysitting.</u>

    A. between the three girls whom she was babysitting.
    B. among the three girls who she was babysitting.
    C. among the three girls whom she was babysitting.
    D. No change

11. <u>Can I please have</u> another piece of apple pie?

    A. May I please have
    B. Can I please get
    C. Gimme
    D. No change

12. <u>The data contradict the hypothesis</u> that Al and Maria had carefully devised for their biology project.

    A. The data contradicts the hypothesis
    B. The data contradict the hypotheses
    C. No change
    D. The data provides a contradiction to the hypothesis

13. I don't know <u>why, but we have less students</u> in the 7:30 class than in the 8:45 class.

    A. why, but there are less students
    B. why, but there have been fewer students
    C. why, but we have fewer students
    D. No change

14. Manny, <u>Pete, Bob and Bill, etc., were going</u> to the park on Sunday afternoon.

    A. Pete, Bob, Bill, etc., were going
    B. Pete, Bob, Bill, et cetera, were going

C. Pete, Bob, Bill, et al. were going
D. No change

15. <u>The enormity of the pay raises excited</u> the team.

    A. The huge size of the pay raises excited
    B. The enormitude of the pay raises excited
    C. The pay raises were so big that they greatly excited
    D. No change

16. <u>Can Maria hit the baseball further than</u> Ellen or Natalie?

    A. May Maria hit the baseball further than
    B. Can Maria hit the baseball as far as
    C. Can Maria hit the baseball farther than
    D. No change

17. "<u>Irregardless of how you feel, you had</u> no business skipping work today," said Bob's boss in disgust.

    A. Irregardless of how you might feel, you have
    B. Regardless of how you feel, you had
    C. Regardless of how you feel, I had
    D. No change

18. <u>Ryan was immensely effected by the letters he found</u> in a big box in the basement.

    A. The affect on Ryan was immense from the letters he found
    B. Ryan was immensely effected by the letters found
    C. Ryan was immensely affected by the letters he found
    D. No change

19. <u>I wanted to quickly clean out my desk</u> and get out of there.

    A. Quickly, I wanted to clean out my desk
    B. I wanted to clean out my desk quickly
    C. I wanted to clean out, quickly, my desk
    D. No change

20. The moment I saw her, <u>I knew that she was the most unique person I've ever met.</u>

    A. I knew that she was unique.
    B. I know that she is the most unique person I could ever meet.
    C. I said, "Wow, she is the most unique person I've ever met."
    D. No change

21. <u>If I were to start my own business,</u> I think I would be very successful.

    A. If I was to start my own business
    B. If a business were to be started by me
    C. If a business was to be started by me
    D. No change

22. First the conductor <u>dropped his baton when he stooped to pick it up</u> he stumbled badly.

    A. dropped his baton, secondly when he stooped to pick it up,
    B. dropped his baton, and then, when he stooped to pick it up
    C. dropped his baton. He stooped. To pick it up
    D. No change

23. Everyone of our <u>guests bring</u> either a casserole or a dessert.

    A. guest brings
    B. guests brings
    C. guest bring
    D. No change

24. She could <u>neither make her bed nor tie</u> her shoes.

    A. neither make her bed or tie
    B. either make her bed or tie
    C. either make her bed nor tie
    D. No change

25. <u>His comments inferred that I had</u> cheated.

    A. His comments implied that I have
    B. His comments implied that I had

C. His comments infer that I have

D. No change

26. Andie all ways participated in as many extracurricular activities as possible.

    A. In all ways possible, Andie participated

    B. All ways, Andie participated

    C. Andie always participated

    D. No change

27. You seem disinterested in hearing about my project for the science fair.

    A. I hope you are interested in hearing about

    B. It's interesting to hear about

    C. You seem uninterested in hearing about

    D. No change

28. She said she'd like to do farther research on that area of biology.

    A. She said she'd like to do further research

    B. She'd like to do farther research

    C. She said she'd like to do research farther

    D. No change

29. She was sort of ungruntled after she got her low grade in World History I.

    A. was rather ungruntled when she got

    B. was somewhat disgruntled after she got

    C. was sort of ungruntled when getting back

    D. No change

30. Hey, look at my free gift from the hardware store!

    A. Hey, get a load of my free gift

    B. Hey, look at my cool gift

    C. Hey, they gave me this gift freely

    D. No change

31. First, I want you to sit and listen to the instructions. <u>Second, I hope you'll feel free to ask questions after I've finished.</u>

    A. Secondly, I hope you'll feel free to ask questions after I've finished.
    B. Secondly, ask questions when I'm done.
    C. Next on my list, I hope you'll feel free to ask questions after I've finished.
    D. No change

32. <u>We tried to effect a change in the school policies, but it was</u> awkward for us to feel like rebels against the administration.

    A. We tried to affect changes in the school policy, but it was
    B. We tried changing the effect of the school policies, but it was
    C. We changed school policies effectively, but it was
    D. No change

33. <u>The Senator started his speech by saying that</u> he was sorry to have been late.

    A. The Senator starts his speech by saying that
    B. The senator started his speech by saying that
    C. The senator has started his speeches by saying that
    D. No change

Part 2

The sentences below test grammar, usage, punctuation, etc. Some are correct as written, and others have one error apiece. Choose E if you think the sentence is correct.

34. The net weights of the curio boxes, crafted from bamboo and <u>lacquer, is not the same</u> from item to item.

    A. lacquer, are not the same
    B. lacquers, are not the same
    C. lacquer is not the same
    D. No change

35. When it comes to charities, <u>I donate to whoever I want to support.</u>

    A. I donate whoever I want to support.
    B. I donate to who I want to support.
    C. I donate to whomever I want to support.
    D. No change

36. <u>Do you think that Henry and her</u> will be able to catch the 5:00 train to New York?

    A. Do you think Henry and her
    B. Do you think Henry and she
    C. Do you think Henry and she herself
    D. No change

37. "Who's there" called the thin voice. <u>"It's I," I replied.</u>

    A. "It's me, "I replied.
    B. "It's I," I reply.
    C. "It's me," I reply.
    D. No change

38. <u>Us football players are unusually tense</u> this evening before our big game against Twin Rivers High School.

    A. Football players are unusually tense
    B. We football players are unusually tense
    C. Us football players are usually tense
    D. No change

39. <u>Whomever you think promised you this job,</u> you're mistaken.

    A. Whoever you think promised you this job
    B. Whomsoever you think promised you this job
    C. Who you think promised you this job
    D. No change

40. <u>After I come home from school, I just need to lay down on the couch</u> for a few minutes before I tackle my homework.

    A. After I come home from school, I just need to lay on the couch
    B. After I leave school, I need to lay down on the couch

C. After I come home from school, I just need to lie down on the couch

D. No change

41. <u>Patti and Jack was wrong to protest</u> the decision of the Student Association without having their facts straight.

    A. Patti and Jack, they were wrong to protest

    B. Patti and Jack were wrong to protest

    C. First Patti, then Jack, was wrong to protest

    D. No change

42. After I went to Europe, I <u>got hungry just thinking about all the great food I had ate,</u> especially in Italy.

    A. got hungry and thought about all the great food I ate

    B. got hungry just thinking about all the great food I had eaten

    C. got hungry whenever I thought about all the great food that had been eaten

    D. No change

43. <u>"Its time to go,"</u> called my sister.

    A. It's time to go

    B. Its time has gone

    C. It's time. Go.

    D. No change.

44. The dog <u>stepped carefully on its injured paw and tried</u> to avoid putting any pressure on it.

    A. stepped, on its injured paw, and tried carefully

    B. stepped careful-like on it's injured paw and tried

    C. stepped carefully on it's injured paw, which tried

    D. No change

45. <u>Eric mowed the lawn. Taking care to clean up all the cuttings.</u>

    A. As Eric mowed the lawn, he took care to clean up all the cuttings.

    B. Eric mowed the lawn, took care in cleaning up all the cuttings.

    C. Taking care to clean up all the cuttings, Eric mowed the lawn.

    D. No change

46. <u>Monty loved fast food, he was also fond of Chinese food,</u> especially wonton soup.

    A. Monty loved fast food; he was also fond of Chinese food
    B. Monty, loving fast foods, also were fond of Chinese food
    C. Loving fast food, fond of Chinese food, Monty ate, and liked
    D. No change

47. I want you to get the <u>following items at the store, eggs, cereal, milk, and some flowers</u> for the table.

    A. following items at the store. Eggs, cereal, milk, and some flowers
    B. following: items at the store (eggs, cereal, milk, and some flowers)
    C. following items at the store: eggs, cereal, milk and some flowers
    D. No change

48. Her hairdo <u>as well as her dress was</u> perfect.

    A. and her dress was
    B. as well as her dress were
    C. on top of her dress could not have been more
    D. No change

49. <u>Will Betsy or her be hired</u> by the pool for a summer lifeguarding job?

    A. Will Betsy or herself be hired
    B. Will her or Betsy be hired
    C. Will Betsy or she be hired
    D. No change

50. "Sir," he said in an irritated voice. <u>"Who are you addressing?"</u>

    A. Whom are you addressing
    B. Who is you addressing
    C. Who is addressing me
    D. No change

51. <u>Dishonesty and sloppiness May could not stand.</u>

    A. Dishonest and sloppy, May could not stand.
    B. Dishonesty, sloppiness, May can't stand.

C. Dishonest sloppiness, May couldn't stand.
D. No change

52. <u>The mass media is always distorting things, as far as</u> my uncle is concerned.

A. Distorting things, the mass media always did, as far as
B. The mass medium is always distorting things, as far as
C. The mass media are always distorting things, as far as
D. No change

53. <u>After practicing so much, the concert went perfectly for Ellen.</u>

A. After she practices so much, the concert went perfectly for Ellen.
B. After she practiced so much, the concert went perfectly for Ellen.
C. Ellen was glad she practiced so much. The concert went perfect.
D. No change

54. <u>I have lain the jacket on the bed, and you can get it</u> whenever you're ready.

A. I have lain on the bed in the jacket, and you can get it
B. I have laid on the bed the jacket, and you can get it
C. I have laid the jacket on the bed, and you can get it
D. No change

55. <u>He had left the left</u> side of the ocean liner.

A. He left the
B. He had left the
C. He can leave the left
D. No change

56. <u>One time, Pete and Jack flown to Antarctica, which was</u> reachable only a few months of the year

A. One time, Pete and Jack flew to Antarctica, which was
B. One-time Pete and Jack flew to Antarctica,
C. Pete and Jack has flown one time to Antarctica, which was
D. No change

57. <u>I've fallen for this person, even though</u> I don't know him that well.

    A. I am falling on this person, even though
    B. I fall for this person, even though
    C. I've fell for this person, though
    D. No change

58. <u>You done well when you helped</u> those people get settled in their new home.

    A. You do well when you helped
    B. Doing well, you help
    C. You did well when you helped
    D. No change

59. <u>The store had repaired bikes for 70 years for thousands of riders at that location.</u>

    A. At that location for 70 years, the store had repaired bikes for thousands of riders.
    B. At that location for years, the store had repaired bikes for 70,000 riders.
    C. The store, for 70 years, had repaired bikes at that location for thousands of riders.
    D. No change

60. <u>"Its no skin off of my teeth,"</u> said Dwayne.

    A. Its skin is off my teeth
    B. It's no skin off my teeth
    C. My teeth are skinny
    D. No change

61. <u>Your's is the best test prep book I've ever used.</u>

    A. Your's is the very best test prep book I've ever used.
    B. Yours is the best test prep book I've ever used.
    C. Of all the test prep books I've ever used, your's is the best.
    D. No change

62. I cant see paying that much for insurance.

    A. I am having trouble seeing why your paying
    B. I can't see paying
    C. I can't see how to pay
    D. No change

63. Do you like Rembrandts paintings?

    A. see Rembrandts paintings
    B. liken this to Rembrandts paintings
    C. like Rembrandt's paintings
    D. No change

64. Weisses motorcycle was in the shop more than out.

    A. Weisses motorcycles were in the shop more than out.
    B. Weiss's motorcycles was in the shop more than out.
    C. Weiss's motorcycle was in the shop more than out.
    D. No change

65. Mary tried the door. it wouldn't open, so she went back to the car.

    A. Mary tried the door. It wouldn't open, so she
    B. Trying the door, but finding it won't open, Mary
    C. Mary tried the door, wouldn't open, so she
    D. No change

Part 3

Some problems on the SAT may have the format of a first draft of an essay. Your job is to figure out what changes might be made to improve the darn thing. Here's an example. The sentences are numbered so we can refer to them later:

(1) The study of etymology (which is the study of word derivations and families) is really, really fascinating. (2) Many of our common names of a person derives from such common professions as barrelmaker (Cooper), one who forges metal with a hammer (Smith), housebuilder (Carpenter), cook (Cook!), or Taylor or Miller. (3) Common colors (White, Brown, Black) too. (4) The translations of those into other language gives us names like Bianca (white),

Weiss (white), Schwartz (black), or Midori (green). (5) The same name might have slightly different permutations from languages to languages. John, Juan, Jean, Ivan, Ian, Ewan, and Yanni really the same name. (6) There are lots of different forms of "the son of," from the most obvious in English, Jackson, Peterson, etc., to forms in other languages ibn, ben, ovich, owicz, ewicz, Mac-, Mc-, ete. (7) Names deriving from physical characteristics: Small, Little, Short, Tall were also common. (8) Location names popped up: Hill, Rivers, etc. (9) Since there were not standardized spelling, you may see variants of a common name: Smith, Smithe, Smyth, Smythe; or Cooper, Kuper, Kuiper, Cuper. (10) When you start to think etymological-like, you can see a lot of common words whose meaning become obvious to you, in names and elsewhere. (11) An example might be the word *kneel*, which means *to get down on one's knees*. (12) It's simply the word *knee* with a big old *L* on the end. (13) Another example might be the word *parasol*, meaning, literally, *to ward off the sun*. (14) That's exactly its use, so the derivation of the word tells you it's meaning.

66. In sentence (1), what is the best way of expressing the thought?

    A. The study of etymology is fascinating. Etymology is the study of word derivations and families.
    B. Etymology is the study of word derivations and families. The study of etymology is fascinating.
    C. The study of etymology (which is the study of word derivations and families) is fascinating.
    D. Etymology, which is the study of word derivations and families, is fascinating.

67. In sentence (2), what is the best way of expressing the thought?

    A. People's names often derive from professions. Barrel-maker (Cooper), metal-forger (Smith), housebuilder (Carpenter), cook (Cook!), or Taylor or Miller.
    B. Professions are a common source of people's names. Some examples are: barrel-maker (Cooper), metal-forger (Smith), housebuilder (Carpenter), cook (Cook!), or Taylor or Miller.
    C. Peoples' names come from professions commonly. Examples? Barrel-maker (Cooper), metal-forger (Smith), housebuilder (Carpenter), cook (Cook!), or Taylor or Miller.

D. Many of our common people names derive from such common professions as barrel-maker (Cooper), one who forges metal with a hammer (Smith), housebuild (Carpenter), cook (Cook!), or Taylor or Miller.

68. Sentence (3) can be improved. Pick the best way.

A. Common colors (White, Brown, Black) too.
B. Some names come from colors (White, Brown, Black).
C. Colors is the source of some names (White, Brown, Black).
D. White, Brown, Black are common colors.

69. How might one better tie in sentence (4) with sentence (3)?

A. One also finds "color" names in other languages; for instance, Bianca (white), Weiss (white), Schwartz (black), or Midori (green).
B. The translations of the latter into other languages gives us names like Bianca (white), Weiss (white), Schwartz (black), or Midori (green).
C. Translations of colors can give us names like Bianca (white), Weiss (white), Schwartz (black), or Midori (green).
D. Bianca (white), Weiss (white), Schwartz (black), or Midori (green).

70. How would you write Sentence 5?

A. The same name might have slightly different permutations from language to language; for instance, John, Juan, Jean, Ivan, Ian, Ewan, and Yanni are all forms of the same name.
B. From language to language, we have different versions: *e.g.,* John, Juan, Jean, Ivan, Ian, Ewan, and Yanni. These are all forms of the same name.
C. John, Juan, Jean, Ivan, Ian, Ewan, and Yanni. What do these have in common? They're all the same name, different languages.
D. Different languages capture the same names. For instance, John, Juan, Jean, Ivan, Ian, Ewan, and Yanni.

71. Edit sentence (6) and insert correct punctuation:

A. Another instance of this phenomenon is that there are lots of different forms of "the son of," from the most obvious in English:

Jackson, Peterson, etc., to forms in other languages: ibn, ben, ovich, owicz, ewicz, Mac-, Mc-, etc.

B. Likewise, there are lots of different forms of "the son of," from the most obvious in English: Jackson, Peterson, etc., to forms in other languages: ibn, ben, ovich, owicz, ewicz, Mac-, Mc-, etc.

C. Another instance of this phenomenon is that there are lots of different forms of "the son of." Besides the obvious—son (in Jackson, Peterson, etc.), there are the following in other languages: ibn, ben, ovich, owicz, ewicz, Mac-, Mc-, etc.

D. Another instance of this phenomenon is that there are lots of different forms meaning the son of. Besides the obvious-son (in Jackson, Peterson, etc.), there are the following in other languages: ibn, ben, ovich, ewicz, Mac-, Mc-, etc.

72. How might you edit (7) and (8)?

A. Some names derive from physical characteristics (Small, Little, Short, Tall), and others came from locations (Hill, Rivers).

B. Names deriving from physical characteristics: Small, Little, Short, Tall were also common. Location names popped up: Hill, Rivers, etc.

C. Physical character and location figured prominently. Small, Little, Short, Tall, Hill, Rivers all are names.

D. Small, Little, Short, Tall, Hill, Rivers all come from locations or physical characteristics.

73. Does sentence (9) need to be altered? If so, pick a choice below.

A. Because people couldn't spell the same, names changed: Smith, Smithe, Smyth, Smythe; or Cooper, Kuper, Kuiper, Cuper.

B. Since there was not standardized spelling, you may see variants of a common name: Smith, Smithe, Smyth, Smythe; or Cooper, Kuper, Kuiper, Cuper.

C. Smith, Smithe, Smyth, Smythe; or Cooper, Kuper, Kuiper, Cuper are all spellings of the same two names.

D. One might wonder why Smith, Smithe, Smyth, Smythe; or Cooper, Kuper, Kuiper, Cuper are all different; hundreds of years ago, the changes happened.

74. Put sentences (10) through (12) into better form.

A. When you start to think etymologically, you can notice a lot of common words whose meanings become obvious to you, in names and elsewhere. An example might be the word *kneel,* which means *to get down on one's knees.* It's simply the word *knee* with an L on the end.

B. Thinking in etymologies, one notices common words suddenly reveal their meanings. For example, kneel, *to get down on one's knees.* It's simply the word *knee* with an L on the end.

C. When one starts to think etymologically, you can notice a lot of common words whose meanings become obvious to you, in names and elsewhere. An example might be the word *kneel,* which means *to get down on one's knees;* it's simply the word *knee* with an L on the end.

D. When one starts to think etymologically, one can notice a lot of common words whose meanings become obvious, in names and elsewhere. An example is the word *kneel,* which means *to get down on one's knees;* it's simply the word *knee* with an L on the end.

75. Combine sentences (13) and (14) more effectively.

A. Another example might be the word *parasol,* meaning, literally, *to ward off the sun.* That's exactly what it's used for, so the derivation of the word tells you its meaning.

B. Another example is the word *parasol,* meaning, literally, *to ward off the sun.* That's exactly what a parasol is used for, so the derivation of the word tells one its meaning.

C. Parasol means to ward off the sun. Etymology tells the meaning.

D. You see the same phenomenon in the word "parasol." "Parasol" means "to ward off the sun." So you get the etymology and the meaning all in one.

Part 4

Note: Some questions show formats that may not occur exactly in these ways on the current test. However, they are highly valuable and instructive questions for students as exercises to build strong grammatical and writing skills. So please do go through all of them extensively and repeatedly in order to learn material that will stand you in good stead during the real test.

76. Once <u>they overcame</u> their shyness, Madeleine <u>and her</u>
             A   B

were <u>willing to try</u> hard to get a part in the school play.
              C

<u>No mistake.</u>
    D

77. <u>Anyways,</u> Peter and Lynn <u>were afraid</u> <u>to look</u> at their grades,
    A   B   C

despite the fact that <u>t</u>hey were both sure they'd aced the test.

<u>No mistake.</u>
    D

78. <u>If anybody</u> <u>was</u> to sneeze, <u>it would totally ruin</u>
    A   B   C

the peacefulness of the pageant. <u>No mistake.</u>
                                          D

79. The game <u>was irretrievably</u> lost; <u>even if everything went</u>
                   A   B

right, <u>there was simply no way in which</u> our team
                      C

could rescue itself from the debacle of the previous 3 quarters.

<u>No mistake.</u>
    D

80. <u>He thought</u> the job was a <u>piece of pie;</u> therefore, he
    A   B

<u>didn't even bother</u> to try very much. <u>No mistake.</u>
      C   D

Grammar Worksheet Answers

And Explanations

1. D (Wendy and Bill form a plural subject, so a plural verb is required.)

2. A (*Usage* is the subject, so a singular verb is needed.)

3. C (the correct format is the simplest, *to know.*)

4. B (As written, the enchiladas are aware that *we were all hungrily awaiting her return.*)

5. D (Correct as written. Substitute *she* for *who* and switch the phrasing around and you get *we suspect she will receive*, with *she* being the subject of *will receive.*)

6. C (*I* instead of *myself* is a proper subject.)

7. A (As written, the sentence is saying that Amy's teachers are a person wise beyond her years, and of course that isn't what the sentence is supposed to say.)

8. B (You want to put *by* in front of all three methods, or only in front of the first one.)

9. C (Both clauses need to have the same verb tense.)

10. C (When you have two people, you divide something *between* them. When there are three or more people, you divide *among* them.)

11. A (When asking permission, you want to use "May I . . . .")

12. D (Data are facts, so a plural verb is needed. The singular of *data* is *datum*.)

13. C (You could say *We are learning less today*, but you'd say *I have fewer headaches. Less* modifies a measurable quantity, but *fewer* modifies something that you count individually. So you could have fewer dollars or less money.)

14. C (*Etc.* means *and other things. Et al.* means *and other people.*)

15. A (*Enormity* means *extreme wickedness*, not *something huge.*)

16. C (*Farther* is the word you want to describe physical distance when you're hitting a baseball.)

17. B (*Irregardless* is not a word. *Regardless* is the correct word.)

18. C (The way the sentence is written, it says that Ryan was caused by the letters he found. *Affected* is correct.)

19. B (Split infinitives are usually not acceptable.)

20. A (*Unique* means *one of a kind*. So you don't ever modify with *most* or *very.*)

21. D (Correct as written.)

22. C (Run-on sentences are incorrect. They can be corrected in a variety of ways through adding punctuation or words like *and, but*, etc. to connect clauses.)

23. B (*Everyone* is the subject. It requires a singular verb.)

24. D (Correct as written.)

25. B (The comments imply. Whoever is listening would infer or derive meaning from them.)

26. C (You might say that all ways of learning are equally valid. But if you are trying to say that something happens all the time, *always* is the word used.)

27. C (*Uninterested* denotes *not having a desire to do something*. *Disinterested* means *not having a preference*.)

28. A (You want *further*, because it means *more of something*. *Farther* is used for physical distance. You travel farther to a wedding. You study a subject further.

29. B (The correct word is *disgruntled*. *Ungruntled* is not a word. If you're disgruntled, you're unhappy or dissatisfied. No matter how happy you are, you never get to be gruntled, since that's not a word. Go figure!)

30. B (Despite decades of advertising copy to the contrary, a gift is by definition free, so it's redundant and incorrect to say *free gift*.)

31. D (Correct as written.)

32. D (*Effect* brings *to cause or bring about*, so this is the right choice.)

33. B (You should only capitalize the word *senator* when it is followed by the name of the senator, *e.g.*, "Senator Freeman submitted the bill that recommended extending services to former foster children.")

34. A (The word *weights* is the subject, so a plural verb is required.)

35. C (You need the objective form after the word *to*. *Whomever* is proper.)

36. B (The words *Henry and she* are the plural subject, so a plural verb is needed.)

37. D (Even though people colloquially say, "It's me," the form in the sentence is correct.)

38. B (Leave out the words *football players*, and you'll see that it is correct to say *We are . . . .*)

39. A (Switch the sentence around in A. and substitute *he* or *she* for *whoever*, and you get *you think she promised you . . .* which is correct.)

40. C (You lay your backpack down on the table. You lie down on the couch.)

41. B (Plural subject, plural verb.)

42. B (It's either *I ate* or *I had eaten.*)

43. A (*It's* means *it is*. *Its* is a possessive word form meaning *belonging to something.*)

44. D (No problem here in the original.)

45. A (*Taking . . . cuttings* is not a full-fledged sentence. It needs to be merged with *Eric . . . lawn.*)

46. A (This is a run-on sentence. It can be divided into two clauses separated by a semicolon.)

47. C (This screams for a colon. Everything after the colon is a list of specifics that are needed from the store.)

48. D (If this said *Her hairdo and her dress,* we would need a plural vere. *As well as* still requires the singular.

49. C (*She* is the subjective form.)

50. A (*Whom* is the subjective form. Substitute *him* for *whom* and switch the sentence order around and you get *you are addressing him.*)

51. D (This is ok. It's stressing those things that May can't tolerate.)

52. C (The word *media* is plural. It requires a plural verb.)

53. B (As written, the sentence says that the concert practiced so much. But Ellen is really the one who practiced.)

54. C (You have lain on the bed. But you have laid the jacket on the bed.)

55. D (It would be better to use the word *port* for left side of the boat, so you don't have such a stupid-sounding sentence!)

56. A (You could say *had flown* or just *flew.*)

57. D (This is fine.)

58. C (The form of *do* that you want here is *did*.)

59. A (You want to change the order of things so that it reads more smoothly. Also it's the store that is at that location, not the riders, except at the moment when they're having their bikes repaired.)

60. B (*Off* is sufficient.)

61. B (The correct possessive form is *yours*, with no apostrophe. This is similar to what you do with *its*, the possessive, which has no apostrophe.)

62. B (Here you need the apostrophe for *can't*.)

63. C (Another apostrophe needed for the possessive. *Rembrandt's* is right.)

64. C (*Weisses* is the plural. You need the possessive.)

65. A (You need a capital *I* at the beginning of the second sentence unless you are e.e. cummings.)

66. D (*Etymology* means *the study of word derivations and families*. So you don't repeat the words *the study of.*)

67. B (This is a far less clunky expression of the ideas, and it eliminates the incorrect singular verb.)

68. B (We had a sentence fragment and turned it into a legitimate sentence.

69. A (When you start playing with sentences, you want to try different things to see what sounds better. This is not a perfect science, or a rigid set of rules. You might create a wholly different sentence, but the idea is to clarify the thought and express it grammatically, eliminating errors like the vague *those* and singular word *language*.)

70. A (You don't need the plural *languages*. And the second phrase lacks a verb.)

71. D (*Jackson, Peterson* needs to be set off as examples. Ditto for *ibn, . . . etc*.)

72. A (Sections 7 and 8 above look more like someone's hastily written notes. We need to combine them into a sentence that gracefully merges the two sources of names.)

73. B (You need to eliminate the plural verb *were.*)

74. D. (*Etymological-like* changes to *etymologically. Big old L* is too folksy for this essay. The last two sentences can be better merged into one thought rather than being separated.)

75. B (*It's* should be *its. Tells one* is better than *tells you.*)

76. B (*and she* is the correct wording, since this requires the subjective form).

77. A (*Anyway* is the word you want.)

78. B (The subjunctive requires *were.*)

79. D (Nothing is grammatically incorrect here.)

80. B (The expression is *easy as pie* or *piece of cake.*)

Essay Writing

This part of the book addresses essay writing in general and two usages in particular: the essays that you'll write for college and the essay on the SAT. Review the grammar material in Section II and do the grammar worksheets repeatedly.

Your Writing Sample on the SAT

You will find that writing, like anything in life, gets easier the more you do it. It's a skill, and skills are learnable. Writing also gets easier if you read more, especially if the reading you choose is of literary quality.

During the SAT you will be asked to take a topic and write a short essay. If you practice writing some essays before that day, you'll get better at the task. Also, get used to going back over what you write and correcting things two, three, four times. You won't have time to do much correcting during the SAT, but if you are used to exercising an eagle eye for mistakes, you'll make fewer of them, and correct them more swiftly.

You probably won't have the chance to write more than 3 - 7 paragraphs. In your booklet, you'll want to scribble quickly ideas of what you'll write, as in the sample below. Then it will be important to organize your thoughts and come up with cogent, clear examples from literature, your own life, or elsewhere. Giving examples goes a long way toward bringing a passage alive, and you will do well not to bore your readers, who are judging a lot of essays. Putting them to sleep is a no-no!

A lot of students tend to write run-on paragraphs: a wall of prose, as some call it. For most people, staring at super-long paragraphs is exhausting. Try to break up longer paragraphs into smaller units when appropriate.

When you write, be yourself. Your job is not to emulate Shakespeare or Hemingway, though it can be an interesting practical exercise to imitate the style of a well-known writer. But in general, it's a good idea to be plain-spoken and to write simply and clearly.

During the SAT you won't have time to rewrite, but when you write essays, papers and so forth at home, it's a good idea to edit and rewrite, to go back at intervals and see whether what you meant to say is, in fact, what you *did* say.

Don't use vocabulary to show off. I know it's tempting, especially if you've gone to the trouble of learning all the vocabulary in this book. But the point of knowing vocabulary isn't to be pretentious; it's to speak and write with a degree of precision not possible with a smaller vocabulary, to think more clearly, and to strengthen reading skills.

Example Essay Question and Response

Let's walk through the process of a sample essay question.

Topic: Discuss pros and cons of taxes in the United States.

Strategy: Scribble notes quickly, since you only have a short time to develop a finished essay. Make pros and cons columns in your test booklet, making sure that you write fairly small so that you have room for everything.

Sample pros:

1. Taxes pay for public services, roads, infrastructure, welfare systems.

2. Taxes provide a systematic way of collecting revenues from the public.

3. Tax structure encourages philanthropy, since charitable giving is tax deductible.

4. Our tax structure takes a lot less money from individuals than happens in many other countries.

Sample cons:

1. Taxes take money that could be invested by individuals.

2. Tax structures are often inequitable, with big corporations paying little and the middle class paying a lot.

3. Government sometimes wastes money.

4. Taxes penalize people for innovation and therefore stymie/stifle creativity.

Now develop an introductory statement and start writing. When you have expressed the core ideas, it's a good idea to end with a paragraph that wraps things up.

The Finished Example Essay
(which took under 20 minutes from start to finish, including the sample pros and cons)

It is often said that only two things in life are certain: death and taxes. While people have to be philosophical about their inability to avoid death in the long run, the subject of taxes evokes strong mixed feelings among citizens.

Those who decry taxes point out that taxes stifle creativity by penalizing those with entrepreneurial or inventive ideas by taking away some of the reward, and thus some of the incentive to create. Yet the U.S. has a relatively low taxation rate compared with, say, England and other European countries. And taxes must not really discourage creativity very much, since we have a high rate of innovation in American industry and society.

Others point out that tax structures are often inequitable, with big corporations paying relatively little and the middle class paying a lot. Certainly, one can debate that the tax structure ought to be altered to make it work better and make corporations pay their fair share, but that is not an indictment of taxes themselves.

Taxes do take some money that individuals could have spent or invested, but they also provide invaluable services and essential infrastructure (bridges, roads, hospitals, libraries, and safety nets for the elderly, poor and sick) in the society, neither of which can most individuals create on their own. While those who deride taxes complain about the government taking "their" money, the reality is that there is real value created with our tax dollars, and few of the complainers would like to function without the services paid for by taxes. Furthermore, the Internal Revenue Service provides a systematic method for collecting revenues from the society.

Sometimes we read of wastefulness in using tax revenue, and no one should be complacent about such carelessness or corruption. But it would be wrong to throw out the baby with the bath water in this case.

We need stringent controls on expenditures, but most money is budgeted judiciously to create infrastructure and pay for services, and we cannot abolish the need to pay for those important items.

One further plus of taxes is that the tax code encourages philanthropy, since charitable giving is tax-deductible. Many wonderful organizations are able to secure donations and accomplish important work in the society because of this aspect of tax law.

Taxes are a fact of life. Unlike death, which appears to confer no advantages to the person tagged by it, taxes provide a quality of life that is enviable, even to those who gripe about the very existence of those taxes.

College Application Essays

The information on essay writing in the book is meant to help you not only with the SAT essay, but with essays required for college applications. It's important that you not write something at the last minute and just slap it together. Start early, and look at it over and over again. Ask an English teacher, counselor or parent to review it for you and make suggestions.

Try to think of something about yourself that will make colleges think more highly of you, and that they wouldn't otherwise know. This is not a place to reiterate your extra-curricular activities list. It's not a place to confess that you're a slob and a procrastinator! It's a place to shed a favorable light on yourself. Maybe you can discuss a difficulty you've overcome, an experience that changed your attitude, or a special family member or friend. Remember that whatever you write about, you must answer the question asked. I've seen many otherwise excellent essays which don't answer the question given!

Make sure you don't have a logical inconsistency in your essay. One example that sticks in my mind: A student wrote an essay about how his father had told him to be proud of his first name because it had also belonged to his father and grandfather from another country. But the problem was that while he insisted he'd learned to take pride in his heritage via his name, the student had changed his name to something very modern. The name change didn't fit with the claim that he was proud of his original name!

It's okay to be self-deprecating a bit, but not okay to trash yourself. One brilliant student wrote an essay about how horribly she procrastinated and how poor her work habits were. It was such a negative essay that I urged her to go back to the drawing board. Neither is it a good idea to boast uncontrollably. Find a middle ground.

Write about what you know. Even if you are not a strong writer today, please don't feel as though that's your permanent fate. You can get much better with practice.

Sometimes people don't know how to get started in writing an essay and in organizing material for the college application. One thing that helps enormously is to write things down, either on paper or on your computer if you have one.

Create a file with all your activities and awards. List anything you remember, including years of involvement, officer positions and chairmanships, both in school and in outside organizations like Scouts, volunteer groups, religious organizations, summer and part-time jobs, internships and seminars, educational or other camps, etc. Whenever you think of something, add it. You can always organize it later, but the first goal is simply to list it. If you do this, then when it's time to let a college know this information, you'll simply retrieve it and put it into whatever format is desired. The file on activities and awards can also include experiences you've had, like travels, and notes on what you've learned. Put as much into it as you like; you can always edit out the excess later, but this way you'll have a fleshed-out list about your life.

The activities and awards file listed above can be a jumping-off point for essay topics too. Sometimes an essay question is open-ended and you need to develop your own topic. If you have a list of what you've achieved, you will better be able to develop an answer. One student phoned me to say, rather plaintively, that he needed to write an essay on something he'd accomplished of which he was proud, and he said, "The problem is that I'm a very average person and I haven't accomplished anything in my whole life!" I said, "Well, let's just talk for a few minutes," and I asked him about activities in school, summer jobs, etc. All of a sudden he said, after mentioning full—and part-time lifeguarding jobs, "Do you think it would count that I saved a child's life?"

Yup! I did, very much so, and proceeded to relay to him a Talmudic saying that, if you save one person's life, it's as though you've saved the entire world. He wrote an excellent essay. So contrary to his initial claim that he'd accomplished nothing, he'd really accomplished something quite stellar! Use your experiences in life to jog your memory.

Another file might be on your family history or genealogy. Interview relatives to learn stories about your family's past or your own personal past. Ask what you were like as a baby and small child and record those stories. They're your personal biography!

Sometimes students need to make personal statements or tell their personal philosophies in essays. Some students will think, "Gee, I don't think I *have* a personal philosophy." But if you set up a file and ask yourself key questions, you will probably discover that there are ideals and attitudes that are important to you. Sample questions for this file: Do you believe in the death penalty or not? Do you think people should play all the time? Work all the time? Are there any circumstances under which it is ok to lie? To steal? Again, you are just trying to jog your mind in order to write better. If you keep these files, then when it's time to write, not only will it be easier (because you've done some thinking in advance), but you'll often be able to create a richer essay since you can use the examples you've recorded.

Another file might be difficulties, setbacks or challenges you've experienced, with which you've coped. Yet another might be goals. Again, you are not expected as a teenager or young adult to have a full-blown idea of what you want to accomplish in your life, but if you start thinking about this topic, it will help you write and help you sort out your interests, goals, strengths, etc. You might even learn more about yourself! You can also write about how these goals might be achieved, or what steps you might take. It may be a good idea to go online or to a library and research the areas in which you are interested, so you can find out about opportunities of which you were unaware.

Instead of looking at the creation of these files as a tedious bunch of work to be avoided, look at the exercises as ultimately saving you time and energy and teaching you something about your life, thoughts, emotions and goals. Socrates said, "The unexamined life is not worth living." It's a good idea to think about your life and your goals at a young age, so you don't just get carried along for years and not know what's important to you.

Essay-writing and the whole college application process can be approached as drudgery or as an opportunity, and I think you'll do better if you try not to go crazy over the whole thing. Virtually everyone gets into some college, and the worst-case scenario (which hasn't happened all that often with my students) is that someone hates the initial school, keeps grades up, and transfers. If I had it to do over again, I wouldn't waste two milliseconds of my life agonizing over getting into college. I'd work hard and give it "the old college try," as they say, but I wouldn't spend any time at all being overwrought, anxious or unsettled by the whole process.

Further advice: lots of people wonder how to start. It took me years to learn this and it sounds simplistic, but it's true. *Just start.* When you get those first words down, leave them. Maybe you'll eventually switch everything around, but it's the act of getting started that eventually gets the whole job done. In writing this book, I simply had to make myself start. Once something is written, it leads to the next thing, and the next thing, and at some point, you're done. But you can't get done unless you start!

This works for anything: a diet, an exercise program, a painting you're doing, course reading, renovation of a room, etc. You just put those first dabs of paint on a canvas or cut out some calories today, and eventually, you'll get where you're going. The old saying that "Rome wasn't built in a day" means that you can't accomplish big chores in a short amount of time. But if you just start, you can eventually get where you want to go.

Sample Essays

Many of our students have written fine essays highlighting their experiences, attitudes, difficulties that they've overcome, and so forth. This chapter will highlight some essays so you can get an idea of the breadth and depth of topics that work when you are writing your own essays for college and elsewhere, including on the SAT.

Obviously, if you are given a specific topic assignment, you must use that topic, not improvise. If you are given a choice, you can go in many different directions.

One student took her love of history and family and created a beautiful essay. This is a perfect example of the fact that one can take a seemingly small event (in this case, a box of letters) and create something quite moving. Notice especially the last paragraph, with the vivid image of "a sun-kissed collection of stamps and scratches."

> *Somewhere amidst schedules, work, homework, chores, rules, and chaos, American subculture has somehow lost the sacred bond of family. The house has become a meeting place, a metro station, instead of a home. In the ever-moving world of suburbia, stress is pervasive and the role of family is reduced to a present circumstance, if not forgotten entirely.*
>
> *This past summer I was fortunate enough to realize my dearth of knowledge regarding the generations who had ultimately begotten me. It became apparent that I was deeply enraptured by my own life without any personal understanding of those who came before me and even of those by whom I am surrounded daily. I was aware of little more than a mere set of desultory facts. Whether it is because I have recently stepped into a more matured perception or because of the once-in-a-lifetime opportunity with which I was presented, I was finally able to learn about something other than mathematics and history texts.*

The opportunity of a lifetime stemmed from my mother's fondness for world travel and cultural exploration, which she has effortlessly propagated to all her children. The chance arose to spend a portion of the summer in Norway, whence came my mother's family two generations before her. The trip became a project that I was immediately engrossed in. I began studying the geography and the sights, but most importantly the history that the nation held. While my mother contacted the Norwegian library of genealogy and located family documents, I allowed the past and present to converge in a more personal way, through the correspondence of my great-grandmother.

My mother was fortunately able to recover a wealth of letters that her own mother had received and avidly collected and preserved. The boxes of envelopes, crisp and browned with many years passed, immediately piqued my interest. I plucked the first letter from one of the boxes and noted the date marked in the postage: 1943. I felt like a literary character ensconced in an adventure as I began to struggle with the handwriting, etched in the World War II era. It was previously a world that I had only known in history texts; now I settled into this world through the eyes of my great-grandmother. I found myself constructing these years in my head through her eyes, becoming a part of the family that had come before my own mother. Letters from friends and other relatives, one of whom was stationed in Germany during the war, brought dimension to the past. I was feeling the excitement of receiving mail with the start of each letter from "Mother." I bit my nails when the prices of fabric fell, and gasped at the events of the women in her society. I hoped for her to have good weather for the garden show and I even missed her company when I read about Christmas Day. As if I were her own daughter, I cried when the neighbor's son was lost to the war and laughed with delight when the couple down the street had a newborn girl.

Lost in the world of "Mother's" correspondence, I met the characters of a real life, whom I had never gotten the chance to meet. I also grew fond of the children that grew up to become my distanced extended family. I might have even called myself a close friend of the writer's, caught up in her profound love for her family. I watched her personality emerge in the words that she sent lovingly to her daughter Ruthie. I learned of the love that flourished between my mother's parents and got to know my grandfather, who never even dreamed of my existence. Learning especially about the women who came before me has given me a much deeper understanding of the people who shaped my mother growing up, who in turn played a major part in molding my individual character.

All from a sun-kissed collection of stamps and scratches, I brought these people, who have become pictures and memories, back to life in my head. Drawing connections, I resurrected their world. Traveling to Norway to discover my family history has reawakened their legacy and although I was never a part of their lives, I can never fully express the gratitude I have for my awareness of their presence in my life.

The same student composed a courageous essay about standing up to the administration of her school on an issue in which she strongly believed.

I became involved with journalism when I was a freshman because of my knack for writing. I was immediately taken with it and have held various responsibility-laden positions on the newspaper staff over the past three years including Opinion/Editorial Section Co-editor, Features Page Editor, Centerspread Editor, Production Manager, Editorial Board member, photographer, and writer. One specific incident sticks out in my mind that brought my study of journalism off the pages of textbooks and into practice. Last year, I pursued an article regarding the soundness of an election held by my class officers. Some students were concerned about the election procedures, and I was zealous about tackling the issue with tact and responsibility. Almost immediately I was confronted with the first of many journalistically ethical questions on a long road to the end product.

I pursued the story diligently from all angles, interviewing a wide sampling of the student body about the manner in which they had voted. I then approached an extremely defensive executive board, made up of my peers and friends in student government. It became evident that the executive board, including their sponsor, did not want the story to run. They bombastically affronted me on a personal level for pursuing the article and refused to be interviewed. I was discouraged, but proceeded in writing the article. The class sponsor attended an editorial board meeting with me present prior to the story's publication. Representing the student government to the leaders of the newspaper staff, she brought up various complaints to which our responses mirrored our thorough education in our rights and responsibilities as a newspaper. The assistant principal, overseeing the student government, went so far as to go to the principal and request that she exercise her right to prior review.

Thankfully, our principal supported the newspaper staff and myself, provided our facts were accurate. Subsequently, the trial of my journalistic ethics culminated in an intimidating meeting that I was embroiled in with the assistant principal, the class sponsor, and two members of the executive board. Each with a copy of a draft of the story I had written, we went over it together and I was put on the spot to defend and justify my writing and my knowledge or journalism, despite the opposition of authority figures. Though I found the process to be trying, it caused my enthusiasm for journalism to burgeon. I was ultimately very proud of the manner in which I handled the situations and the article that was ultimately published. This experience, among others over the past four years, caused me to progress in personal development and has made Journalism particularly significant to me.

Asked about discrimination, a student wrote of sexism:

Prejudice, bigotry, and discrimination are unfortunately ever-present in our society. From centering on race and ethnicity, age and sex, or physical characteristics, it exists. Some forms of discrimination are more conspicuous. Even though I am Hispanic, and therefore a member of an ethnic minority, the form of discrimination that I am most concerned with is sexual discrimination. It not only affects both men and women, but also prevents them from achieving their full potential as successful members of our society. More importantly, it prevents both from gaining from each other's experiences and perspectives.

Women have fought to have equal opportunity for a long time, and it is still yet to be achieved not only in the United States, but in many other parts of the world. There are laws and regulations that dictate equality, but actions and thoughts of everyday life prove that there is resistance to these laws. It is unfair in every way that women should receive less income than men because of their gender. Those who believe one gender is better than the other are on a path that will prevent them from getting the benefits of differing viewpoints. Women and men can both benefit greatly by living in an equal world. Both genders have different things to offer in their experiences and approaches to life.

Men are not excluded from this type of discrimination. They are said to be weak if they walk away from a fight, or "acting like

*a girl" if they show any form of sensitivity. Boys are taught from
a young age to be tough, show no fear, and never surrender (or ask
for directions). Boys should be encouraged to show sensitivity and
compassion, and these limiting stereotypes should be erased. Men
should be allowed to explore their fullest potential, just as women
should be free to develop their talents.*

*Men and women have so much to offer one another that it
is hurtful to hold one another down. Each gender is unique and
special in its own way, and by constricting our abilities, we are only
constricting our own possibilities as a society.*

Yet another student took this same question and focused on genetic
discrimination. When you are given an essay assignment, there is more
than one way to approach it. Be creative, and brainstorm different
approaches before you settle on a specific angle.

*Society as a whole has made tremendous advances with
regard to equality in recent years. Civil Rights and gender equality
legislation have made significant strides in preventing social and
economic discrimination.*

*However, new discoveries in science have opened up the flood
gates for a contemporary display of prejudice: genetic discrimination.
The mapping of the human genome and the identification of
specific chromosomes allow geneticists to determine a person's
genetic predisposition to a particular disease. This information is
undoubtedly beneficial as it could be essential in determining a
person's survival by allowing early treatments and preventative
measures to be taken.*

*When a chromosome map falls into the wrong hands, we find
the origins of genetic discrimination. Predisposition to a debilitating
disease like Huntington's Chorea or Alzheimer's Disease may be used
to exclude certain people from obtaining insurance or to disqualify
them from jobs. A significant amount of genetic discrimination is
occurring presently and it will magnify with the scientific advances
that stand to make widespread genetic testing feasible.*

*The location of pathogenic genes is happening much faster
than the development of preventative treatments or cures. This
situation leaves open a window for genetic discrimination. The
denial or elimination of health coverage is a dreadful consequence
of genetic discrimination, as it can eliminate the patient's core
chance of survival.*

> As the magnitude of this discrimination increases (a situation
> that can almost be guaranteed), it will be up to the nation to ensure
> rights and equality down to the very last chromosome.

The following essay was written by a student asked to describe the best gift she'd ever received. Rather than choosing something material, she wrote a touching essay about a difficult but important experience.

> "Bill," my Aunt said to my dad by phone, "your father had a stroke in the middle of the night." He has to be okay, I thought. This is the same man who magically pulled tootsie rolls from my ears, slurped his spaghetti by pulling his ears, made up songs like "The Old Family Toothbrush," and slipped me money when Grandma wasn't looking. A World War II veteran and two-time Purple Heart recipient, he taught me about war, life, and history. He was my role model, my favorite person.
>
> But somehow, in my heart, I knew Grandpa wasn't going to recover this time. My dad took a plane to Florida to see him. I wanted to go, but Dad said to stay home because my grandfather wouldn't want me to see him dying, but rather to remember him how I did. Grandpa was unconscious, in critical condition. On Saturday morning, my dad called in tears: Grandpa had had three heart attacks and wouldn't make it another hour. I begged him to let me come to Florida, but he said by the time I got there it would be too late. I stayed home and went to my Homecoming dance. But when I got home, my mom said Grandpa was still alive!
>
> When we got to Dulles Airport the next morning, our tickets said "Dallas," not "Dulles," and there were no seats. After almost giving up hope, we found two seats to Jacksonville. My cousin met us and drove straight to the hospital. The Jaguars game was on and I sat by my frail grandfather and watched with him. His eyes weren't open but he knew I was there. I talked to him and rubbed his arm; he even squeezed my hand twice. I stayed all day.
>
> The next morning when I arrived, his oxygen mask was gone; he had passed away ten minutes earlier. I stayed strong as I hugged my crying father, my Vietnam-Veteran-Citadel-graduate-Army father. I didn't shed a tear until my cousin gave me a hug. She whispered, "He waited for you, you know."
>
> I loved that man, and when I look back I smile. I have closure. I know how he died, how he looked, and most importantly that he didn't suffer. I know this from my own experience, not from

someone phoning me from 14 hours away, and that is the greatest gift I have ever received.

Another student chose to highlight her struggle with Obsessive-Compulsive Disorder (OCD), a brain-based illness where patients dwell incessantly on thoughts or perform repetitive actions like washing, counting, checking, etc. The student showed great bravery and forthrightness in this essay, which discussed the difficulties she'd fought and conquered. It is a perfect example of using an essay to highlight a personal hardship or challenge and of showing a side of oneself that the admissions committee might otherwise never see.

My Battle with Myself

I think the worst part was thinking that something horrible would happen to me at any time. My head was perpetually telling me that something dire would happen to me or to someone else I cared about. That feeling that I consistently had is known to some as Obsessive Compulsive Disorder or OCD. Obsessive Compulsive Disorder is a mental disease that is triggered by abnormal chemistry in the brain. The person who is stricken with this disease cannot help the senseless thoughts that are going through the mind.

I developed OCD when I was about twelve years old. My family and I were moving for the first time in my life. When I found out we were moving, I became very anxious about meeting new friends and going to a new school. When we first came to Virginia, I adjusted well and made lots of friends, but something was just not right in my mind. I started to become paranoid that something bad would happen to me. I thought that at any moment I could be killed or my house could catch on fire. To make myself feel better about all this, I began checking things.

I had to make sure that all doors were locked and appliances were shut off. During the day was not as difficult, but going to bed was a different story. My blankets had to be a certain way, my window had to be closed, and my alarm clock had to be set at a certain angle. All of these needed to be checked in a certain order and checked twice. Two was my "number" that I used to check everything; it just seemed like the right number. At night I was only getting three to four hours of sleep because I was up so late perfecting my obsessions and compulsions. My grades began to go down because I was so tired in school every day. Every night

I would be determined not to give in, but somehow my brain just kept taking over.

At some point I realized that this was all becoming too much for me and that I had to tell someone. I decided to tell my mom and she was very understanding. She was surprised that I had waited so long to say something to her. We decided that to overcome this battle I needed to understand what was wrong with me. We went to the faithful internet to help us. I found out ways to treat Obsessive Compulsive Disorder. I did not want to go on any type of medication or go into therapy, so it was all up to me.

Every night I would eliminate something from my "routine." It was probably the worst feeling in the world lying in bed thinking that something was going to happen to me because my closet door was not shut. Even if I did not go through with my "checks," I would wake up in the morning and be fine. I began to realize that things would be ok. Also, if something did happen it would not be because I did not do something.

Overcoming this battle with my mind has shown me how much courage and strength that I really have. I now know that, when I put my mind to something, it can get done. I think an old Chinese proverb is the best fit for how I feel each day: "Be not afraid of growing slowly; be afraid only of standing still." I know that this disease takes time to get over, but I would rather get beyond it slowly than not get over it at all.

A battle over a fear of heights is described by another student. The writer vividly recreates a difficult episode in which confronting a lifelong fear leads to vanquishing that fear and then to exhilaration. The student takes the lesson and extrapolates to another challenge, which is no longer seen as a dreaded activity, but as "an opportunity to prepare for the future."

As soon as the harness came down, I asked myself, "What am I doing?" The attendant pressed the button, and off I went. I looked straight ahead into the seat in front of me. "What am I doing? What am I doing?" I asked myself a hundred times as the roller coaster tilted up and began the ascent to the top. With my feet dangling in the air, we very slowly climbed toward the first drop. Thinking we were almost done with the climb, I looked up expecting to see the drop. We had only gone about half way up, and the people walking around the park were getting smaller and smaller.

When we reached the top of the incline, my heart stopped. I was dangling 170 feet off the ground. Time froze as I watched the coaster switch tracks to begin descent. There was a slight drop, and we began to plummet. Down, Down, Down, and then Up, Up, Up. Flying left and right, we did loops and corkscrews. I was trying to scream, but the combination of fear and excitement had taken the wind out of me.

As we pulled to a stop at the end of the ride, I wiped tears, which had been blown out of my eyes, off my face and fixed my hair, which had been blown upright by the 70 mph speeds. I sat there in shock; I was deathly afraid of heights, yet I wanted to ride the ride again.

The next time, and the time after that, the height became less of an issue, and I realized what joy and excitement I had been missing for the first 15 years of my life.

My first roller coaster ride showed me that embracing something for its good aspects can help overcome the fear brought on by its bad ones. For example, I am taking AP Government this year, and the teacher is notorious for giving overwhelming amounts of writing. Rather than fearing the writing, I looked at it as an opportunity to prepare for the future.

While riding a roller coaster might be a regular activity for some, it was a life-changing experience for me.

One student wrote, with a mix of good humor and insight, about an AP English summer assignment: reading the Bible. In the first paragraph, the juxtaposition of the student's summer activities and the episodes in the Bible are vivid, expressive, and charming: " . . . I spent the summer before my senior year lying on lounge chairs, basking in the sun, while Adam and Eve experienced expulsion from paradise. My feet dangled in the swimming pool as Moses parted the Red Sea." Then this teenager, who had not had a religious upbringing, developed an understanding of various friends' religious involvements and went on to have a desire to learn more in the realm of theology.

I was confused and disheartened when I discovered that the prerequisite for advanced placement English literature was reading the Bible. Wasn't that against some obscure county regulation? To my dismay, I spent the summer before my senior year lying on lounge chairs, basking in the sun, while Adam and Eve experienced expulsion from paradise. My feet dangled in the swimming pool as Moses parted the Red Sea.

My enthusiasm for the piece grew as I got further into it, and the purpose of the reading began to make sense. It allowed students to identify allusions that, in many cases, have biblical connotations. However it also allowed me to make connections with people that had been previously barred. I lack a religious upbringing; my values and beliefs are based on what my parents instilled in me, not necessarily supported by religious doctrine.

I have surrounded myself with a diverse group of friends with regard to religious background, but I never fully understood where their positions on issues originated. Completion of the Bible, though not the primary doctrine of all faiths, allowed me to identify the forces that moved many of my companions. I learned what made my friend Heather rise at 5 in the morning and go to seminary before school, why Angie fasted during the month of Ramadan, how temple could be more important than the district football game on a Friday night, and the belief that made many a student rise early on a Sunday morning, no matter how long the previous Saturday night had lasted.

The required summer reading that I had originally dreaded, provided me with a knowledge that I otherwise would not have been able to attain. It sparked my interest in religious philosophy as a whole, leaving a desire to read other theological doctrine, perhaps to find something to fill the void left by a lack of spirituality.

Another student wrote of the hold time had on her and on people in general in this society, and chronicled her day from the alarm clock at 6AM to a bedtime at midnight. She mused that "[o]n planet America, everyone is on a schedule." Touching on wristwatches and traffic lights, she pondered what an alien might think of "rolling pieces of metal, stopping at red lights and going through green ones."

Beep. Beep. Beep.

Its simple presence and soft screech results in the day's scheduled hardships. It comes and goes at the most impolite, yet crucial times. I call it my best friend: the inevitable alarm clock, of course.

It's 6:00 AM. I look at my window and I can't make out the blinds from the birds. It's pitch black outside, but somehow I need to create artificial light and artificial energy. It's a school day.

All right, so what if 6:00 AM is about six hours earlier than the average teenager wakes up? In this world, timing is key. On planet America, everyone is on a schedule. If people break away from their schedules, it's as if they somehow escaped earth's gravitational pull. People nowadays live their lives according to the ticking of a clock.

It's 6:05 AM. If I don't get out of this bed soon, I'm going to be late for first period. One minute of tardiness could ultimately result in my failing the class. I'd better hurry; "time does not grow on trees."

Whenever I'm walking down the street, I constantly see people looking at their watches. I find it humorous that, for some reason, the second after most people glance at their watches, they begin to pick up their pace. It is as if time has somehow jumped ahead of them, and they have to hurry up to find their lost time. What if their watches were confiscated, and they had no way of seeing when they were going to get to their next appointment? Maybe they would just have to trust their own biological clocks.

It's 7:25 AM. I made it to class on time, as always. Timing is so important to everyone. If I am late and disrupt someone's schedule, I disrupt the person's life. Time is life; without time, there would be no life. The minute hand jumps to 7:26 AM, and shockingly the morning announcements appear on the TV screen.

I always set times for activities I plan. I cannot just "pencil things in." Penciling things in is like driving into a foreign city, with a certain destination, but lacking a road map. It simply should not be done. If, for instance, I were to plan an activity for 4:00 PM, I do not expect people to show up at 4:00 sharp. On-time is late! If they show up any later than 3:58, I will hold an everlasting opinion of them as unreliable and incompetent. Time is not for wasting; it is for savoring. It is the clay that is used to build out a day. There are 24 cubes; use them wisely.

It's 2:10 PM. School is out for the day. Now, I have approximately 8 hours before I should go to sleep. In those eight hours there are certain tasks I must accomplish. I must set out a couple hours for doing homework, surfing the internet, relaxing, running, etc. Each activity takes time, and time is of the essence.

There is, however, a certain machine that seem to grab some time, chew it up and spit it out into the atmosphere. It is called the traffic light. Granted, traffic lights do make the roads a safer place, but people get places much more efficiently by using their own feet for transportation. There is nothing to do at red lights; they are too brief to do anything significant, yet too long to just waste time and sit there. The person who comes up with the perfect red light time-saving activity will make millions.

It's 10:00 PM. A beeping goes off in my head: it is time to become tired. I still have homework to finish, so it's a good thing

I plan on making time to do it tomorrow. At 10:15 PM, I turn off the light. The sun has long since gone down. Perhaps if I followed nature, I would be sleeping more and working less, but that's just not the way Homo sapiens has chosen to live life.

Imagine what the alien witness must think, as he flies overhead in some sort of spacecraft. He sees millions of rolling pieces of metal, stopping at red lights and going through green ones. At yellow lights, the things either zoom up to twice their speed or stop short, either way endangering the mechanisms around them. These colorful lights, each in perfect timing with each other, appear to communicate to the beings how they should be moving and when. He must think, "Wow, what kind of strange, dependent creatures live on this planet?"

It's midnight. I'm asleep. If someone needs me to do something, just tell me now. My subconscious has become very good at scheduling my events for me; it's like a net I can fall onto. Sometimes on Sunday nights I forget to set my alarm clock. But on Monday morning, alarm clock or not, I will somehow be awake by 6:20 AM. On Saturday mornings, it never even occurs to my body that it is possible to wake up before 9.

Maybe my biological clock isn't as far off from my everyday schedule as I would think. Maybe through evolution, humans have acquired the precise ability to train their own bodies to live according to the clock. The subconscious could be constantly sending messages to its host body about timing. Perhaps boredom is just the body's way to say that it is wasting time. I'm not sure, but I do know that it is 6:35 AM and if I do not leave the house this instant, I will be late for school.

Another essay touched on diversity and proceeded to talk about the writer's long-time passion for learning Spanish. An amusing anecdote about using the wrong vocabulary word while in Costa Rica demonstrated a self-deprecating good-humoredness.

Attending a diverse elementary school where more than 60 countries were represented, I have always been exposed to different languages. Throughout elementary school, on Monday mornings I took Spanish classes that introduced me to the language, culture, and food. I had the opportunity to practice speaking and listening to the language often when I would go to my friend Carolina's house to play. Sometimes we would watch movies in Spanish, and although I didn't understand most of what was said, I used the pictures and animation to associate the words I knew with the plot.

By the time I began high school and was entering Spanish 1, I was comfortable listening to the language, but I was eager to learn grammar, more vocabulary, and writing skills.

When my sophomore year schedule arrived in late August 2000, I was apprehensive upon finding that I had the "dreaded" teacher for Spanish 2. My friends warned me that I should switch out before classes even started, that she would only give passing grades to her favorite students (of which there were few), and that I wouldn't learn anything the whole year. I entered her classroom on the first day with the goal of succeeding, and I accomplished far more than that goal throughout the year.

When I stayed after school for extra help in Spanish, my teacher advised me to "dive into the language, head first." This advice was invaluable because it taught me to think in Spanish, rather than think in English and translate into Spanish. As a result, my grammar, vocabulary, and overall sense of the language improved immensely. As my skill level increased, so did my teacher's expectations, so I was pushed the whole year to improve.

I seized the opportunity to "dive into the language, head first" that year when I took my first trip to a Spanish country with my parents. We went to Costa Rica for a week, and I was lucky to encounter many friendly natives who were patient with my attempts to communicate with them in Spanish. Through casual conversation with Costa Ricans, I surprised myself with how much I knew. By the end of the week, it was natural for me to speak the language and I even started having dreams in Spanish. I learned from this trip that diving into the language does not guarantee perfect results. When I was talking to a shop owner in a village, I tripped; I immediately said "Estoy embarazada," thinking that I was saying "I am embarrassed." But what I had really said was "I am pregnant." I will always remember that "embarazada" is not a Spanish cognate for the English word "embarrassed"!

I have had two other opportunities to immerse myself in Spanish with a week-long trip to Mexico and a week-long trip to the Dominican Republic. These experiences gave me the chance to listen to people speak with native accents and to communicate with people on the streets. An important lesson I learned from being in other countries is that people speak quickly, and in order to understand them, one needs to listen to the whole sentence they are saying, rather than focusing on translating and understanding every word. This lesson goes back to the advice that I got from my 10th grade teacher-to "dive in."

At the end of my junior year, my Spanish teacher asked me to join the National Spanish Honor Society. I am currently a member and I look forward to a year of projects in and out of school that will deepen my knowledge of the language and culture.

My true passion for the language was sparked when my 10th grade Spanish teacher advised me to dive into the language, because it allowed me to succeed in her class and in the language. I plan to pursue Spanish in college and continue traveling to Spanish-speaking countries so that I have the opportunity to continue learning about the culture and the people that make up the Spanish language.

The following essay was a light-hearted answer to a question asking for the pupil's favorite word. Given that there were thousands upon thousands of English words that could be picked, there were numerous potential answers and an opportunity to display something of the student's personality.

I love "cinnamon." I love the way the spice tastes, smells, and looks. My mom used to joke about how she would have to hide the jar of cinnamon or it wouldn't last more than a couple of months. In grade school, while other kids would eat their applesauce plain or with a dash of cinnamon, my applesauce would be nearly the color of coffee.

Not only does the word remind me of the rich and spicy flavor that I love to add to just about every food, but I love the word as well. Cinnamon! As a kid I could never remember how many n's and m's were in my word, and it would come out something like "Cinnammonnan." It's like trying to say "Worcestershire sauce," which most people I know still can't say, but more fun.

Try saying "Cinnamon" ten times fast! Not only is cinnamon fun to eat, but also it's amusing to say.

A different favorite word occupied this essay by another student. The question didn't specify a word in English! Again, this presented a chance for the pupil to demonstrate personality and spirit.

"Verklempt" conjures up visions of wrinkled old ladies wearing bright oversized sweaters, perhaps sitting on a couch covered in plastic wrap. I'm a seventeen-year-old girl who does not seem to be the "verklempt" type. To be perfectly honest, I'm not sure exactly what "verklempt" means, but I do know that it's Yiddish and German, and I'm certain that I am in love with it. I heard it on a Mike Myers'

SNL sketch, "Kawffee Tawk," where Barbara Streisand comes on and the ladies all shriek that they're "verklempt!""

Somehow, this word has made it into my everyday vocabulary. Most people would spew some delightful four-letter words or a religious reference, but I prefer "verklempt." I use it when I'm excited, surprised, anxious, apprehensive, terrified, happy, emotional, tearful, hurt, or when I'm stuck in rush-hour traffic or watching a Giants football game. "Verklempt" is that moment when you cannot say everything you need to say, when you are all choked up and startled. When I say it, I always throw my hands up in the air with a sharp jerk; I think it conveys the power of the word more effectively. When I see other people say "verklempt," their eyes tend to get wider and their mouths gape open a little, and they too make a motion with their hands. On occasion I wonder if I look like that when I exclaim "I'm all verklempt!"

At first my friends thought I was nuts when I started saying it, but now whenever I say "verklempt," they know exactly how to mollify me. Maybe there's something in my tone of voice that lets them pick up on what's going on, you know, like how mother cats can recognize their kittens based upon their unique sound. I love to say "verklempt" because one little word can encompass so many emotions that I just cannot seem to define in English. Then again, I am just a seventeen-year-old girl with many complicated emotions, and it is nice to have a word that makes something in life simple.

The same student wrote about her first experience with failure. Even though it had happened long before, she managed to bring in enough detail to make the story seem as fresh as if it had happened yesterday. The initial paragraphs set the stage. Note the vivid image of the teacher standing at "the green blackboard, tapping her fake red nails."

Winter always seemed to drag in February. I would always start to think to myself, "God, just get it over with!" In sixth grade, every day seemed to take its sweet time, the second hand languishing for eons on the clock that hung on the Language Arts room wall. Each day faded into the next, none with any particular distinguishing factor that might jog my memory. English, or Language Arts, was the worst-what an elementary joke that class appeared to be. But it proved to be the one lasting memory from that bleak winter of 1997.

I had just gone to my locker, put on more mocha lip gloss, and brushed my hair as I hurried down to my classroom with Jenna. Our teacher, Mrs. H–, yelled at our class for being late even though

*she had unlocked the door after the bell rang. That should have been
the first sign that something was terribly wrong. She stood at the
green blackboard, tapping her fake red nails.*

*"I've graded your last grammar quizzes," Mrs. H—chirped,
tapping her heel loudly on the floor. "I was not impressed," she added
curtly as she turned around sharply and grabbed the papers from
the shelf. She proceeded to go around the room, handing papers to
people with eyes gleaming with a mixture of terror and confusion.
Whispers began to flutter around the room, buzzing in my ear. She
stopped at my desk.*

*"Ms. M—, I'm very surprised," Mrs. H—said, placing the
paper face-down on my desk. Uh oh, face-down can't be good . . . I
tentatively turned the quiz over with one hand. There on the paper
was a small red "F" and a circled "15/30" points. My eyes filled
with hot wet tears; I had just received my first failure.*

The author of the cinnamon-is-my-favorite-word essay showed
another equally good-natured side while musing about a college-level
summer course, Microeconomics 103. Drawn in by "the alarming green
background color" of a boxed-off area in her textbook, she wondered
if she'd become a Schumpterian like so many of the other economists
described therein.

*It was quite a sunny day in July. I looked out the window
and couldn't see anything except clear, blue skies. Well, that and
the GMU library across the street. Here I was, inside a classroom
learning Microeconomics 103 at George Mason University, while
the rest of my friends were probably tanning at the pool. It wasn't
that I didn't love the class; it was just that it was so sunny out.*

*Since I had just turned in my quiz, and the scene outside the
window grew boring, I had a few minutes to look in my book to
see if I had just answered a question correctly on my quiz. Not
finding the right page, my eyes wandered to a bright green box
entitled Schumpterian competition. Now that's a mouthful. But the
alarming green background color drew me in " . . . He questioned
the very concept of equilibrium." Well, that's interesting, I thought.
I just finished a quiz based on the very theory of the competitive
equilibrium model. Nevertheless, with the rebellious thought that
everything I had learned was wrong, I read on.*

*In summary, he believed that the economy was always in flux
and there was never just one equilibrium. Yet, his work alarmed me.
How do we actually know that the market can be this predictable?*

Who says that what we're learning is a representative model of the real world? I know these questions were almost as far-out as the "what if" questions that students ask to throw their teachers off on tangents. Yet, I truly believed in what Joseph Schumpter said. "As respect for and understanding of the importance of innovation have grown, so too have the number of economists who think of themselves as Schumpterians."

Break time. I shut the book and got up from my seat. Yet the thought lingered in my head. I wonder if I'll turn out to be a Schumpterian. I guess we'll just have to wait and see.

Volunteering can be an excellent essay topic. Here a teenager traveled to a small town in Mexico where she "raced the sun to begin my work down the road in an area devoured by poverty." Building two homes for total strangers was a life-changing experience indelibly imprinted on this student's mind: "I flew back to D.C. with new eyes that night." The striking opening sentence sets the tone for the rest of the essay:

The scent of mixed mortar and fresh paint would linger in my hair for days, but the memories would last forever in my heart.

Six hours on a plane filled with people of all walks of life would land me in a place that would change my outlook and my life. While many know it as a place for sunbathing and exotic adventures, I have come to know it as a dwelling for both the physically—and spiritually-hungry. I arrived in Mexico as a young girl looking for fulfillment, and I left as a young woman truly hopeful and undoubtedly blessed.

I unloaded my luggage in the add-on of a small Christian church in Rio Bravo. The next day, I raced the sun to begin my work down the road in an area devoured by poverty. The filthy road was inhabited by scrawny dogs and chickens and children played by burning heaps of trash. I would have knocked on the door if one had existed, but instead I waited for a resident to appear behind the sheet of cloth which hung above the door frame. A grandmother, a mother, and six children were found crouching in the back room of the improvised shack, awaiting our arrival with apprehension.

The sun beat down upon my team for hours upon hours as we spent an entire week creating two entirely new homes for people we had never met before. Children and adults alike came from all over town to inspect what the Virginians were laboring over. I had the chance to make lunches and snacks for over 30 people every day and the opportunity to play Simon Says in a foreign tongue with the neighborhood kids. "Simon dices," I would start in Spanish, and they would listen intensely and follow whatever I said with immediate reactions and then laughter at my pronunciation of their language.

What I cannot forget, though, are the faces and the emotions I encountered. We blessed the two new houses, with families inside, at the end of the week. I was approached by the mother, plastered with tears and a grateful smile, who told me that I was a blessing to her and her family, that I would never be forgotten; I wish she knew just how much she has done for me. My trip ended with pictures of our new houses, new friends, and new hope.

I flew back to D.C. with new eyes that night. Because I was given unwavering hope, I am determined to provide it to others. Since then, I have started a club at school dedicated to helping the community however possible. As of now, my peers and I mentor at a local elementary school once a week, bake for servicemen in the hospital, and even raise awareness about worldwide hunger. One might assume that I provided a lot for a family in Mexico during my one-week trip, but they have filled me with hope and determination to last a lifetime.

A single poem, *The Road Not Taken,* by Robert Frost, influenced another student greatly:

The one piece of poetry that challenged me from the first moment I read it is "The Road Not Taken" by Robert Frost. The poem encourages me always to follow my heart and not be frightened of going my own way, though it may not be with my friends. Frost describes the two roads as being two different paths one may take in a lifetime. He speaks of taking the road that "was grassy and wanted wear." Frost took the road that others would not because it was harder, unfamiliar, and it would offer more interesting challenges.

Frost has been a role model for me through his poetry. He challenges me to think and take chances in life because one may never have that opportunity again. Quite often I think about this poem and ask, "Am I taking the road less traveled? Am I being the person I want to be and seizing all opportunities I might have?"

Another lesson Frost taught me through this poem is to be proud of my decisions and myself. The choices one makes are the choices that shape one's life. To regret is a decision, a decision that can make life crumble before one's eyes. Be proud and certain when making choices.

This poem is the most touching and liberating piece I have ever read. It reaches me on a personal level. I no longer want to be what everyone else is, but to be myself and carve my own path across this world.

The same student had had the opportunity to travel to China with a high school dance team as Goodwill Ambassadors for the United States. The team was filmed and photographed here and in China, so the students learned to cope with a level of celebrity and pressure they'd never experienced before. Viewing the cultural, economic, and environmental differences between China and America, the pupil came home with greater compassion for others and a new understanding of "myself, my great country, and the rest of the world."

Representing the United States in China with my high school dance team for ten days in September 1999 was my strongest achievement and it greatly influenced my world view. This trip, sponsored and paid for by the Chinese government, allowed me to experience a different culture while sharing mine with others. The preparations and work were exhausting, but the lessons learned will last a lifetime.

Although I had trained since age three in dance and gymnastics, the summer of 1999 consisted of long, excruciating practices. They were filmed and photographed by The Washington Post and local television stations, so I learned to work well under pressure and fine-tune my ability to focus in extreme situations. This opportunity also taught me time management, an important skill I use daily to juggle my busy schedule. When we weren't practicing, we were consumed with planning music, dance costumes, and choreography. We had to ensure passports were valid and immunizations updated. Although that summer the team felt that our work might be in vain, once the school year started we received encouragement from peers, faculty, parents, and even the President, Bill Clinton.

Upon our arrival in Beijing, we were escorted by the mayor's assistant, translators, and representatives of the company that coordinated the trip. We participated in parades and exhibitions in Beijing for the first few days. Our job, as Goodwill Ambassador for the United States, was to bring smiles to the Chinese people as we danced down the streets of Beijing and Dalian and performed in Beijing's stadium to an audience of eighty thousand.

Chinese newspapers photographed our team, and we were the front-page story of the main Beijing newspaper. The Chinese people climbed onto bridges, balconies, and the tops of buildings to cheer and wave. Their excitement is what helped us with the fact that we were in very unfamiliar surroundings in a communist country with an archaic infrastructure. The standard of living was much below what we take for granted. The general population was poor, with few modern items or facilities. These realities truly caused a deeper appreciation of the United States. In particular, I gained greater respect for my freedom and the modern, sanitary infrastructure of my homeland.

We were given the privilege of attending dinners with Chinese officials and visiting a talent school where we met children our age. These wonderful, talented, intelligent teenagers amazed me with their friendliness and excitement. Besides meeting important official and students, we were allowed to tour such sights as the Great Wall, Forbidden City, and Tienenman Square.

The collective experience of my visit to China taught me the meaning of both human dignity and human suffering, and I developed considerable compassion for the world's less fortunate people. Quite often, I find myself thinking of the conditions I experienced, and the people I met and observed, as I take advantage of the modern infrastructure of the United States. This journey changed my view of myself, my great country, and the rest of the world.

Another teenager was asked to describe the scene outside his window. He wrote of waking up to a mysterious, disturbing landscape, but he created a bit of a surprise ending:

Upon waking, I find that the entire outside world is nondescript. I take a gander, but I only am able to see mounds and shapes of unadorned objects. I wonder to myself what apocalyptic event could have transpired. Did an atomic bomb explode and leave ashes on top of our town? Why did God forget to use his paintbrush in the heavens today? Whatever the case, a gloomy mood is set by the colorless landscape.

I find myself aghast at how the vivid colors of trees, rolling hills, and beautiful houses that usually fill the view from my bedroom window have been replaced by a dismal setting that makes me feel that I am living inside a cloud. I used to gaze outside and see my young neighbors frolicking and talking with friends in the cul-de-sac. On this fateful day, however, I cannot tell the street from the roof of my next-door neighbor's house.

I hit myself in the forehead and rub my eyes to verify that this is not an illusion. I long for another 24 hours of the bucolic scenery that customarily envelops my home. As I progress to my parents' room to find out what has occurred, I hear a sudden loud thump on my window.

My heart is pounding with fear as I retrace my steps back towards the glass pane that is seemingly under siege. Releasing the tension in my biceps, I quickly snap my window open only to witness my buddies screaming:

"Snowball fight!"

Essay Topics

There are two types of essays I definitely do *not* recommend:

1. essays on how you learned teamwork from being on a team;

2. essays on how you learned responsibility from your summer or other job.

Now, this doesn't mean that you can't write about your team or your job, but please don't write a generic essay on those topics. Why? Well, let's say you are applying to a university accepting 3000 freshman and your application asks for 3 essays. The university only accepts 1 out of every 4 students, so those 12,000 applicants produce 36,000 essays. When you write on topics (1) and (2), you are writing an essay the admissions officers have seen before. You don't want to bore them! You don't want one of them rolling his eyes and saying, "Hey, Joe, another one who learned responsibility from his summer job!"

You can write about topics large or small, from a pack of letters to a revolution rally, from a word you like to your philosophy of life. Please do not write a reiteration of achievements listed elsewhere in your application. The essay is an opportunity to show the admissions committee a side of yourself that they wouldn't otherwise know, and to make the committee say, "We must have this student in our school!"

Boasting often creates a poor impression. It's better to be mildly self-deprecating, but please don't go to the point where you sound as though you're dredging up your worst traits. One student wrote an essay in which she talked of how big a slob and procrastinator she was; this amounted to shooting herself in the foot. Even if you are asked to find your worst trait, please pick something that sounds like a flaw but can be seen as a positive trait. An example? Let's say you were asked "What's your worst personality trait?" You might elaborate on the fact that you're a perfectionist and that you can't stand to turn in anything but your best work. See? You've managed to parlay a seeming weakness into a strength.

It's okay to mention hardships or difficulties you've encountered overcome, but the essay isn't a therapy session, and you have to be careful in how you do this.

If there is anything negative in your application (poor grades, low test scores), you may use essays to explain extenuating circumstances. Examples might be family or personal illness or disability, economic hardship, divorce of parents, etc. Admissions committees are perfectly within their rights to reject a student for poor grades or low test scores, but if there's a reason for them they can, and often will, make allowances.

The essay is a chance to stand out, but gimmicks like writing the essay in red or gold ink or drawing a border of smiley faces will probably backfire. Although there are people who get into schools by doing something outrageous, there is a real risk that such behavior will not endear you to the admissions committee.

Sample Essay Topics

You might try to do a few of the following essays as a way of prepping for the Writing section of the SAT, or use some of the ideas as a way of jump-starting your own essays for the college applications you're filling out. Whatever you write about, make sure you use vivid examples to support your essay. Remember: practice will help!

1. Some people believe taxes are evil and the government is stealing people's money when it collects taxes. Others believe taxes pay for necessary services that promote the common good. Justify the function of taxes.

2. Many young people don't vote even when they're old enough. Please write on this topic, explaining either why there's no point for young people to vote or explaining why young people should vote, or even telling both sides.

3. The trend in schools is for teachers to give more homework. Discuss this phenomenon in terms of how it affects student learning and quality of life.

4. You find a wallet stuffed with cash. What will you do?

5. What will you be doing in the year 2030? Give vivid illustrations.

6. Someone you thought was a friend has lied about you to others. How will you handle this?

7. It is said that Americans are restless people. Do you agree or disagree? Give clear evidence.

8. Many problems in the world are a function of tribal conflicts. Do you agree or disagree and why?

9. In the 2000 Presidential election, the election was essentially decided by the Supreme Court. Discuss why you agree or disagree with that statement.

10. America is a youth-oriented society. Describe what you think it will be like to grow older in such a society.

11. Choose a person you admire and tell why.

12. What is the best gift you ever received and why?

13. Agree or disagree with the following statement and support it: "A fair society is one in which there are not huge gaps between the haves and the have-nots."

14. What is your favorite saying, slogan or song? Tell why.

15. The foster care system replaced orphanages. At age 18, foster children are pushed out of the system with no families to fall back on. Discuss this problem.

16. The Civil Rights movement produced some changes in laws. Discuss how successful or unsuccessful those laws have been in producing parity among races.

17. Separation of church and state is an American ideal. Discuss how this ideal affects your school or community.

18. If you could pick any career, what would you pick?

19. If you could speak to any famous person alive today or in history, who would it be; why? What would you say?

20. *Brevity is the soul of wit.* Discuss this saying.

21. *Let no good deed go unpunished.* Discuss this saying.

22. *The love of money is the root of all evil.* Discuss.

23. What do you think is the biggest problem facing our country? How would you address it if you were President?

24. What do you think about the idea of a female President? Give specifics.

25. If you had three wishes, what would they be and why?

26. Imagine you go up into your attic and find, buried in a remote corner, a diary from 100 years ago. Describe differences in our lives today from 100 years ago.

27. If you could be a person in history, who would you be?

28. Some people say the concept of marriage harkens back to a time when people didn't live as long, and that *til death do us part* was an easier vow to keep. Do you think marriage has value and pertinence in the 21st century?

29. An acquaintance shoplifts and wants you to hide the object in your room for a few days. What do you do?

30. Imagine you are offered a huge sum of money with the stipulation that you could never see a loved one again. Would you accept this?

31. It is said that labor unions in California created a class of people with enough money to buy homes, thus fueling the development of California. Others feel unions damage a business's ability to function efficiently. Please discuss.

32. *Love is blind.* Do you agree? Why?

33. *A bird in the hand is worth two in the bush.* Discuss.

34. Many people have plastic surgery to change their appearance. What do you think of this trend? What does it say about those who have it?

35. Haiku is a form of poetry in which there are three lines. The first line has five syllables, second line has seven syllables and the third line has five syllables. Do five verses of haiku about your life.

36. Do five verses of haiku about your political views.

37. The Americans with Disabilities Act (ADA) protects the rights of those who are disabled. Discuss how the ADA affects schools and the workplace.

38. Someone you know has been diagnosed with a serious illness. What do you say to that person or how do you help?

39. Your school has a student population of 2000 and it holds a big fundraiser every year. People donate $35,000 in goods and services for an auction, and after expenses, the auction nets $7000. The next year, someone says, "Hey, why don't we just charge each kid in school $10.00 and we'll raise $20,000?" What do you think?

40. Immigration is a hot topic. Discuss problems, issues.

41. The principal of your school awards a big scholarship to one student every year. You and two friends are the finalists. When the winner is announced, it's one of your dearest friends. How do you feel and how do you behave?

42. Taking the previous question, how about if you win? How do you feel and how do you behave?

43. If you have siblings, talk about them. If you are an only child, talk about the pros and cons of that.

44. There have been many corporate scandals in the news. Discuss how these affect our day-to-day lives.

45. You are offered a big promotion if you will lie about sales figures in a document. Discuss how you handle this.

46. What is your favorite book and why?

47. What is your favorite character in a book and why?

48. What is your favorite TV show? Why?

49. What is your favorite movie and why?

50. Who is the person you'd most want to be like? Why?

51. If you could change anything about a person you know, what would it be and why?

52. Graduation from high school involves a commencement ceremony. Yet *commencement* means *beginning*. Why is this word appropriate or inappropriate?

53. When you are 28, will you go to your 10th high school reunion? Why or why not?

54. You are a famous author. What do you write about?

55. Aging can be seen as a process of attrition, since people often diminish in physical and mental ability. But people can choose to focus on what they *can* still do and not on what they *can't* do. Discuss.

56. Discuss your experiences with a person who has a physical disability, and how it made you feel or see life differently afterwards. (I once saw a triple amputee wearing prostheses on both legs and one arm. He was, interestingly, one of the most poised people I've ever seen.)

57. There are entrance exams for college, graduate and professional schools, and jobs. But there are no entrance exams for parenthood. Discuss.

58. Some schools have students carry around a lifelike doll to teach them how much attention a child requires. The idea is that

it might discourage some from having children prematurely. Discuss such programs.

59. If you volunteer in your community, please discuss.

60. Tell about a person whom you've helped. Give details.

61. Tell about a person whom you feel you've harmed. If you made amends, discuss.

62. If you were stranded on a desert island, what three books would you take? Why?

63. Spin doctors are people who try to put a good gloss on news. How do you feel about people who do this?

64. What is your favorite food and why?

65. Did anyone ever throw you a party? What was it like?

66. You've stayed up until 2:30AM writing your term paper, due tomorrow. At the end of the session you shut down the computer and accidentally delete it. The next morning, you discover your error. What do you do?

67. What is your favorite Shakespeare play? Why?

68. The Harry Potter books are an international sensation. Discuss why they are so popular, giving specific examples.

69. J.K. Rowling was almost penniless when she started writing these books. Imagine if she had simply taken a job as a clerk instead of risking writing the books. Describe choices that people make in picking careers.

70. You are in law school. You have learned that African Americans convicted of crimes get harsher penalties in court than Caucasians convicted of those same crimes. Discuss how this might affect your choice of career.

71. You have a perfect attendance record in high school. You are offered a chance during senior year to take a few days off and

go skiing with your best friend's family in Colorado. Would you go and why?

72. What are your two favorite words and why?

73. Some people mistrust teenagers. What would you say to them?

74. *Fool me once, shame on you. Fool me twice, shame on me.* Discuss this saying.

75. If you wrote a screenplay, what would it be about?

76. There have been many movies about people losing their memory. How would you deal with someone you knew who suddenly didn't remember you?

77. What's your favorite color? Why?

78. What's your favorite song? Why?

79. Many WWII veterans are dying. What kind of project could you suggest in your community that would help capture their memories before it's too late?

80. Every person is a repository of experiences. If you went into a nursing home to talk to a resident, what would you ask that person? What would you tell that person?

81. Steven Spielberg started a project to have Holocaust survivors be interviewed on tape so that their stories won't be lost. What kind of individual investment in such a project can you imagine for yourself?

82. Your next door neighbor has lost his job. What can your family do to help? Be specific.

83. Have you ever been involved in local politics? If so, how?

84. Imagine there were a way, at the end of your life, to download all your memories into a storage medium so that you could still "live on" as a robot. Would you do it? Why or why not?

85. Technology changes so quickly that commonplace things become obsolete (phonograph records, for instance). Imagine what technology will be like in 30 years.

86. Take the previous topic and imagine what it will be like in 1000 years.

87. Who is your favorite actor or actress and why?

88. Imagine you are planning a party for a relative. Describe what you will do.

89. Describe something that you thought was a waste.

90. Tell about a time when you economized.

91. The earth has some major problems environmentally. Discuss at the world and local level.

92. Some people give 10% or more of income to charity. Some people give nothing. Discuss philanthropy and what it means to you individually or in your family.

93. Tell about an adversity that you overcame and how.

94. Many families assign chores to children. Discuss your chores and why you feel it's an important contribution.

95. *Honesty is the best policy.* Do you agree?

96. Have you found an exception to the above saying? If so, discuss.

97. What do you think about the space program?

98. There are numerous goodwill programs that have Americans travel to other countries and vice versa so that people can understand each other more at the individual level. Do you think these programs have an effect on international relations?

99. The Japanese have a fairly homogeneous society. We have great diversity. Please discuss how you feel about diversity in our society and in your community.

100. What is the first page of a novel you've written?

101. What is the 43rd page of a science fiction book you've written?

102. Many American companies are closing plants here and relocating overseas. How do you think this will affect our economy in the short run? In the long run?

103. If you were given a free trip anywhere in the world, where would you go and why?

104. What is the most interesting place you've ever been and why?

105. Who is the most eccentric person you know and why?

106. Should parents pay their children for grades? Why or why not?

107. Imagine you are an artist having a retrospective exhibit. Describe your favorite painting or sculpture that you've done, and the inspiration for it.

108. What is your favorite piece of artwork, and why?

109. Imagine you are the hero or heroine of a book. Tell what you do.

110. Are you for or against the death penalty? Why?

111. Discuss the advisability or inadvisability of adding new amendments to the Constitution of the United States.

112. What is the highest honor a person can receive? Why?

113. If you could live forever, would you? Would it make any difference if others you know were also immortal?

114. Discuss your worst trait.

115. Discuss your best trait.

116. Is the jury system outmoded or still useful? Why?

117. Do wealthy people get breaks in the legal system?

118. What do you think about mandatory penalties for crimes?

119. Suppose you can get a year of once-a-week free meals at your favorite restaurant. How much trouble would you go to in order to get that? Would you, for instance, stand outside in the rain for 1 hour? 2 hours? 7 hours?

120. If you could get any present, what would you pick?

121. Lottery winners often find that, after the first exhilaration, their lives become more difficult in ways they never imagined (people resenting them for their wealth, people pretending to befriend them, etc.). If you won the lottery and had $100,000,000 after all taxes, what would you do with the money and why?

122. A new medicine has been developed that they think will allow people and their pets to live twice as long. Nobody knows the long-term effects of the drug. Would you take it?

123. A new medicine has been developed that cuts the risk of getting cancer by 50%. No one knows the long-term side effects. Would you take it?

124. A doctor gets a test result. How quickly should the doctor let a patient know and are there instances in which a doctor should keep a diagnosis a secret?

125. The Human Genome Project has mapped human genes, so it may be possible to do things medically that were only dreamed of. Diseases might be cured, and people might be able to avoid passing conditions down to their children. Discuss ethical concerns.

126. If genetic testing shows that a person is more likely to develop an illness or condition, should an employer know this? How about an insurance company? Should people be turned down for health insurance or life insurance on this basis? What

safeguards to privacy might be installed? Might the Americans with Disabilities Act apply to this?

127. We have a two-party system. Discuss the merits and downsides.

128. In some elections, a person runs in a third party and siphons off votes from a candidate closer to his ideals and ideas. Discuss how this can affect the outcome of a race.

129. A President nominates members of the Supreme Court. Since these members serve as long as they wish, until they retire or die, this power to choose nominees has a huge lasting effect on the nation. Discuss.

130. *Live in the moment.* Discuss this as a philosophy.

131. Have you been influenced greatly by a teacher? How?

132. Have you been influenced greatly by a book? How?

133. Have you ever had a grandparent or anyone at least 50 years older than you whom you really enjoyed spending time with? Discuss in detail.

134. Has anyone done you a favor that touched you emotionally?

135. Have you ever done anyone else a favor that touched the person emotionally?

136. Have you ever received a letter or note from someone that touched you emotionally?

137. Have you ever made or built something with your own hands that you were exceptionally proud of?

138. Have you ever tried an activity that you wanted to give up on but didn't, and then achieved something great?

139. If you cook, what is your favorite thing to cook?

140. If you bake, what is your favorite thing to bake?

141. Have you ever bristled at a rule? Tell how you handled it and why.

142. Have you ever had a mentor (someone who guides you)?

143. If you could solve one large problem in the world, what would it be? How would you do it?

144. If you could discover one thing scientifically, what would you discover?

145. If you live to be 100 years old, you will get 10,400 weekend days approximately. Tell about something you do on a weekend that makes you feel fulfilled.

146. Have you ever kept a secret?

147. Imagine you are decorating a hat to express your personality. What things will you put on it?

148. What slogan would best express who you are?

149. Is there any saying that you completely disagree with or don't understand?

150. Really loud noise (music, construction) can destroy hearing. What is the loudest place you've ever been in your life? What is the scariest sound you've ever heard? The sweetest sound?

151. You and your friends all agree to meet once a decade until you are all too old to get around. Where do you decide to meet and why?

152. You have a two-for-one coupon for any restaurant in the world. Where would you go?

153. If you could immediately learn any language, even without studying, which one would you choose and why?

154. Are you a night person or a morning person? How will this affect what you choose to do in your life?

155. The world has always had challenges. Do you agree?

156. *Life is uncertain; eat dessert first.* Do you agree?

157. If you had a choice between a job that would pay you lots of money to live on but it was dull, or, a job that didn't pay well but was fascinating, which would you choose?

158. Do you believe in miracles? Have you ever known anyone who experienced what you would consider a miracle?

159. Sometimes you hear about a reporter fabricating news stories. Discuss journalistic ethics and how important this issue is.

160. The media often inform citizens of injustices. Do you think this is an important role? Why or why not?

161. Someone once said that indoor plumbing was one of the greatest inventions of the past few hundred years. What do you think was the most important invention in the last 300 years? Why?

162. Many people have home computers. How has this affected families?

163. Many people have cell phones. How has this affected you and people you know? Describe a situation that is easier now that people have cell phones. Describe a situation that is *harder* now that people have cell phones.

164. If you could buy any kind of vehicle you wanted, what would you buy and why?

165. Some people like scary movies and some people hate them. How do you feel and why?

166. Some people have trouble controlling their spending when they get credit cards. How can you set up a system so that you won't have this problem?

167. Imagine that your freshman year roommate becomes famous. What will your visits be like?

168. You start a charity. What is the role of that charity?

169. You invent a game. Describe it.

170. You design a reality TV show. Discuss the theme.

171. Your senator has commended you for something. What is it?

172. You are asked to nominate a teacher for an award. Which elementary teacher would you pick and why?

173. Which middle school teacher, and why?

174. Which high school teacher, and why?

175. If you could invent an interdisciplinary course to take, what would it be?

176. You work hard on a project, but you don't reach your goal. What is your next step and why?

177. *Quitters never win, and winners never quit.* Discuss.

178. Is there ever a time to quit something, and why?

179. Bad habits are hard to break. Have you ever broken yourself of a bad habit, and if so, how?

180. *The Lord of the Rings* discusses a world divided between good and evil. Do you see our world that way?

181. *It's not whether you win or lose, but how you play the game.* Discuss.

182. *The meek shall inherit the earth.* Discuss.

183. Someone is praising you. How do you respond?

184. Some people think it's rude to brag. Others say you have to toot your own horn. How do you feel and why?

185. What is the most embarrassing thing you've done?

186. If you could tell a college one thing about yourself, what would it be?

187. Do you have a guiding principle or philosophy of life?

188. *Do unto others as you would have them do unto you.* Discuss the Golden Rule, giving examples from your life.

189. Have you ever done someone a favor and found that the other person didn't appreciate it at all?

190. What is your favorite season and why?

191. What is your favorite day of the week and why?

192. Who is the person who makes you laugh the most? Why?

193. Who is your favorite professional comedian and why?

194. Have you met someone famous? What happened?

195. Have you ever been in a situation where you didn't know the proper etiquette? How did you cope?

196. Who is the funniest person in your family? Why?

197. Who's the most honest person you've ever met? Why?

198. Do you give yourself pep talks? What do you say?

199. Have you ever had a job or chore you hated? What was it, and why was it the worst?

200. Has someone ever disappointed you?

201. Have you ever disappointed someone else?

202. What is the most important room of your house?

203. If you had to pick a president based on one issue only, what would that issue be?

204. If you only had enough lunch for yourself, would you share it anyhow with a friend?

205. What is your favorite thing about high school?

206. What is your least favorite thing about high school?

207. Name some ways in which the Internet has transformed life for the better. For the worse.

208. If you were a doctor, what specialty would you pick and why?

209. If you were a teacher, what subject would you teach and why?

210. Talk about freedom versus responsibility.

211. Talk about national security versus individual rights.

212. What is the worst food you've ever eaten?

213. Interview a relative or friend about the person's life.

214. See if anyone will talk to you about a war experience, and discuss the effect this conversation has on you.

215. Research the history of your town and write about it.

216. Pick a prominent person locally and discuss.

217. What is the most exciting place you've seen?

218. If you had one place on earth you could visit, what would it be and why?

219. Have you ever seen something that changed your attitude about life?

220. Interview a relative about your early childhood.

221. If you have family photographs, interview someone about who the people were and what their lives were like.

222. Have you taken a community college course?

223. If you've done a summer program, tell about it.

224. Consider women's roles in modern-day America.

225. Discuss changes in women's roles in the past 500 years.

226. Have you ever tutored another person in a school subject? How did it go? Do you think you were effective?

227. Discuss a hobby.

228. Discuss the subject in school with which you have greatest difficulty.

229. If you have a career choice, tell how you came to that choice and why.

230. Talk about a place in terms of what has happened there, either in your own life or in history.

The Panic-Level Module

(also good for last-minute cramming for everyone)

Let's say you have only a short amount of time until your SAT. If it's ten minutes or less, grab a snack, your No. 2 pencils and calculator and hustle into the test room. There's not really time to master any material. If you have a day or two or a week or two, the situation is different. Memorize the Tips section that follows, and the first three items listed below.

The most important things to study and memorize are:

1. the Top 100 Words;

2. MathFacts™ 1 - 7 and New Math to Know;

3. the Math Worksheets: repeatedly work the math problems on separate sheets of paper until you've memorized the questions, answers and explanations for every single problem.

4.   material you missed on tests taken in *The Official SAT Study Guide* (the current title, but they may change it back to *10 Real SATs* or another title; always make sure it's by the College Board).

If you want to go further or you've mastered 1 - 4, above go on to:

5. Words You Must Know!: learn as many as you can of that vocabulary list;

6. Word Building and Discovery™: study this section for etymology tips, and do the worksheets with the aid of the Latin dictionary;

7. the Latin dictionary: try to learn as many of the words in boldface as you can, a job that is easier if you try to connect the words to simple words you already know in English or another language; and

8. Vocabu-toons™

Remember that making flashcards or having someone quiz you is an especially good way to study vocabulary.

Get enough sleep, stay (or get) healthy, eat right, and don't drive yourself crazy. But if you do the homestretch work outlined here, I think you'll be grateful when you see your scores! It may be tedious, but it can pay off handsomely!

I find when students learn that material cold, they do very well. The trick is to study and test oneself repeatedly, not merely look at it and say, "Yeah, I know this." It is amazingly easy to *recognize* the material and not really put it into long-term memory. But repetition really does help.

TIPS!

Everything in here is *extremely* important to know. You should read this section 6, 8, 10, 12 times, and you should test yourself on it. You *will* see much of this stuff on the SAT.

Even if you're taking the dreaded test soon, there's still probably time to affect your scores! Please read (peruse) below.

[Speaking of scores, you can get SAT scores 12 or 13 days after the test by phone or online; PSAT scores take longer to arrive. Maybe the scores will make you happy (or *ecstatic, exultant, blissful*) or sad (*morose, forlorn, bereft,* even *lachrymose,* meaning *teary-eyed*) or maybe you just don't care (are *blase, nonchalant, apathetic*). It is necessary (*imperative, essential, requisite*) to develop a game plan. I hope the game plan will be that you can retire (*withdraw*) from SATs for the rest of your life, and you can just jump up and down, but maybe you'll have to do some further study.]

It's going to be important for you to eat breakfast the day of the SAT and be hydrated (have some liquid, though not so much that you're *inundated*: flooded with liquid!). If you skip breakfast, you'll be quite hungry (*voracious*) and you'll feel a lack (*dearth*) of energy (*vitality, pep*) and operate slowly (be *torpid, sluggish, enervated*). Take a snack (solid and liquid) with you to the test so you can replenish (*revitalize*) yourself during a break (*intermission, respite, breather*); vending (*selling*) machines may be empty, broken, or far from your test site (*locale*).

Now this section may look like a sneaky (*sly, surreptitious, wily*) way to get in a few extra vocabulary words, and in a way it is! But I'm hoping I can cram in a few last-minute tips that will help you.

Perhaps you're not a beginner (*tyro, neophyte, novice, greenhorn*) in terms of the SAT anymore. I hope you've been working hard (been *diligent, assiduous*) just like all of your *contemporaries* (people who live at the same time as yourself) or peers (*equals*). And I think you'll do well on the test, but I want you to think about (*contemplate*) a few items (*particulars* or *details*) . . . .

Please remember to use your time well. Pace yourself and ditch any problem or question that seems tough (*arduous, laborious, troublesome*) or looks as though it's going to take a lot of time. Just make sure you track where you should be on your answer sheet. Please check your work. Please circle relevant (*pertinent*) things in the problem like fraction, integer, perimeter, area, sum, product so you don't make pointless (*inane*) or laughable (*ludicrous*) mistakes.

When a problem says "A circle's area is 15," the first thing you do in your test booklet is write down the formula for circle area and set it equal to 15. If you don't recall the formula (πr^2), it's often in the reference info at the beginning of the math section. Whenever you become aware you are dealing with perimeter of a rectangle, area of a triangle or whatever, write down that formula! It will help you solve the darn problem, redundant as this may sound! (And by the way, when you have a wheel going around or the tip of a fan blade going around an axis of rotation, that's a circumference problem).

Remember that many geometric figures can be puzzled out by two facts: there are 180 degrees in a straight line and 180 degrees in a triangle on the SAT. If they put a figure (square, triangle, or rectangle) within an x - y axis, you can figure out the lengths of the sides and thus perimeter and area as follows: if the x coordinates of 2 points are the same, find the difference between the y coordinates, and that's the length of the line segment; if the y coordinates of 2 points are the same, find the difference between the x coordinates, and that's the length of the line segment.

Please note when you have one or more right angles in a figure; there are lots of things you can figure out if you notice that (for instance, area of a triangle, Pythagorean calculations, etc).

Sometimes you can't figure out what one angle is by itself, but you can figure out what 2 or 3 angles are together and that will *suffice* (be enough) to solve the problem.

What if something is a complete puzzle (*conundrum, enigma*) to you? Leave it blank (*void*)! You do not have to answer every question on the test to get a great (*grand, superior, admirable*) score!

Know MathFacts™ 1–7, New Math to Know, the Math Worksheets, all grammar rules, anything you missed on any sample tests you've taken in *The Official SAT Study Guide* and the Top 100 Words, at the minimum.

Get a good night's sleep. Sleep deprivation causes careless (*lax, negligent, incautious, inattentive*) mistakes.

Play with equations, always doing the same thing to each side of the equal sign. Remember to substitute real numbers for variables. Sometimes you can solve things by substituting the answers A through D and seeing which works. If you have two fractions equal to each other, cross multiplication is your friend (*ally*). Ratios may be expressed as fractions.

When you have variables, unless they give you more specific information, try substituting three things: (1) positive versus negative numbers, (2) fractions or decimals versus whole numbers or integers and (3) zero. If they tell you x is a positive integer, you have to follow directions. Often the following numbers will help you in substituting: -5, -4, -3, -2, -1, -$\frac{1}{2}$, 0, $\frac{1}{2}$, 1, 2, 3, 4, 5. Obviously if they say x is more than 5, you have to use a number more than 5. If you already have a number used (*utilized, employed*) in a problem (an exponent of 2, say), don't substitute that number unless you're told to in the problem.

Speaking of exponents, when you have parentheses or brackets, you multiply the exponents inside and outside the parentheses. With no parentheses, add the exponents.

Remember: a cube has 6 equal sides (think of dice). If they give you total surface area of a cube, you divide by 6, then take the square root of that number and then cube that square root to get volume. If they give you volume, you take the cube root of it, square that number and multiply by 6 to get total surface area. Important cubes to know: 1^3 is 1, 2^3 is 8, 3^3 is 27, 4^3 is 64, 5^3 is 125, 6^3 is 216, 7^3 is 343. Use your calculator for the rest! The reason it helps to know these is that it speeds up (*expedites*) solving cube problems. π is 3.14, $\sqrt{2}$ is 1.4, and $\sqrt{3}$ is 1.7, for faster (*swifter, more rapid, accelerated*) calculations.

Remember that dividing by a fraction is the same as (*is tantamount to*) multiplying by the inverse or reciprocal of the fraction, *e.g.*, dividing by $\frac{1}{2}$ is the same as multiplying by 2.

If they say, "The average number of chickens that 4 farmers have is 300," the first thing you must usually do is multiply those two numbers. So there are 1200 chickens total. If they ask, "What is the greatest number of chickens that any farmer can have if each farmer has at least 50 chickens and no farmer has the same number of chickens?" you will want to set aside the one (*sole, lone, solitary*) farmer that's going to have the most chickens, and make the other 3 have the smallest number they can have: 50, 51 and 52. So add 50, 51, and 52, get 153 and subtract that number from 1200 to get 1047.

With a positive number, when you square it and then take the square root of the resulting number, you get back your original number. When you take the square root of a positive number and then square that resulting number, you get back your original number.

Remember that each square contains two equal isosceles right triangles, created by the diagonal. You can put a square within a circle in such a way that all four corners of the square will be on the circumference of the circle. Then the diagonal of the square, which is the hypotenuse of the triangles, will also be the diameter of the circle, and you can use that information to figure out circumference and area of the circle.

There are agrarian words you have to know on the SAT: *arable*: suitable for farming, plowing, tilling or cultivation and *arid*: dry (think of the deodorant; they added an extra R, but the idea is that it's supposed to keep you dry).

Make sure you fill in your answer sheet as you go, and make sure your answers are entered in the proper places on the answer sheet!

Use everything in your brain to help you. Do you know simpler English words or Spanish, French, Latin, Italian, Romanian or Portuguese words that might help you get the answer right? If you have *florid*, meaning *flowery or fancy*, but you don't know that word, think of *florist*, a place/person that sells flowers, and that might help. If you have *facile* (*easy, or too easy*), think of the Spanish and French words that resemble it. If you have had time to memorize some of the prefixes, roots and suffixes in the Latin dictionary, you can break down words into component parts and figure out what the words mean, as in Word Building and Discovery™. If you have a word starting with *sub-*, think of *submarine*, which means *under the sea*. So *sub* means *under*. If you have *circumnavigation*, think of a circle being round and *circum*—meaning *around*, and *nav*—being part of *navy*, which consists of ships that sail around, so *nav*—means *ship* or *sail*. Thus *circumnavigation* is sailing around the world.

People panic when they see words that have 15, 16 letters in them, but you can often break them down into a more manageable size!

If you see a word like *reductive* that you've never used, you know the word *reduce*, and *reductive* means *tending to diminish or reduce to simplest form*. If you have *wily*, think of Wile E. Coyote who was always trying to be tricky; *wily* means *tricky, crafty, mischievous*.

If you have a word that starts with *ultra*—like *ultraconservative*, think of the spectrum, where ultramarine is above the marine (blue) color. An ultraconservative, therefore, would be a highly conservative person. If you see the word *infrasonic*, remember that infrared is below red, and *infra*—means *below*, so *infrasonic* means *below the level of perceptible sound*.

There are lots of words meaning *condescending* or *looking down on someone* on the SAT (hmm, are the people in Princeton trying to impart a message?): *patronizing, deigning, sneering, scoffing, deriding, gibing, scorning*.

Remember that if you know one word form (*e.g.*, *aesthete*, a person who appreciates or seeks beauty), you might have *aesthetically, aesthetics*, or another form on the test. Please don't be rigid (*inflexible, unpliant, unyielding*) in your thinking.

A common thing in etymology is that related words sometimes have the same consonants, but different vowels. Take *camaraderie*, which means *comradeship or friendship*. See the C, M, R, D in both words in the very same order? The order is important. That's a tip-off that they mean the same (*identical, equivalent*) thing. Ditto for *effective* and *efficacious*, which both mean *getting results*. F, F, C in both words. Thus, when you have the word *retain* and *retention*, they are different forms of the same word; *ten, tain* both mean *hold or keep*.

The word *eclectic* means *coming from a variety of sources* and it will in all likelihood show up on your test. So will *charlatan* (a *fake*), *dupe* (to *fool*) and *totalitarian* (pertaining to governments that control what people think and do, often using *propaganda*, which is information that tells people how to think about something). You are likely to have *egregious*, which refers to behavior so terrible that they threw the person out of their group or herd (*greg* means *group or herd*). A *virtuoso* is *a skilled expert*, often in music, and a *bard* is a poet (they call Shakespeare the Bard of Avon). *Frenetic* means *agitated* (think of *frantic*, a similar-sounding word). *Compliant* means *going along with something* (think of it being the opposite of *complaint*, where you're not going along with something. Reverse the *a* and *i* and you get different word senses). Words meaning *mental*: *cerebral, intellectual*. Words meaning *small*: *diminutive, bantam, lilliputian, petite*. Words meaning *large*: *enormous, immense, colossal, prodigious, vast*. Words meaning *charitable*: *munificent, philanthropic*. Words meaning *poverty*: *penury, indigence, meagerness, pauperism, impoverishment*.

Lay out clothes (*garments, raiment*) the night before the test and dress in layers (*strata*) since the room can be cold (*gelid, glacial*) or hot (*thermal, torrid, sweltering, stuffy*); pick comfortable clothes. Charge your calculator or have good batteries, and take several sharp No. 2 pencils with good erasers. Have your ticket and picture ID (driver's license will *suffice*, or be enough). Make sure you know which test center you are going to, and make sure you know how to get there if it's a new (*novel, alien*) location.

During the test, I'm hoping your mind will be clear (*lucid*) and all your work (*effort, industriousness*) will pay off. Before the test, please use your time to both maximize your knowledge and to relax (opposites, I know). It's not a time to be a *hedonist* (pleasure-seeking person) or focus only on aesthetics (beauty) in your surroundings (environs)!

Best wishes (with good will, or benevolence),
Marcy Denmark Manning